Chengdu

A City of Paradise

Jack Quian

CHINA INTERCONTINENTAL PRESS

图书在版编目（CIP）数据

天府成都：英文／（美）少君著．—北京：五洲传播出版社，2007.3
ISBN 978-7-5085-0969-3

Ⅰ.天…　Ⅱ.少…　Ⅲ.游记－成都市－英文　Ⅳ.K928.971.1

中国版本图书馆 CIP 数据核字（2007）第 030877 号

责任编辑：荆孝敏　王　莉
封面设计：缪　惟　刘豪亮

图片提供（以汉语拼音为序）：

陈元峰、迟阿娟、郝康理、何海洋、胡大田、江宏景、金世宗、李祥云、
李绪成、李　豫、孙立新、王达军、王瑞林、王若冰、王　效、吴晓桐、
杨永赤、姚　远、张登伟、张全能、周孟棋、周勇良

天府成都

出版发行：五洲传播出版社
社　　址：北京市海淀区莲花池东路北小马厂 6 号华天大厦
邮政编码：100038
电　　话：010-58891281
传　　真：010-58891281
制版单位：北京锦绣圣艺文化发展有限公司
印　　刷：北京尚唐印刷有限公司
开　　本：215x215　12 开
印　　张：15
印　　数：1-4000 册
版　　次：2007 年 3 月第 1 版　2007 年 3 月第 1 次印刷
书　　号：ISBN 978-7-5085-0969-3
定　　价：136.00 元

Contents

I. A Panda City — 1
Giant pandas are the generous gifts that nature has given to Chengdu and the best calling card and trademark of Chengdu as well…

II. A Relaxing City — 23
Jinli Street highlights Chinese characteristics and the local color of Chengdu and impresses you as a space-time where reality and history join together…

III. A Gourmet City — 48
If you want to figure out everything about Chengdu, you must learn to taste it with your "tongue"…

IV. A Tea City — 71
Teahouses in Chengdu are like bars in Paris and cafés in Vienna…

V. A Historic City — 87
Three thousand years of wind and rain have nurtured the cultural profundity of this city…

VI. A Water City — 104
Thanks to water, Chengdu has developed a character of its own: leisurely, tolerant, and enterprising…

VII. A Romantic City — 121
This city is like mist, full of mysterious allure and tender feelings…

VIII. A Nightless City — 138
A bar is a second living room for urban young people, which reflects the living habits and public feelings that permeate this city…

IX. An Unforgettable City — 153
Already an image on my atrium, Chengdu has captured my yearning…

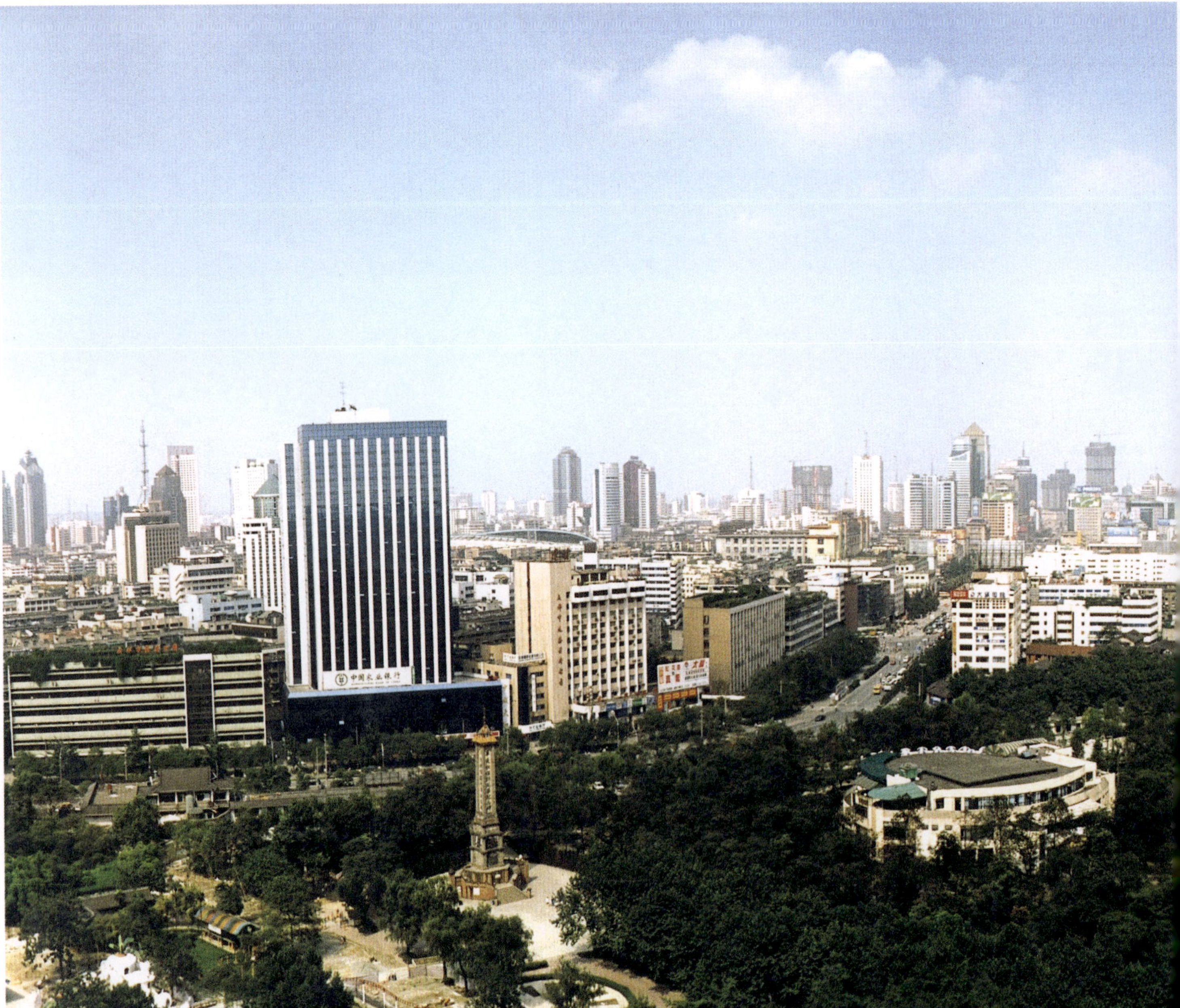
中国农业银行

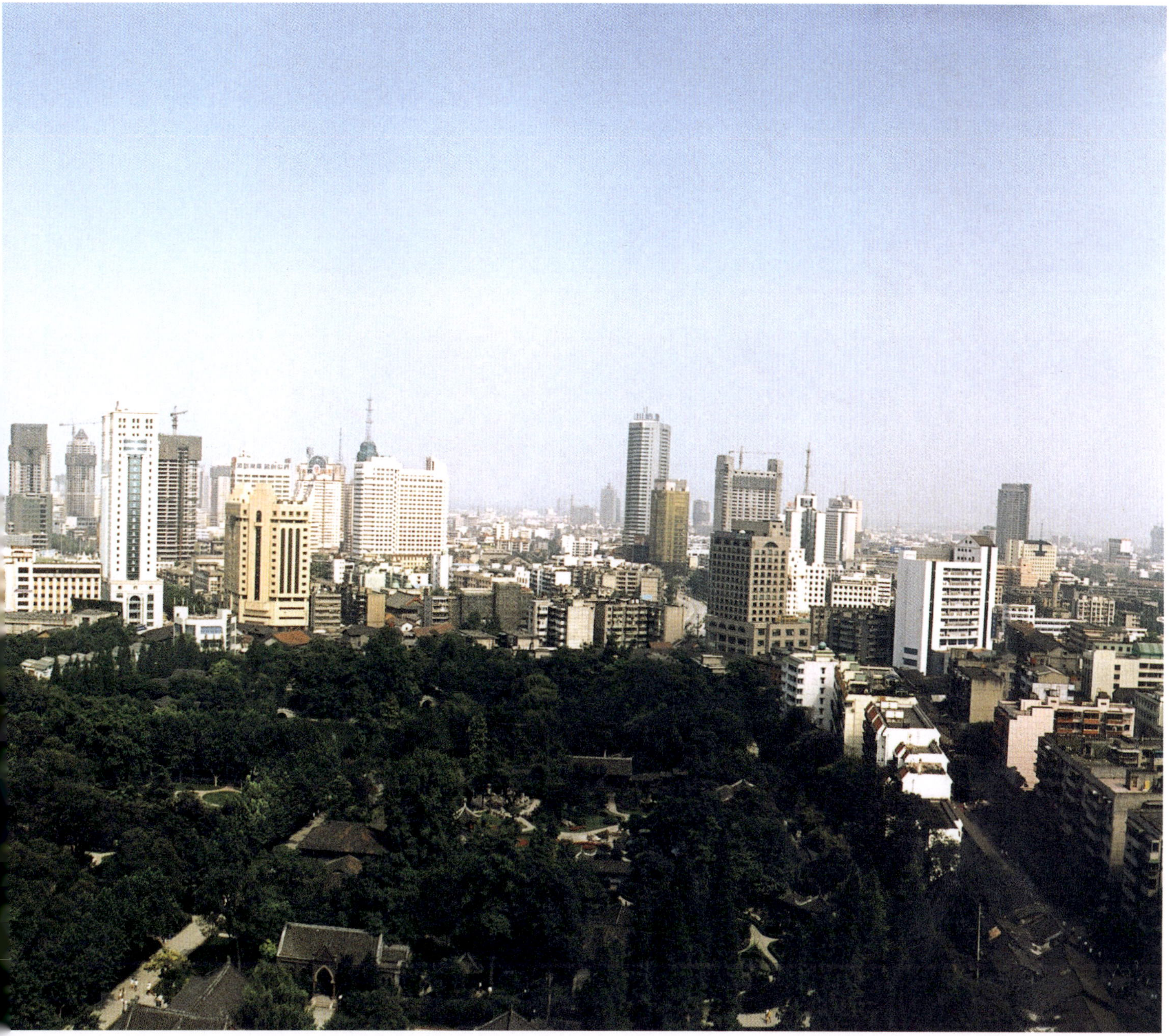

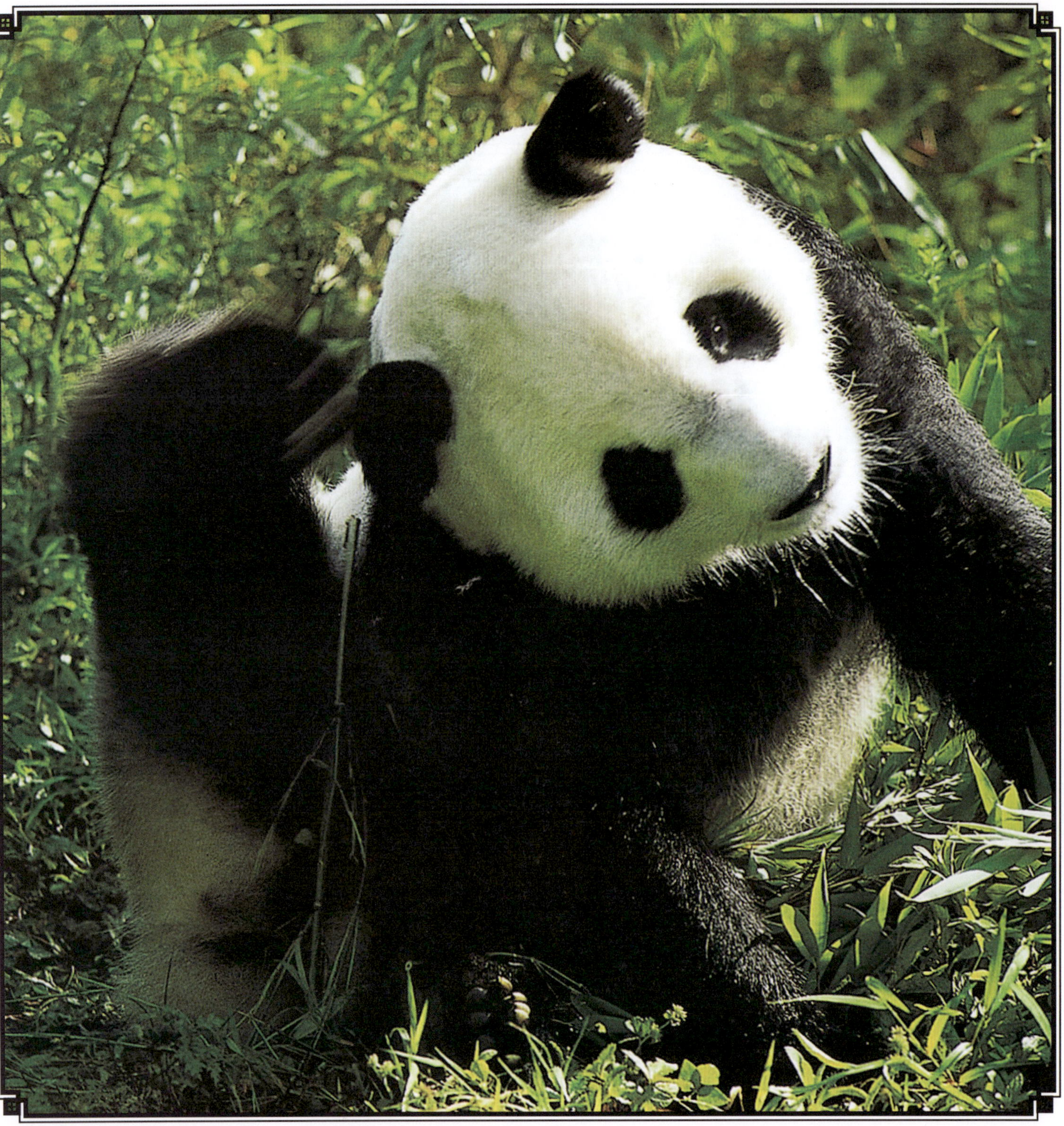

1. A Panda City

It was spring, 1936. Ruth Harkness, a fashion designer and a socialite in Manhattan, New York, unfolded a map of China drawn by the Operations Command of the Royal Army of Britain in her upper-city apartment. Her fingers were moving slowly westward from Shanghai along the Yangtze River, searching carefully for a city. Bill, her late husband and an outstanding explorer, had told her that this city was located in a basin on the eastern edge of the Qinghai-Tibet Plateau, not far from the other end of the Yangtze River…

Seventy years later, it was also spring. Danny and I googled this city and nearly 3,000,000 items appeared on the computer screen…

This city is Chengdu, with an area of 12,400 square kilometers and a population of about 11,000,000. It is not just the biggest provincial capital in west China, but also the only city in the history of China whose name has remained the same for 3,000 years since its establishment.

Chengdu was the starting point of China's famous southern Silk Road, which ran past Ya'an, Lushan, Xichang, Panzhihua to Zhaotong, Qujing, Dali, Baoshan, Tengchong, Dehong in Yunnan Province, then entered Burma and Thailand, and finally arrived in India and the Middle East; thus Chengdu was the most important stopping place along this bridge between Chinese culture and world civilizations.

In Chinese, "cheng" means "success or successful" and "du," "big city or capital." This "Successful City" not only boasts a long history, but also holds an unusual position: latitude 30 degrees north. An imaginary circle marked out by geographers, it nevertheless possesses a magic power that no other longitude or latitude could possibly rival. It is on this circle that the highest mountain, Mount Everest, and the lowest trench, Mariana Trench lie; and it is on this circle that the Yangtze River, the Mississippi River, the Nile River, and the Euphrates River all pour into the sea. It is also a mysterious circle, on which stand the pyramids and Sphinx of Egypt, the "god of fire and kindlings" mural in the Sahara Desert of North Africa, the Bermuda Triangle in the Caribbean Sea, The Hanging Gardens of ancient Babylon, Mount E'mei, Mount Huang, and Mount Lu of China. It was on this circle that the four civilizations of ancient China, ancient Babylon, ancient Egypt, and ancient India all developed. Why are there so many coincidences? We felt even more puzzled and curious than ever when another wonder—the Sanxingdui-Jinsha civilization created by the ancient Shu people in Chengdu Plain of latitude 30 degrees north—was discovered…So many unsolved mysteries through the ages have kindled many people's interest in and even fascination with this city…

It was 1287. The mountain wind was blowing hard and a brass bell rang like crystal. A caravan was trudging among lofty and precipitous mountains, and at the lead was a foreigner with an aquiline nose and big eyes. He was Marco Polo (1254-1324), who later became a world-famous traveler and adventurer. This Italian merchant, who was born in the "City of Water" commonly known as Venice, set out from Beijing, passed Zhuozhou, Taiyuan, and Xi'an, to get to Chengdu; he was the first European to have reached the southern Silk Road. When Marco Polo first set foot on the mountain roads on the plateau in the southwest, he was impressed by the precipitous mountains, deep valleys, and untold difficulties. After many travel-worn days, he felt his abilities falling short of his wishes amid all those continuous mountains. It was right then as if by magic, a lovely and peaceful plain spread out suddenly before his eyes. And more importantly, he saw a flourishing and bustling city that was Chengdu. Marco Polo walked in the streets and saw rivers, big and small, merging by the streets, boats shuttling back and forth on the rivers, and people moving in an endless stream over the bridges. All the small bridges, flowing waters, and signs of everyday life, enveloped in a wet cloudy mist, reminded him of his faraway hometown Venice. "Thank God," Marco Polo said, "after such a long distance of difficult and dangerous walk, I finally saw a city of water and a view similar to that of my hometown."

In Chapter 44 of *The Travels of Marco Polo* that he wrote later, Marco Polo described Chengdu as follows: "Chengdu is a beautiful city on a flat land. There are quite a few rivers flowing around or through the city. They emanate from the remote mountains and supply Chengdu with abundant water. In the city there is a big bridge on a river. All along its length on either side there are columns of marble to bear the wooden roof, which is decorated with red paintings and covered with tiles to keep out wind and rain. And on this bridge there are neatly-arranged houses and stores, in which a great deal of trade and industry is carried on…"

Marco Polo was the first European to have introduced Chengdu to foreign people so Chengdu is one of the cities in China that people in Europe got to know first.

In 1870, Ferdinand von Richthofen, a German explorer, came to Chengdu to confirm Marco Polo's account. By then, Chengdu had "become the biggest city in China, incomparably flourishing in culture, elegance, and style…Paintings hang on the walls of every teahouse, hotel, store, and residence…The artistically consummate steles win prodigal praise from merchants and travelers coming and going…Yet what best displays the refined culture of this city is the courteous manners of the local inhabitants and in this regard, Chengdu is far ahead of the other parts of China."

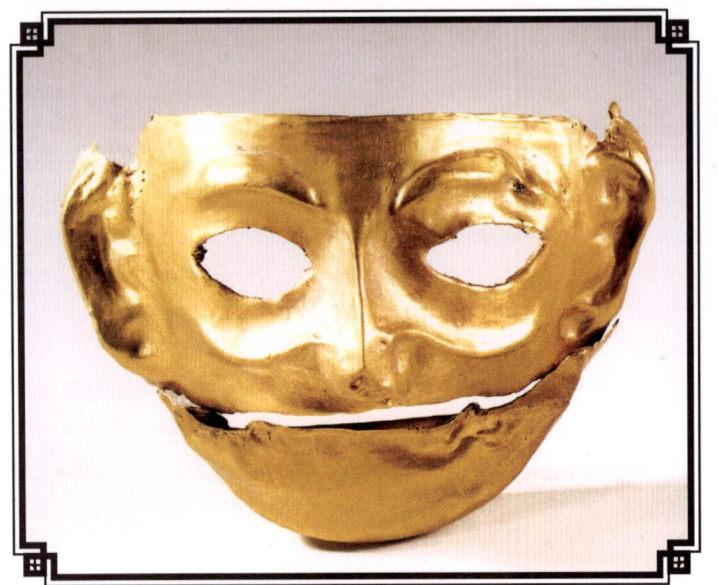

While examining the molecular formula of camphor in a chemical laboratory in John Hopkins University, Luther Knight read the above description and made up his mind to go to Chengdu. This American professor, who had grown up in Iowa, started to teach in Sichuan Institute of Higher Learning in Chengdu in 1910. He died of illness in 1913 and was buried in Chengdu. But within this short period of two years and ten months, he had traveled to every mountain and river, every high street and back lane in Chengdu and left to posterity several hundred photos, which amounted to a complete record of his work and life in Chengdu and the sights of every place where he had been. These old photos exhibited the natural sceneries, folk customs, and architectural highlights in Chengdu at that time and fully registered the historical conditions almost a hundred years ago. From Luther Knight's correspondence with his family, we can see that he harbored a deep respect and admiration for this land and its inhabitants...

Joseph Beach, an explorer who arrived in Chengdu coincidently with Luther Knight, wrote in his *Visiting the Alps in West China, 1911*: "Chengdu is one of the most beautiful cities in China. Chengdu is the biggest city in the basin in west Sichuan, the capital of Sichuan, and perhaps, the best city in China other than Beijing, the capital of China. The beauty of Chengdu is not limited to its appearances; its thirst for knowledge is also most fascinating..."

As a matter of fact, Sichuan Province, to which Chengdu belongs, has been called "a land of abundance" in the history of China and Chengdu is not only the biggest city in Sichuan, but also one of the earliest city in China. It is situated in the middle of Sichuan and adjacent to Longquan Mountains on the east, the Yunnan-Guizhou Plateau on the south, Qionglai Mountains on the west, and Qinling Mountains on the north. A bird's-eye view from the sky shows that Chengdu is a basin coated in green, nestled in a vast fertile land, and entwined by two rivers, fairly peaceful and cozy. Embraced by a plateau, mountains, and hills, Chengdu boasts a three-in-one beauty plus a mild climate and plentiful rainfall; therefore it has a reputation for being "a city of paradise" where "floods and droughts are under control and the inhabitants know no famine." From historical works as vast as the open sea, Chengdu is found to be a mysterious city. The developing of mountains 360 million years ago resulted in the special physiognomy of Sichuan Basin and Chengdu stood right in the middle of this Basin. Early in the 4th century B.C., Kaiming the ninth, a king of the ancient Shu Kingdom, moved the capital "to Chengdu" and allegedly, "built a village in the first year, a town in the second year, and a city in the third year."

On April 17,1936, when Ruth Harkness boarded the "American Trader" ocean liner that would depart from New York for China, all her friends believed "[s]he's as mad as a hatter." It was because very few people had heard of giant pandas, and if they had, none of them had seen the "living animal fossil," one of the last rare mammals in the world. And what was worse, Ruth was neither a zoologist nor an explorer and knew very little about animals, except for the little family of kittens that she was leaving behind.

Before her husband Bill told her what he knew about giant pandas, she, in common with most of the world, had never heard of a giant panda. And Bill's information was mostly gleaned from *Trailing the Giant Panda*, a book that the Roosevelt brothers, Kermit and Theodore, had written.

For me, Chengdu is a seemingly familiar yet very remote place, as well as a dream-world that has existed for more than twenty years in a half-asleep state...In the early 80s of the last century, as a recent college graduate, I was given a chance to visit Chengdu and stayed there for the short period of one week. Then, Chengdu was an ancient but shabby city composed of dilapidated gray compounds and matchbox-shaped simple buildings. Every morning I woke up, I heard hawkers crying out for customers in various ways: some shouted to the accompaniment of bamboo clappers or a gong, and some simply yelled at the top of their voices; whether in a high-pitched voice or a low-pitched one, whether in quick rhythm or slow rhythm, they always called out melodiously: "Oil tea—"; "*Guokui, Guokui* with sesame, aromatic and crisp—"…The high-pitched voice poured out as rapidly as a waterfall fell down to the ground in torrents, and the low-pitched voice floated about as unhurriedly as a white cloud drifted out from a cave; together they composed a marketplace ditty that was hard for me to forget. The most unforgettable was the shouting in Sichuan dialect of the hawker who sold bean jelly: "Salty bean jelly, hot bean jelly, hot and tongue-numbing bean jelly—" With the end sounds lingering, it made my ears tingle, just like the high tune in Sichuan opera, melodious and agreeable…

I believe every one of us has developed a sort of complex, which knots, tightly or loosely, at the bottom of our hearts, and this knot will remain intact until it is given a chance to unfold itself. After such a long time, it was the hand of chance that set my eyes on Chengdu again; otherwise, my memory of Chengdu over twenty years ago would probably keep me company for the rest of my life…That day, I went to Arizona State University to do some errands and ran into a lecture on China. On the platform, a beautiful young doctor was speaking with fervor and assurance about Chengdu, a city with a long history. She never bothered to conceal her laudation and love of Chengdu and was brimming over with feelings for her hometown. I had thought of leaving a few minutes later, but her ardor affected me to such an extent that I could not help but listen attentively…After a detailed introduction of Chengdu's history: status quo, and investment situation, she added, "The following short movie is directed by Zhang Yimou, the most famous movie director in China, and it is a mirror of the present Chengdu. I'm sure you'll like it…" On the screen first appeared a modern airport, Shuangliu International Airport. Then a young man with a heavy backpack walked down an airplane. The voice-over said, "My grandma told me: 'Chengdu is a place where once you go, you don't want to come back!' She's old now and can't travel far from home, so she asked me to videotape Chengdu for her." I looked at the magnificent expressways in the movie and high-rise buildings fleeting by one after another, and could not help feeling amazed: Is it Chengdu? Is it the provincial capital in southwest China where I've been? Those seemingly familiar places on camera—Chunxi Street, Wangjianglou Park, Du Fu's Thatched Cottage, and so on—did not fit in with my memory. Not to mention the bustling downtown streets, towering buildings, carpet-like grass, and bamboos with supple twigs and tender leaves…The voice-over said, "I can't believe it's the place my grandma has told me about again and again." And in my ears it sounded like this: "I can't believe it's the place where I've been."…

"You're welcome to visit Chengdu again. The present Chengdu has developed into a central city in west China. If there's something in good preservation, that's Chengdu's cultural tradition, such as the emphasis on leisure and human warmth and its cultural profundity," Doctor Tang Hua said to the audience at the end of the lecture and in a certian way I was tempted. Amazingly, that evening I received an e-mail from Sophia, a French friend of mine, who I had been out of contact with me for quite a long time. She told me that she was now teaching French and studying Chinese at the same time in a university in Chengdu and felt overwhelmed with admiration for the beauty and affluence of Chengdu.

"How about China this time? There's a city called Chengdu. Let's go and have a look," I said to Danny, who was going to have a spring break. In the USA, many parents look forward to their children's holidays, but sometimes they are big headaches for them. There are four holidays every year and you have to arrange different trips or programs for each; it is really very difficult to come up with a fresh and interesting suggestion for your kids who have been to Disney Land and Sea World many times.

"Chengdu? See What?" Danny asked absent-mindedly, busy playing an online game. For a fourth-grade primary school student, "Chengdu" sounded not just odd but unfamiliar. So I went to his computer, suspended the game window, googled Chengdu, and all of a sudden, millions of items appeared on the screen.

"So?" Danny asked impatiently, hoping, with the game in mind, to end this conversation as soon as possible.

Then I googled panda for relevant pictures and immediately, pandas in various poses displayed themselves on the computer screen. Danny was nicknamed "Panda" at school, and his room was full of things related to pandas, from wall calendars to all the ornaments on the bookcase.

"Are there pandas in Chengdu?" He asked me doubtingly.

"Of course. Of all the pandas in the world, eighty percent live in or around Chengdu."

"Really? When can we go there?" Nothing interested a ten-year-old kid more than seeing a giant panda with his own eyes.

Thus with the prospect of seeing giant pandas, I tempted Danny, who had never been to China, into embarking on a trip to Chengdu on a sunny spring day…

In 1936, it took Ruth Harkness more than two weeks to arrive in China from the USA by sea and more than ten days to get to Chengdu from Shanghai by water; and even "the arrangements for the three-hundred-mile trip from Chungking [Chongqing] to Chengtu [Chengdu]" were "not made without difficulty." Here is a recollection of what she saw near Chengdu in her book: "The flooded rice paddies reflected lazily floating clouds, or were muddy from the slow-moving water buffalo that, nose deep in the water, dragged their wooden plows through the mire. Little villages dozed in the sunshine…Our way lay through…past hamlets where life went on as it had for centuries. Glimpses of women weaving in ancient fashion on their doorsteps, dyeing the blue cotton cloth universally used by the peasantry, old women tottering on bound feet to market with pigs, goats, even geese on lead strings. The chair traffic, the groaning wheelbarrows that carried all sorts of burdens, including human ones, and the coolies with great loads carried in baskets, suspended from poles, across their shoulders"; "Every turn and bend in the road presented a new picture of peace and beauty…"

Now, it takes less than a day to fly from Los Angeles to Chengdu and reportedly, there are already more than ten direct flight courses connecting Chengdu with big cities in Europe and America. There are also many flights from Chengdu to all the other big cities in China and those linking Chengdu to Beijing, Shanghai, and Guangzhou come and go as frequently as buses and you can take one at any moment. In Ruth Harkness's days, it was a two week ride from Shanghai to Chengdu by water, but the flight now takes two hours, no longer than the duration of a football game or a movie. If you happen to take a flight of Sichuan Airlines, you will have the opportunity to eat typical Sichuan dishes, learn about local conditions and customs, and chat with pretty stewardesses.

On the flight to Chengdu, outside the porthole there were lofty mountains and precipitous peaks everywhere; the physiognomy of Sichuan is similar to that of China as a whole: It is high in the west and low in the east. With an English book on Sichuan in his hand, Danny asked me why Sichuan was also called "Shu." I told him the name "Shu" appeared first on inscriptions on bones and tortoise shells of the Shang Dynasty (the 16th-11th century B.C.). The ancestors of the Shu people were allegedly a division of the Qiang nationality who lived in the upper and middle reaches of the Yellow River. They migrated southward along the Minjiang River Basin, entered the Sichuan Basin, and established a country of their own in Chengdu Plain. As for the origin of "Shu," some history books say it refers to silkworms, for the king of ancient Shu Can Cong taught his people to plant mulberry trees and rear silkworms and made Sichuan the first silkworm-rearing place in China. From the cultural relics unearthed in Sichuan it can be inferred that as early as 4000 years ago the ancient Shu people had already established a slave-holding country on the plain in west Sichuan. Since the emperors and kings of later dynasties all seated the local government of Sichuan in Chengdu, which was the capital of the ancient Kingdom of Shu, Sichuan has been called "Shu" for short.

"So Chengdu is the biggest city in Sichuan? There're too many pages of introduction to Chengdu in this book. Could you please make a shorter one for me?" A ten-year-old child liked to inquire into the root of everything and I must be patient enough. I opened a magazine offered on the airplane and told him what I learned on the spot: Chengdu is not only the biggest city of Sichuan but also one of the metropolises in China. Its earliest names also include "the city of brocade" and "the city of hibiscus." From historical works as vast as the open sea, Chengdu is found to be a mysterious city. The mountain developing 360 million years ago resulted in the special physiognomy of Sichuan Basin and Chengdu stood right in the middle of this Basin. Early in the 4th century B.C., a king of the ancient Shu Kingdom named the place "Chengdu." And for more than 2000 years, Chengdu has been the seat of the local government of Sichuan, whether it was called Jun, Zhou, Fu, Dao, or Sheng in Chinese. What is more worthy of note is that her name has remained the same till now, which is very rare in the history of place names in China. Chengdu can be said to be one of the cities with the longest history in China.

Although I had condensed Chengdu's 3000-year history into something that could not be simpler, it was still too difficult for Danny, an American-born American-raised primary school student to understand fully. Although I did not know how much he understood, I did learn much myself. The process of learning about a city is actually like reading a thick and heavy history book. Although before our departure, I had made a concentrated effort to read its history, the very soul of Chengdu, a city with such a long history and profound cultural tradition, could not possibly be touched by trivial fragments and data.

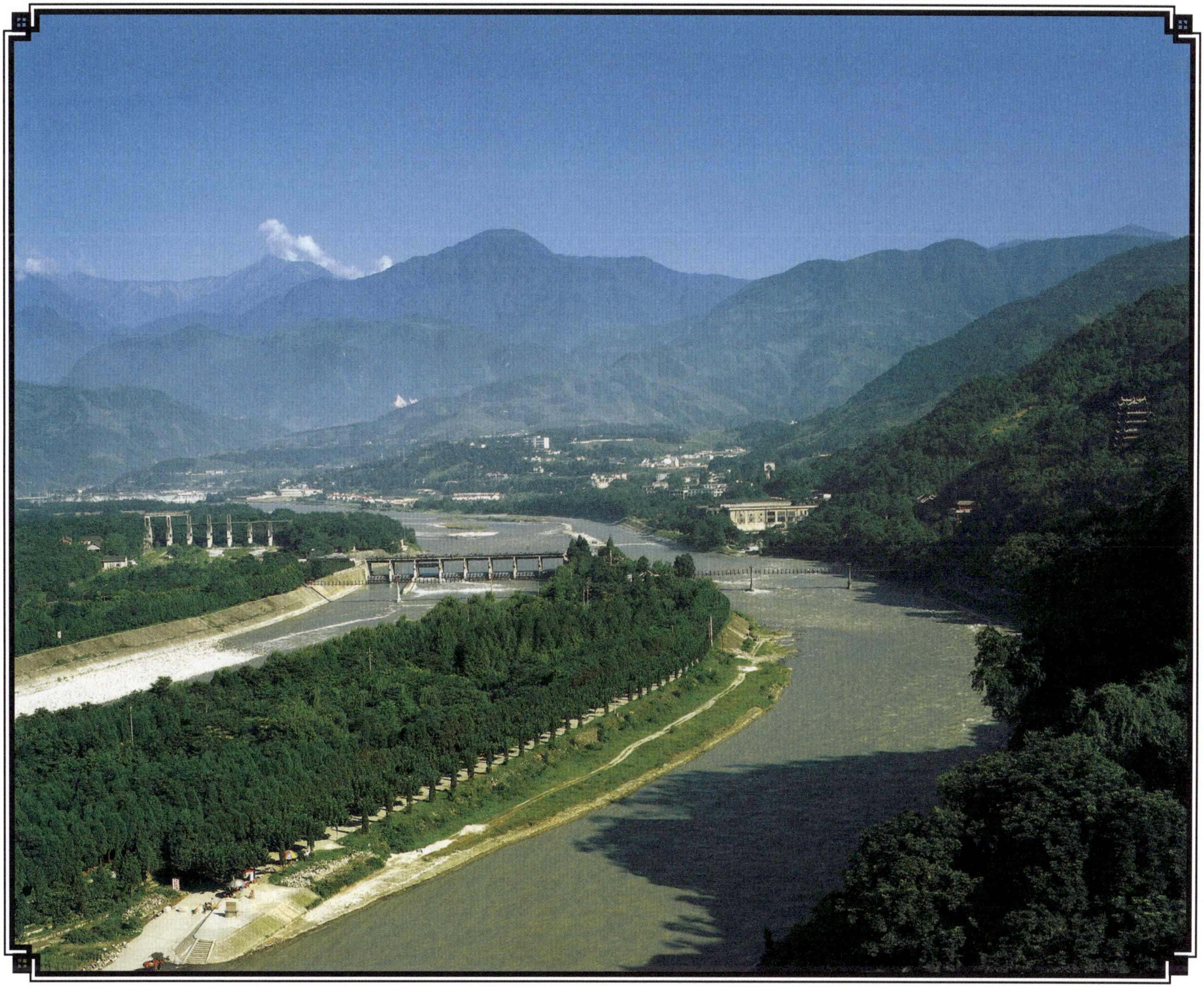

"Why can giant pandas live in places near Chengdu? Why not in other places?" Danny asked curiously as he closed his book..

The question nearly daunted me, for it was not long ago that I had got from books a limited knowledge about giant pandas. But parents are parents and in their children's eyes, they are an encyclopedia. In the simplest words that I could manage, I told Danny, in terms of zoology, giant pandas belong to the Carnivora order and are members of the Stegodon Genus. This Genus is mostly extinct now and the only survivors are giant pandas with a history of eight million years; hence the laudatory title "the living animal fossil." Its ability to survive such a long history of evolution proves that it once possessed an indestructible life force. But due to the environmental changes, it has now become an endangered specie. At the present, there are only about 1000 giant pandas in the world and most of them live in Chengdu and its surrounding country. The reason that the natural conditions and human culture in Chengdu are fit for the living and breeding of giant pandas: Chengdu boasts many a river, a warm and damp climate, complex and varied landforms and vegetation, and plenty of wild life. Besides, in and around Chengdu there are range upon range of verdant mountains, dense and beautiful forests, valleys of unfathomable depths, and four nature reserves with a total area of 1,100 square kilometers—the Anzihe Nature Reserve in Chongzhou, the Heishuihe Nature Reserve in Dayi, the Longxi-Hongkou Nature Reserve in Dujiangyan, and the Baishuihe Nature Reserve in Pengzhou.

These nature reserves provide giant pandas with many fit conditions for their living and breeding: there are not only golden monkeys, takins, lesser pandas, rhesus macaques, Asian black bears, sambars, crimson-bellied tragopans, and many other wild animals, but also gingkoes, katsura trees, Taxus chinensis, and hundreds of other primitive plants, which constitute a complete natural eco-system. In addition, the inhabitants of Chengdu are exceedingly fond of and protective toward giant pandas and kindly treat and feed those that chance to enter some villages, thus making Chengdu the best habitat for this species of animal with a history of eight million years…

As we walked out of Shuangliu Airport, a damp breeze blew on my face and I felt as if a puddle of water could be breathed from the air. My cheeks and lips, which had already got used to the dry climate of Phoenix, USA, sensed a damp heat all of a sudden and a tender wetness rippled slowly across the bottom of my heart. Bathed in such watery air, girls in Chengdu certainly find it hard not to grow pretty and charming and no wonder giant pandas also like to live here. Around us there were people everywhere, so many people: tour guides who spoke loudly in Sichuan dialect, trendy girls in name-brand dresses and high-heeled shoes, foreign travelers with a huge backpacks on their backs and helpless expressions on their faces, and domestic travelers pulling big and small pieces of luggage. I looked up at the sky and saw a boundless gray haziness, which was able to breed in your heart some romantic feelings at first sight. And lazily, the breeze was blowing on my face, bringing along the leisureliness and ease that had accumulated in this city for thousands of years.

It was from the south along South People's Road that we drove to the downtown area. South People's Road is Chengdu's "Chang'an Street," broad and straight, stretching far, its vehicle traffic leading all the roads in Chengdu. On both sides of the road, gigantic billboards and signs in both English and Chinese flashed by; bicycles, motorcycles, yellow-and-green taxicabs, tricycles with a canvas roof surged forward one after another; old people leading a dog, running children, stubborn-looking young girls wearing a uniform, eyeglasses and earphones each went his or her own way at the crossroads…Every face savored of Chengdu; these people, along with the tall buildings, bridges, and highways under construction everywhere, constituted a picturesque view peculiar to this city…Passing a grand cable-stayed bridge shaped like the Chinese character "human," I found an emblem similar to Phoenix's city emblem where the two strokes of the character meet; of a lucid and lively design, the emblem looked quite impressive. Our driver told me, it is Chengdu's city emblem, the "divine sunbirds": the sun's twelve rays of light form a fast-turning wheel of light and four gold birds dance around the sun, which exhibits the ideal state of "harmony between man and universe." The emblem was designed in imitation of the gold foil of "divine sunbirds" unearthed in Jinsha Ruins, which was a masterpiece of the ancient Shu people who lived in Chengdu more than 3,000 years ago. It suddenly occurred to me that an understanding of Chengdu perhaps should start with this gold foil, for she not only reflects Chengdu's historical and cultural profundity and aptly embodies the local inhabitants' pioneering, innovative, persistent, and striving spirit that has endured for thousands of years, but also represents the bewitching charm and mysterious allure of the ancient city of Chengdu…

In years past, every time I tried to persuade Danny to go to China with me, he came up with a lot of excuses: there was a training session in the swimming team, there would be no one at home to take care of the tortoise, and so on. But this time when I said I was going to take him to see giant pandas in Chengdu and he could even have his photos taken with a giant panda, my son responded, his eyes sparkling with excitement, "Are you kidding?" and then followed me to China without a second thought. The year before last, in order to have a look at the giant panda Hua Mei (China-America), he "forced" me to drive him to the Zoo of San Diego, which took six to seven hours. And we had to stand in a queue under the scorching sun and when it was finally our turn, we had to settle for a several minutes' stare at Hua Mei from a distance. This, however, was enough to keep him excited for several days.

Therefore, as soon as we put down our luggage in the magnificent Sheraton Chengdu Lido Hotel, when Danny urged me to go straight to Chengdu Research Base of Giant Panda Breeding, which is located on a side hill of Mount Futou in the northern suburb of Chengdu, about ten miles from the downtown area. There are complete facilities for giant panda breeding: living quarters, feeding rooms, medical stations, and laboratories; and there are thousands of bamboos and shrubs to feed giant pandas and tens of giant pandas are captive-bred or captive–raised here. In years past, researches on giant pandas in this base have made quite a few breakthroughs; especially those concerning artificial breeding of giant pandas have attracted worldwide attention. Ever since 1980 when the base succeeded in using frozen semens for artificial insemination, nearly 100 giant pandas have been born and bred here. What is worthy of note is that Mei Mei produced 11 babies in 9 births and 7 of them have matured; and Qing Qing, Mei Mei's daughter produced 10 babies in 6 births, and all of them have matured. The third generation of captive-bred giant pandas have already been born and brought up in the base.

Cases of successful protection of endangered species of rare animals at home and abroad suggest that the protection of wild giant pandas and captive-bred ones must be carried out simultaneously. Chengdu Research Base of Giant Panda Breeding was established to fulfill the task of multiplying captive-raised giant pandas by way of artificial breeding and returning them to nature after being trained for and adapting themselves to a life in the wild; in this way, wild giant pandas can be multiplied and rejuvenated, the species' genetic diversity can be maintained and improved, and ultimately, the whole species can survive and coexist with humankind as long as possible. Now Chengdu is planning to expand the Panda Base and build a semi-domestic park in imitation of the habitat of wild giant pandas for the purpose of preparing captive-bred giant pandas for a life in the wild. The Panda Base provides a favorable environment for the living and breeding of giant pandas as well as lesser pandas, golden monkeys, black-necked cranes, pheasants, and other endangered rare species.

There is a Giant Panda Museum in the Panda Base, exhibiting the history and status quo of humankind's knowledge, research, protection, and salvation of giant pandas. According to the guide, on exhibition there are nearly 1,000 pictures of every description, over 2,140 specimens, over 100 fossils and models, several thousand printed works by writers both ancient and modern, both Chinese and foreign, and what not.

In ancient times, giant pandas were a valiant species; they dominated the world together with machairodonts, stegodons, and quite a few other ancient animals when humankind was nowhere to be found. In struggling for existence over a span of millions of years, giant pandas seemed to have got a sudden inspiration and radically changed their habits and characteristics: unable to beat meat-eating animals, they began to eat grass; unable to defeat plant-eating animals, they turned to bamboos. In order to survive, they endured humiliation and stooped to eat bamboo branches and leaves with their typical meat-eating molars. Dinosaurs fell down and turned into gigantic fossils on exhibition in museums, with every shred of prestige swept away; machairodonts died out, so did stegodons, and their calcified bones were scattered in remote corners of the world—what a pitiful sight!

But with their flexibility, climb-down, and perseverance, giant pandas have survived and become the "living animal fossils" during the evolution of life in the world, which testifies to Darwin's theory: the fittest survives natural selection.

Scientific researches on giant pandas have a short history of over 100 years. Pierre Armand David (1826-1900), a French missionary, was the first to introduce giant pandas to the world. He stayed in China from 1862 to 1874 and did missionary work successively in Beijing, Shanghai, Chengdu, and other places. In March, 1869, he became the fourth priest of Dengchigou Roman Catholic church in Baoxing County, west of Chengdu. Pierre Armand David wrote in his diary: "On March 11, 1869, on the way back to the church, I was invited by a landlord in the valley whose surname is Li to have tea in his house, where I saw an unfolded black-and-white bear skin. The skin looked very queer, almost completely white except the limbs, ears, and the areas around the eyes. It is probably an interesting new species in science!" Ten days later, Pierre Armand David bought from a local hunter a skin of what the locals called "white bear" and mailed it to Melne Edwaeds, director of the Nature Museum in Paris. After a careful study of the skin and bones, Edwaeds pointed out in a paper published in 1870: "It looks very much like a bear, but its bones and teeth are clearly different from those of a bear yet similar to those of a lesser panda or a raccoon. It must be a new species and I call it 'Ailuropoda.'" To commemorate Pierre Armand David's discovery of this new animal, Edwaeds named giant pandas "Ailuropoda melanoleuca David," which is still in use today. And the specimen made from the first giant panda skin is kept well in the Nature Museum in Paris, France.

Allegedly, "panda" is the English abbreviation of "Pierre Armand David." But in the academic circle, there is another theory: in Nepali, giant pandas are called "nigalya-ponya," which means "bears that eat bamboos," and "panda" is its pronunciation variant.

Since then, explorers from western countries kept coming to the surrounding country of Chengdu in search of giant pandas. Among them, the most famous were Kermit Roosevelt and Theodore Roosevelt, Jr., the two sons of President Theodore Roosevelt of the USA. In 1929, they organized an expedition to hunt for giant pandas and became the first westerners to have shot a giant panda. They wrote in their memoir *Trailing the Giant Panda*: "We shot at the back of the giant panda that was getting farther. Both of us hit the target…We fired again. It fell down at the sound, but managed to stand up and run into the dense bamboo grove. We knew it could not possibly get away…" Later, the giant panda shot by the Roosevelt brothers became the first specimen to go on exhibit in a western museum, which caused a panda mania in the west and attracted more and more explorers to China, including Ruth Harkness…

We had just got out of Giant Panda Museum, when Danny, overwhelmed with excitement, asked Miss Qu, who accompanied us, again and again: "Where are giant pandas? Where?" The moment we stood close to several giant pandas, Danny burst into tears… For Chinese children who grew up in the USA, giant pandas are fairy tales in their childhood memories, pixies in cartoons, playmates in their dreams… When we were preparing for our trip to Chengdu back at home, our neighbors and Danny's classmates all asked, Which place are you going to visit in China? When we answered, "The place where we can see giant pandas," they responded mostly with an envious exclamation. To travel to the habitat of giant pandas is also a long-cherished dream of many Americans. We visited Chengdu Research Base of Giant Panda Breeding together with a group of travelers from the USA. In tears, an old couple from Ohio asked me to help them have their photos taken with the giant pandas and they kept saying to me, "How lucky you are to live in Chengdu and watch giant pandas every day." When they got to know that I was also from the USA, the old lady said embarrassedly, "I loved to read a book called *The Lady and the Panda* in my childhood and imagined someday I would visit the hometown of giant pandas. Now my dream has come true. May I borrow your mobile phone to call my son? Just one word, I just want to tell him I'm in the home of giant pandas. You know, he also loved that book in his childhood…"

The Lady and the Panda, which has influenced three generations of Americans, was authored by Ruth Harkness, the first foreigner to take a giant panda out of China and raise a worldwide panda mania. Ruth was neither a zoologist nor an explorer but an American fashion designer. Her husband was a zoologist and an explorer with a keen interest in giant pandas. Unfortunately, he died midway through an expedition in China shortly after they got married. In April, 1936, Ruth came to China with the purpose of fetching her husband's remains back to America. But after reading the diary that her husband had kept before his death, this socialite in New York, a young lady with a bohemian spirit but no experience in open-country adventures, unexpectedly decided to give up her career as a fashion designer in New York and go to China in search of giant pandas in order to fulfill her husband's last wish, that is, to bring the first giant panda back to the USA. On November 9, 1936, Ruth eventually found a newborn giant panda in Wenchuan County in the north of Chengdu, which was recorded in *The Lady and the Panda*: "Quentin stopped so short that I almost fell over him. He listened intently for a split second and then went plowing on so rapidly I couldn't keep up to him. Dimly through the waving wet branches I saw him near a huge rotting tree. I stumbled on blindly brushing the water from my face and eyes. Then I too stopped, frozen in my tracks. From the old dead tree came a baby's whimper. I must have been momentarily paralyzed, for I didn't move until Quentin came toward me and held out his arms. There in the palms of his two hands was a squirming baby *bei-shung*. Automatically I reached for the tiny thing. The warm furriness in my hands brought reality to something that until then had been fantasy…The little black and white ball nuzzled my jacket and suddenly with the sureness of age-old instinct went straight to my breast…"

It was discovered later from Ruth's diary and correspondence that Ruth's adventure did not just aim at taking the first live giant panda out of China, but it was also raised to spiritual heights and even became a religious faith. She was in high spirits throughout the adventure; she liked the simplicity and beauty of Chengdu as well as the quietness and tranquility in the surrounding country; and she even fell in love with Quentin Young, a Chinese who accompanied her in search of giant pandas. Twenty-two years old only, Quentin was already one of the most accomplished explorers and biologists who worked in China at that time. He was also Ruth's greatest help during the course of hunting for giant pandas.

Later Ruth named this baby panda "Sulin," after Quentin Young's elder brother's wife. As Quentin Young was working for the Academia Sinica in Nanjing at that time, he chose to stay in the mountainous area in Wolong and continue his work to find more traces of giant pandas. With Sulin in her arms, Ruth had to say farewell to her lover and finally took the panda out of China in the name of "a Pekingese that she will carry in person"; hence Sulin became the first giant panda to have left China. When Sulin arrived at the American coast by sea, it was the Christmas Day. She gave much rare pleasure to the American people still trapped in the Great Depression. The Americans celebrated this exceedingly happy event in a special way and the Explorers' Club in New York held a welcome ceremony in honor of Sulin. When Sulin was on exhibit at Brookfield Zoo in Chicago, Americans went from far and near to have a look at her; Helen Keller, a famous blind woman writer, also traveled a long distance just to touch her for a moment. It was a pity that Sulin lived a life of less than two years and died of pneumonia on April 1, 1938. It was after dissection that Sulin was discovered to be a "he" instead of "she." …What is worthy of mention is that Ruth Harkness died in Pittsburgh, USA on July 20, 1947 and to fulfill her last wish—"I shall return to China, to the country that gave me so much of its kindness, its friendliness, its hospitality; to the country whose generosity allowed a blundering foreigner to leave with a baby Giant Panda"—her offspring brought her husband's and her ashes to China in 2002 and buried them permanently on the land that they had explored more than sixty years before.

Giant pandas can survive such a long history of evolution and exist till today, which shows that they have an indomitable life force. But, due to environmental and historical factors, they are now faced with the danger of extinction. Among the unfavorable factors, the internal one is the high specialization of food and eating habits, breeding and baby-raising habits, and the extrinsic one is the damaging of their habitat, which was partitioned off from each other like isolated islands and resulted in the division of the animal community, the practice of inbreeding, and the degeneration of the whole species. The other factors include the shortage of their staple food, bamboos, panda hunting by humankind, the assaults of their natural enemies, and the plaguing of diseases. All of them constitute a serious threat against the existence of giant pandas and put them in peril of extinction.

In 1961, Peter Scott and a group of scientists and environmentalists gathered in Geneva, Switzerland and planned to establish a foundation aimed at preventing the deterioration of natural environment, that is, World Wildlife Fund (WWF). At the moment, a giant panda named "Xi Xi" was on exhibition in the Zoo of London in Britain. Peter Scott drew the emblem of what was to become the biggest non-governmental environmental protection organization in the world by modeling it after Xi Xi, that is, a giant panda slightly holding up its head and looking at humankind half suspiciously. From then on, giant pandas have been regarded as the emblem of China and the world movement for the protection of natural environment and the salvation of endangered animals as well. WWF is the earliest organization to cooperate with China in the protection of and research on giant pandas; at present, it is also the most influential environmental protection organization in the world. Peter Scott believes that as far as human feelings are concerned, the protection of giant pandas is very important; if giant pandas should disappear ever and forever, humankind would feel that the world would become infinitely empty. In terms of ecology, giant pandas are an indicator species; that is to say, where 1000 giant pandas live, there are probably 1000 golden monkeys, 1000 takins, 1000 giant salamanders, and many other animals such as tigers, leopards, golden eagles, musk deer, muntjacs, and golden pheasants. The habitat of all these animals is composed of precipitous mountains and dense forests, which, characterized by biological diversity, serve as a natural screen for hundreds of millions of inhabitants in the Yangtze River Basin and the Yellow River Basin. The effort to protect the last 1000 wild giant pandas, therefore, is also an effort to protect human beings themselves.

Inside Chengdu Research Base of Giant Panda Breeding, the ecological environment in the wild is reproduced and conditions fit for the living and breeding of giant pandas and many other rare animals are created and maintained by scientists. Here bamboos and trees are luxuriant, birds are singing, and flowers are in full bloom—it is a combination of natural scenery in the wild and beautiful artificial landscape. There are usually over twenty giant pandas as well as some lesser pandas, black-necked cranes, and white cranes living in captivity here. In terms of the number of captive-bred or –raised giant pandas, the Research Base is second to none in the world.

Danny was most excited when having his photos taken with a giant panda. That lovely naïve-looking giant panda was only half a year old, but it did not bother to behave itself while sitting on Danny's lap; and it seemed so strong that he could hardly hold it in his arms. I only took three precious photos and felt much regret for failing to take more. Yet, these three photos were already enough to put Danny at the center of attention and make him extremely proud for quite a long time after our return to the USA. The day when school began, the principal of Danny's school announced—as if it were very important news—through wired television to nearly one thousand students and their parents in the classrooms: "I'm pleased to share with you something that we should be very proud of. During the spring break, fourth-grade student Danny and his father paid a visit to the hometown of giant pandas—Chengdu and there, he even had his photos taken with a giant panda in his arms. Amazing, isn't it!…" When the photos of Danny with a giant panda in his arms showed on the screen, a storm of applause and emotional exclamations arose inside the classrooms.

On November 10, 2005, the Zoo of San Diego in the USA named a baby panda of 100 days old "Sulin," which had been voted out on the Internet by over 70,000 Americans. As if by magic, 67 years after the unforgettable and sorrowful death of Sulin, his name was readopted by another giant panda. The younger Sulin's great-grandmother is Bai Yun (White Cloud), who was sent to San Diego from Chengdu in 1996, her grandmother is Hua Mei, who was born in 1999, and her mother is Mei Sheng, who was born in August, 2003 and whose Chinese name means "born in America" or "beautiful life." She was named after the deceased Sulin for the purpose of commemorating the first giant panda that Ruth Harkness brought to the USA and signifying the continuance of the giant panda fairy tale between China and America as well…

When we got out of Chengdu Research Base of Giant Panda Breeding, we saw a striking and touching poster, which urges people to care about endangered animals by a simple line, "We CANNOT LOSE THEM!" On the poster, a lifelike giant panda looks at us with a baby-like expression in the eyes, so timid yet alive with longing to get close to human beings. With their innocent, baby-like and pure, gentle and simple nature, giant pandas have won the heart of human beings who treasure them like pets.

Chengdu is the cradle of Chinese Taoism and Yin and Yang are the central principles of Taoism. According to Taoism, black and white are two opposing extremes in nature that, nevertheless, form a balance and a unity. These characteristics are most obviously embodied in the appearance of giant pandas. Giant pandas thus take on a magic charm; their mildness and placidity are so fascinating that people cannot help but like them, love them, and remember them; everyone who has seen a giant panda will surely be touched emotionally.

In the USA, many people may not necessarily know the name of "Chengdu," but no one does not know "giant panda." Giant pandas are the generous gifts that nature has given to Chengdu; they symbolize the protection of wild animals all over the world and more importantly, the love for all living creatures. The effort to save giant pandas not just aims at avoiding the tragic extinction of beautiful things, it also bears the hope of humankind to save the earth and the human race as well. As Mr. Shaler, a zoologist, said, giant pandas have no history but a past. They come from another Age and meet us for a short time. A giant panda brings countless strangers into contact with each other. They form heart-to-heart ties with each other and they are ties of love for giant pandas…

Giant pandas are the best calling card and trademark of Chengdu; every year, millions of people are attracted by giant pandas to spend their holidays here, go sightseeing here, make investments here and even settle here permanently. The reason is that for people around the world, the charm of giant pandas cannot be replaced by anything else. When people are fed up with crowded and monotonous cement buildings and excessive cold glass walls, they will, above all, seek for oases and animals that can be seen, history and culture that can be touched; they are in need of an ecological and cultural environment in which they can walk around and feel the vitality of life and the appeal of living.

Li Bai (701-762), a famous poet in the Tang Dynasty (617-907), described Chengdu of more than 1000 years ago as follows: "Chengdu is a city carved out in the Ninth Heaven / And looks like a beautiful picture dotted with thousands of households." I do not know whether giant pandas appeared in the "beautiful picture" or not, but Chengdu is really a city that ties up with giant pandas in countless ways, which is unparalleled in the world.

Tips:

Chengdu not only boasts abundant tourism resources, it is also an important travel route dak: for tourists who go to the Jiuzhaigou Scenic Area, the Yellow Dragon Scenic Resort, Leshan Giant Buddha, Sanxingdui Ruins in Guanghan, the Dazu Grottoes, the Three Gorges (Qutang Gorge, Wu Gorge and Xiling Gorge) of the Yangtze River, Tibet and other places, Chengdu is an important stopover. There are also many places around Chengdu where it only takes one day to go sightseeing, for example, Shiling Town, Luodai Town, and Longquan Town in the east, Huanglongxi Ancient Town, Xinjin County, and Pujiang County in the south, Dayi County, Qionglai City, Pixian County, and Dujiangyan City in the west, and Pengzhou City, Xindu District, and Jintang County in the north.

Transportation:

By airplane:
There are flights from almost every big city in China to Chengdu, including many direct ones from Beijing, Shanghai, Guangzhou, Xi'an, and Hongkong to Shuangliu International Airport in Chengdu. There are also direct flights to Chengdu from Los Angeles in USA, Vancouver in Canada, London in Britain, Paris in France, Seoul in South Korea, Bangkok in Thailand, New Delhi in India, Sydney and Melbourne in Australia, Tokyo, Nagoya, and Hiroshima in Japan.
Website: www.cdairport.com

By train:
Every day Chengdu Railway Station sees the comings and goings of nearly 100 trains, which can reach almost every big or medium-sized city in China and work best to provide tourists with a view of sceneries along the way.
Website: www.chengdustation.com

Where to see giant pandas:

The Panda Adventure Website:
It is a website that combines information, popular science, academic studies, entertainment, business affairs, and tourism. As the most authoritative website on giant pandas in the world, it enables people to get up-to-date information on the living and breeding of giant pandas as well as the researches on and protection of giant pandas.
Website: www.pandaworld.cn

Chengdu Research Base of Giant Panda Breeding:
It is the best place to see giant pandas. Established in 1987, it possesses living quarters in imitation of wildlife habitat for adult giant pandas, adolescent ones, newborn ones, lesser pandas, and other rare animals, in addition to open laboratories and research buildings with advanced equipments and complete auxiliary facilities. With an area of 35 hectares, it is going to be expanded to 200 hectares. By 2005, there had been nearly 50 births of captive-bred giant pandas. Over 30 giant pandas receive visitors on a regular basis.

Address: Giant Panda Avenue, Mount Futou, the northern suburb, Chengdu
Phone: 028-83516748
Website: www.panda.org.cn

Chengdu Zoo:
With an area of 18 hectares, the zoo presents a tempting view with shady green trees. There are over 30 animal quarters, gardens, enclosures, lakes, and ponds of various descriptions inside the zoo. More than 3000 animals of over 300 varieties are on regular exhibition; and among them, there are over 10 giant pandas of different ages. As a zoo with the most giant pandas reared in captivity, Chengdu Zoo leads the world in terms of captive breeding of giant pandas. Among the ten big zoos in China, which include Beijing Zoo, Shanghai Zoo, and Guangzhou Zoo, Chengdu Zoo ranks fourth.
Address: Chengdu Zoo, the northern suburb, Chengdu
Phone: 028-83516953
Website: www.cdzoo.com.cn

The Giant Panda Research Center in Wolong Nature Reserve:
Located in Wolong Nature Reserve, northwest of Chengdu, this giant panda reserve with the largest area in China is the earliest of its kind. About 10% of the wild giant pandas in the world—or more specifically, about 100—and about 30% of the captive-bred or –raised ones in the world—that is, 44—live inside the reserve. From 1991 to 2000, there had been 50 captive-bred giant pandas in 34 births, of which 33 survived. Wolong Nature Reserve has not only taken effective measures to protect wild giant pandas and stabilize the number of communities, but also has made a great breakthrough in captive breeding of giant pandas.
Address: Wolong Nature Reserve, Sichuan (a three hours' ride from Chengdu)
Phone: 0837-6246754
Website: www.chinawolong.com

Main roads and streets in Chengdu:
The principal road: South People's Road
In New York, everybody knows Broadway; and in Chengdu, there is no reason for local inhabitants not to know South People's Road and Tianfu Square. South People's Road is the thoroughfare of Chengdu, lined on either side by tall trees rising high into the sky, with dense shades able to blot out the sun. Along the road stand Sichuan History Museum, Sichuan Athletics Center, West China University of Medical Sciences, Jinjiang Hotel, Minshan Hotel, and many other office buildings. The vehicle traffic on this straight main road tops all the roads and streets in Chengdu and it is a must route for a drive from the airport to downtown Chengdu.

The most plebeian street: South Qingshiqiao Street
South Qingshiqiao Street is the biggest consumer goods market in Chengdu, full of agricultural and secondary products. Pork, vegetables, seafood, non-staple foodstuffs, flowers, birds, and everything are available here and urban inhabitants are seen to be bargaining with peasants cheerfully. When you see people sauntering through the street with a shopping basket or a rice bag

in the hand, you will surely think that such a lively and bustling scene is the truest panoramic reflection of common people's life in Chengdu.

The most fashionable street: Fangcao Street
"Fangcao" means fragrant grass, which may arouse a pleasant association in your mind: fragrant grass grows everywhere in this street. As a matter of fact, it was originally a plot of land used for the cultivation of flowers and grass, but as the times have changed, now it is an important place of consumption for white-collar workers, where teahouses, restaurants, and beauty salons cluster together. Here you will fully experience the romantic appeal of the Chengdu people's modern life as well as the most fashionable lifestyle in Chengdu.

The most classic street: The Wide Alley
Walking into the Wide Alley, you will feel as if the wheel of time was turned back to the years past. Bungalows, gates with two or four door leaves, and motley rusty spots quietly tell their own histories. Seat stones flank the gates, whose lintels are carved with mascots such as pumpkins and fingered citrons. Cage birds are singing under the eaves of many households and may remind you of young diehards of the Qing Dynasty (1616-1911) who wear a single long pigtail and a long gown, sing ditties, and engage themselves in aviculture and cricket-fight. All the inhabitants of the quadrangles raise various kinds of plants, such as bamboos, trees, and flowers; green vines climb over low walls, which makes an elegant and alluring picture.

The most luxurious road: Qintai Road
It is the most famous "jewelry street" in Chengdu and the ancient-style and antique-flavor buildings that stand one after another on either side mostly sell gold, silver, and jade wares. The interior of the stores look splendid and aristocratic and they are the most convenient places to buy all kinds of gold and silver jewelry or curios.

The best place to go shopping: Chunxi Street
It is a street crowded with the most stores in Chengdu, the majority of which stay open from early in the morning till late into the night and sell everything that you can imagine. From the smallest souvenirs to the most extravagant name brand watches and handbags, from famous snacks of Chengdu to Häagen-Dazs ice creams, everything can be found here. If thirsty, you can have a drink in a café or a bar; if tired, you can beckon for a taxi or a tricycle. It is a street where no visitors to Chengdu will fail to go in any way.

The most intimate street: Tongren Street
This ancient street with a history of about 100 years is lined on both sides mostly by the commonest old-fashioned courtyards inhabited by the common folk. They are spacious inside and seem like another world quite different from this world. There are many small, narrow but tidy snack bars that offer a rich variety of dishes at a reasonable price. The bar keepers' smiling faces and the steaming hot food are sure to make you feel at home even if you do not have a heavy purse with you. Here you can see many things hard to be found in flourishing and busy streets: an old-fashioned store sells stout multi-layer cloth shoes; ancient books in a neat store give off the scent of ink and graceful asparagus ferns and a couple of bamboo chairs reveal the store

keeper's fine taste. Amid the steel-and-cement structures of this city, the strong atmosphere of human warmth that permeates the street can never fail to fill every family here and even every passer-by with tender feelings.

The most heartwarming road: East Binjiang Road
Everyone who has been to Binjiang Road cannot help being touched by its beauty and characteristic human warmth. Flanked by shady green trees and luxuriant grass, the Fu-Nan River flows at leisure. Although the artificial sceneries of systematic and orderly design cannot excel nature, the road can still be counted the best place to return to nature in a big city where cold armored concrete buildings stand in great numbers. Every morning or evening, you can see many a warm and romantic scene on Binjiang Road: some people in casual clothes are practicing shadowboxing; some are dancing in foxtrot to a light music; some are strolling about side by side, chatting about something about themselves or others; the young are supporting the old by the arm, and adults are leading children by the hand. All of them compose a warm picture scroll of human life.

The most officialized street: Duyuan Street
There are several thousand streets in Chengdu, of which Duyuan Street is probably the most officialized and the most legendary. Since the Ming Dynasty (1368-1644), or more specifically, 1748, Duyuan Street has been the political center of Sichuan and now it is the seat of Sichuan Provincial People's Government and Sichuan People's Congress.

The wealthiest street: Zongfu Street
It is the most famous commercial center in Chengdu. Subsidiary banks or small local branches of all the big banks in China crowd the street; Red Flag Department Store, Parkson Shopping Center, Pacific Department Store, Wangfujing Department Store, East Wind Department Store, and the like line the street one after another. Bills flow much faster than a compact bill counter runs nonstop, and you can well imagine how much wealth converges in this street.

Scenic spots near Chengdu fit for a one-day tour:

Leshan Giant Buddha:
A sitting statue of Maitreya sculpted on a riverside cliff of Peak Qixia in Mount Lingyun, it is located in the eastern suburb of Leshan City, 160 kilometers south of Chengdu, where the Minjiang River, the Qingyijiang River, and the Dadu River converge. Started in 713, the sculpting of the statue took more than 90 years. Cut from the precipice, overlooking the river, the Giant Buddha has a well-proportioned figure and a solemn expression. It is 71 meters tall, with a head 10 meters wide, two ears 7 meters long for each, a nose 5.6 meters long, two eyebrows 5.6 meters long for each, two eyes 3.3 meters long for each, two shoulders 28 meters wide in total, ten fingers 8.3 meters long for each, two insteps 8.5 meters wide for each, and 1021 chignons. There is enough room for more than 100 people to sit on the Buddha's insteps. It has a reputation for being the biggest stone Buddha in the world. About it there is a popular saying: "A mountain is a Buddha, and a Buddha is a mountain."
How to get there: There are long-distance buses to Leshan City from Chengdu Railway Station; all local travel agencies also provide tourists with sightseeing buses to Leshan City.

Luodai Town:
The ancient town of Luodai was built during the rule of the kingdom of Shu Han (221-263), one of the Three Kingdoms (222-280). Of the town population, more than 20000 are Hakka, who speak Hakka, a dialect with some of the phonological features of ancient Chinese. Walking in the town, you will feel the presence of a strong Hakka tradition. There are many fine and ingenious architectural complexes, mainly quadrangle in structure with one entrance. Among them the best known are Guangdong Guildhall, Jiangxi Guildhall, and the like. Besides, you may go and visit Fengyi Hall, the museum, the church, and other ancient buildings.
How to get there: Buses to Luodai, which is located about 20 kilometers from downtown Chengdu, departs every few minutes from Wuguiqiao bus station in Chengdu.

Huanglongxi Ancient Town:
Situated in Shuangliu County, about 40 kilometers southeast of Chengdu, it is an ancient town in west Sichuan with a history of over 1700 years. In the ancient town, architectures of the Ming and Qing Dynasties can be found everywhere in good preservation. Streets paved with bluestone slabs, pavilions and houses with wooden pillars and cyan tiles, balustrades and muntins with delicate carvings, all give visitors an impression of primitive simplicity and tranquility. There are 6 big banyan trees, aged more than 1000 years, which, still in leafy profusion, add an aura of immortality and much vitality to the ancient town. The Zhenjiang Temple, the Chaoyin Temple, and the Gulong Temple are three ancient temples in good keep. The ancient street, deep and quiet, wriggles its way through the town, and on either side there are quite a few small restaurants. Milled bean jelly here is very famous, but the town's highlights are its teahouses, which, with their bamboo tables, chairs and stools set on the roadside and river banks or under bamboo groves, make a fascinating view.
How to get there: Every day there are buses to Huayang County from New South Gate bus station in Chengdu and from Huayang County tourists can take a bus to Huanglongxi Town. All travel agencies in Chengdu provide tourists with sightseeing buses to Huanglongxi Town.

Jiezichang Town
Jiezichang Town is located at the foot of Mount Fengqi, back of Mount Qingcheng, and 25 kilometers northwest of Chongzhou City. It boasts the delicate charm of rivers and the sublime beauty of mountains, as well as the historical charm of 32 ancient temples of the Tang Dynasty with the Guangyan Buddha Hall at the center; therefore it may be said that natural sceneries and human culture fuse into one here. The old houses in today's Jiezichang are mostly relics dating back to the Ming and Qing Dynasties. Yulong Bridge is a beauty spot worthy of special attention. There are over ten tall gingko trees standing in leafy profusion by the main dam at the entrance to the town, near Yulong Bridge. A red tower, which was built with great care during the last years of the Qing Dynasty, rises high beside the gingkoes, and every time a mountain wind arises, the copper bell on the tower will ring melodiously; ancient people called towers like this "Word Banks." Jiezichang is a place alive with legends about hermits. According to *A General History of China*, Zhu Yunwen, son of Zhu Yuanzhang, the first emperor of the Ming Dynasty, disappeared mysteriously for a time; and scholars' textual research shows that he actually lived in seclusion near the Shanggu Temple in Guangyan Buddha Hall in Jiezichang Town.
How to get there: There are buses to Jiezichang Town from Jinsha bus station in Chengdu.

The Ancient City of Hibiscus:
It lies in Yongning Town, Wenjiang District, in the western suburb of Chengdu. The inhabitants live in traditional quadrangles that are linked with one another by corridors. A moat winds its way under the tall city walls and on its banks you can see the supple twigs and tender leaves of weeping willows, fragrant flowers in full bloom and hear the singing of birds. Inside the ancient city, the main street is paved with bluestone slabs and flanked with ancient-style and antique-flavor restaurants, teahouses, and snack bars. The layout of streets inside the city is modeled on that of the Ming and Qing Dynasties and the Imperial City, the Mingyuan Building, the Zhigong Hall and other famous traditional architectures of Old Chengdu have been reproduced. In the evening glow, horse-drawn carriages can bring passers-by into the artistic world of countless poems on dusk; crisscross alleys and slabs of flagstones remind them of the lingering charm of ancient times; and they also see brooks and lakes, big or small, that artfully surround the quadrangles.
How to get there: It takes a bit more than ten minutes to get there by car from the Second Ring Road in Chengdu and tourists can also take Bus No. 89 or Bus No. 1 from Jinsha.

Main hotels in downtown Chengdu:

Five-star hotels:
Jinjiang Hotel: No. 80, Section 2, South People's Road, Chengdu
  Phone: 028-85582222
Holiday Inn Crown Plaza Hotel: No. 31, Zongfu Street, Chengdu
  Phone: 028-86786666
Sheraton Chengdu Lido Hotel: No. 15, Section 1, Central People's Road, Chengdu
  Phone: 028-86768999
California Garden Hotel: No. 258, Shawan Street, Chengdu
  Phone: 028-87649999
Chengdu Sofitel Wanda Hotel: No. 15, Central Binjiang Road, Chengdu
  Phone: 028-66808989

Four-Star hotels:
Sichuan Minshan Hotel: No. 63, Section 2, South People's Road, Chengdu
  Phone: 028-85583333
Sichuan Hotel: No. 31, Zongfu Street, Chengdu
  Phone: 028-86755555
Galaxy Dynasty Hotel: No. 99, Xiaxi Shuncheng Street, Chengdu
Phone: 028-86618888
Chengdu Tibet Hotel: No. 10, Section 1, North People's Road, Chengdu
  Phone: 028-83183388
Chengdu Tianren Hotel: No. 18, Sandongqiao Street, Chengdu
Phone: 028-87731111

Jack Quian

Three-star hotels:
Chengdu Hotel: No. 29, Section 2, Central People's Road, Chengdu
Phone: 028-83173888
Chengdu Jinhe Hotel: No. 18, Jinhe Street, Chengdu
  Phone: 028-86642888
Chengdu Pearl International Hotel: No. 329, Section 2, North Liberation Road, Chengdu
  Phone: 028-86429188
New Shulian Hotel: No. 17, West Northern Railway Station Road, Chengdu
  Phone: 028-83172222
Qintai Hotel: No. 2, Qingyangzheng Street, Chengdu
  Phone: 028-86149099

11. A Relaxing City

Lu You, a great Chinese poet of the Song Dynasty (960-1279), once wrote: "Newly-sprung willow leaves are brushing against the window, which reminds me first and foremost of the upper reaches of Jinjiang River." Situated in the upper reaches of the Jinjiang River is none other than the city of Chengdu. During the Han Dynasty (206 B.C.-200 A.D.), Chengdu boasted a thriving silk brocade industry which became an important source of tribute and taxes for the present emperors of China. Since then, Chengdu has been nicknamed "a city of brocade." In Chinese dictionaries, the character "jin" is not only the shortened name of brocade, but also used to describe ways of life in such idioms as "gay with bouquets of flowers and piles of brocades", "an age of charm and beauty like brocades", "an extravagant life with brocade clothes and precious food" and "a future as splendid as brocades."

Permeated by such a hopeful and happy atmosphere, this city surely possesses many unforgettable things. If this is the first time that you have been here or if you can only pay a whirlwind visit to this city, I recommend a place of interest that you should see by all means. If you fail to go, you will surely miss a chance to learn about the past and present of Chengdu and the unique and leisurely way of life there. And I hope everyone blessed with an opportunity to come to Chengdu will not head for hotels or elsewhere upon debarkation but directly for this street: Jinli Street, a small place that will fill your mind with amazing things.

It was on the second day that Danny and I went to Jinli Street. It is not a long street, but it reminds me of Kawaramachi Sanjo in Kyoto, and Odaiba Shopping Street in Tokyo. All of them are imbued with antique flavors, packed with stores and handicrafts of every description, and are busy with people coming and going all the time. But I feel Jinli is more agreeable, more classic, and more typical of Chinese culture, especially because it savors the strong historical appeal of what the Chinese call the "Three Kingdoms". Later on I will explain in detail about the Three Kingdoms, for that historical period has everything to do with Jinli. Many foreign people know of Chengdu, but they have never heard of Jinli Street; and many Chinese people know of Jinli, but not all of them have actually walked into the street…

Jinli was one of the oldest and most commercial streets in the history of Chengdu. In some sense, it is Chengdu's historical memory bank. Currently, this street is built in the style of a town typical of the Ming and Qing Dynasties, producing the great charm of the local traits and folkways of the Kingdom of Shu. Under the high roofed entrance to the street, there are two pitch-black four-meter-tall gates, and over them a horizontal board of the same color, on which are inscribed two shiny and bright golden Chinese characters, "Jinli." The gates appear dignified and imposing and some doornails are about the size of a fist, each arranged neatly into dozens of lines, as if loyal sentinels of ancient times were conscientiously standing on guard at the city gate. The gray brick wall blends into one integral whole with the entrance gates, overwhelming us with a strong flavor of culture. The moment we walked through the entrance gates, it was as if all of a sudden time turned backwards through thousands of years, and for a while, we felt at a loss for where we were. It felt as if we had crossed history, penetrated winds

Jack Quian

and clouds, and were standing on a path unwilling to move on. Looking up, we saw one house after another—with dark cyan tile roofs and black balustrades—stretching onwards like radiant rays and colorful narrow flags with names of various stores printed on them—some are rich and gaudy, and others simple but elegant—fluttering in the breeze, making a splendid view. Looming in the distant section of the path were bamboo groves, lotus leaves, and light smoke as well—these green plants with twisted roots and gnarled branches were growing as freely as the flood, quietly threatening to drown everything. I was in a daze; Has our era crossed the time tunnel to the remote past? Or have the ancient times moved through cyclic eras to occupy the present?

Adjacent to Jinli Street, the Wuhou Temple is one of the most famous museums in Chengdu,(built in memory of Liu Bei, the first king of Shu Han and Zhuge Liang, its prime minister in the Three Kingdoms period (208-280)). Of China's long history of about 5000 years, why do the people of Chengdu only have eyes for this period of nearly 80 years? It is due to the historical novel *The Romance of the Three Kingdoms*—well-known among the Chinese people, both old and young—and particularly to the fact that Prime Minister Zhuge Liang, who wore a black silk ribbon scarf on the head and held a feather fan in the hand, has been regarded as a model of loyalty and intelligence. A great deal of literature and historical relics relevant to him are on display in the museum, and as a result, the Three Kingdoms has become the historical period with which the Chinese people are most familiar.

Undoubtedly, the Wuhou Temple is one of the places that display Chinese masculinity to the utmost. A single Wuhou Temple is enough to do justice to the history and intensity of the tripartite confrontation between the Kingdoms of Wei, Shu Han, and Wu. How many later generations—especially men—have been stimulated to yearn, to decide, and to establish themselves in life and make contributions to society?

Walking on the alley in Jinli, you will be deeply impressed by this "Three Kingdoms complex" of the locals; yet in the meantime, you can feel a sort of feminine elegance and harmony. As you walk on and on, through the reproduced folk customs and living conditions of the Three Kingdoms, under your feet is the mark of history imperceptibly left by time: following a winding bluestone flagging, you will see manor houses, mansions, common residents' houses, inns, stores, and stages on both sides, with black tiles arranged in perfect order on the roofs—all of them fuse into one, with the architecture of the Wuhou Temple dating back to the Qing Dynasty. Along the way, the everyday life of local people in the history of Chengdu will be presented to you in its original form. While lingering and contemplating, you will see a ricksha passing you; while looking around at leisure you will hear the singing of birds and smell the scent of tea. You will feel a delicate fragrance floating everywhere: taverns, inns, opera houses, pawnshops, embroideries, bamboo-woven articles, silk brocades, lanterns, black tiles, gray walls, lichens, bamboos, and what not. Walking on such an alley with a quiet antique flavor, you will come upon Sichuan tea, Sichuan dishes, Sichuan liquors, Sichuan medicine, Sichuan opera, famous snacks, and handicrafts, which represent the quintessence of Shu culture. You feel as if you are in the midst of an ancient marketplace in Chengdu. You will see hawkers set down their *dandan* (carrying poles with its load) call out and try to sell various kinds of local snacks: *tanghua* (sugar paintings), *guokui* (somewhat like scones), *zhengzhenggao* (steamed corn flour cakes), and etc. With a little money, you can not only taste such typical local delicacies as *niurou jiaobing* (Chinese crispy bread with beef) and *sandapao* (a bunch of three pellets made with three sounds from cooked glutinous rice paste), whose aroma lingers on your lips and teeth, but also purchase combs from *Tan Mujiang* (Carpenter Mr. Tan's Store), chopsticks from *Yunhong* (Rhythmic Pond), ancient-looking painted potteries from *Qingyaxuan* (Elegance Store), and batik clothing from *Yelang* (name of a small ancient state in China).

In front of a stand which sold clay figurines, Danny handed over the money and took a lifelike figurine of Sun Wukong (the Monkey King) from the old craftsman. I went closer and observed the row of clay figurines on the rack: red-faced broadsword-wielding Guan Gong, feather-fan-shaking stratagem-minded Kongming (another name of Zhuge Liang), charmingly naive pig-headed Zhu Bajie, flower-burying Daiyu, the inferior-to-no-man heroic woman Mulan, and so on. All of a sudden, life seemed to be breathed into these clay figurines, who were performing dramatic pieces about the First Qin Emperor of the Qin Dynasty (221-206 B.C.) and Emperor Han Wu of the Han Dynasty before my eyes. In front of Zhuge Well, a group of girls in printed-cloth dresses and sleeveless flaxen jackets were clapping their hands and chanting something—the game of "floral-basket-weaving," which had disappeared from memory for a very long time, now reappeared right before our eyes. Here adults were reminiscing about their bygone childhoods, while children were taking pleasure in such past curiosities. I could tell by the tourists' accents that they were from France, Japan, and Germany, and of course, there were more English-speaking tourists. Such a spectacle made a stronger impact on them than on Chinese visitors, so everyone of them kept their digital cameras or video cameras working nonstop.

Danny was a fourth-grade primary school student in the USA and I should say, he knew nothing about Chinese history, which, however, did not impede his finding so much delight in a toy called *Zhuge liannu* (a repeating crossbow allegedly invented by Zhuge Liang) that he could hardly bear to put it down! Every time he shot, he would shout excitedly, "I almost hit the red mark!" The then *Zhuge liannu* had been developed into a toy crossbow. My son took so much interest in this ancient weapon—which could fire ten arrows at once—that he played one game after another and even insisted on bringing one back to America. And there was another kind of toy *xianghuang* (the Chinese yo-yo), which he had never seen before. It consists of two palm-sized thin wooden discs, which form a "little drum" with several grooves inset in the rim and a two-*cun*-long (a Chinese unit of length, 3 *cun* = 10 centimeters) stick connected to the center, and around the stick coils a flaxen string tied to two bamboo sticks. To play *xianghuang*, you should use the string to catch the wooden axle, winding and shaking, until the unwinding force causes *xianghuang* to spin. While spinning, wind will steal through the grooves in the rim of the "little drum" and result in *xianghuang* making a whistling sound. As the hawker shook the string, *xianghuang* jumped and droned overhead like a marble. Danny gazed at it with wonder and did not even bother to blink his eyes. He watched the hawker making *xianghuang* leap over the string onto one of the bamboo sticks and then climb upwards along the bamboo stick. "It's called, "A monkey climbing a tree'," the hawker explained and then bent down, and the "monkey" returned to the string, spinning rapidly from the lower end of the vertical string onto the upper end. "It's called 'An ant climbing a tree'!" *Xianghuang* was jumping and whistling, like a pigeon with a whistle, leading my son into another kind of magical wonderland. Here in Jinli, out-of-towners can view historical specimens of the urban residents' everyday life in Chengdu while locals will be brought back to the hoop-trundling and *xianghuang*-spinning past. Here, life in the past can be slowly wound backwards like a videotape for you to watch…

This ancient-style street evokes old memories, and the wooden benches along the street may remind you of their ancient owners and fill you with a profound sadness. In a primitively simple but elegant store named *Baixing Xungen Tang* (Seeking the Roots of Hundreds of Family Surnames), you can find out information about your roots and ancestors. After you have stated your surname, you will be told that hundreds and even thousands of years ago, one of your ancestors was actually a king or a duke under an emperor who ruled a certain region. In the store, you can hear a hubbub of voices asking about ancestors in order to find out where their roots and hearts lie. As a matter of fact, one's root lies right under one's feet, but no one seems willing to think so. Outside by the window, a *jigong* cart (a wheelbarrow in the shape of a cock's head) leans quietly against the foot of a wall, though its squeaks seem to linger by your ears to the accompaniment of *suona* horns.

Without being informed beforehand, we were invited to attend a wedding ceremony so we went into Jinli Hotel, a hotel with antique flavors halfway through Jinli Street. This hotel is a three-building complex based on the architectural style of the late Qing Dynasty and the early Republic of China (1912-1949), composed of *Kezhan* (the hotel proper), *Yinlu* (the secluded cottage), and *Furong* (the hibiscus mansion), each with its distinctive features. Walking into the courtyard you will see winding corridors and lanes, lesser courtyards, flower gardens, rockeries rising aloft, green trees affording umbrage, and streams murmuring, all of which constitute a tranquil and serene environment amidst the hustle and bustle of Jinli Street. The interior of the hotel is decorated with a simple, classic and elegant taste and equipped with whole sets of antique-like mahogany furniture. How could anyone expect to see such a classically beautiful and tranquil hotel in such a busy street? The wedding ceremony looked like a traditional Chinese one. The bridegroom was an Englishman and the bride, a girl from Chengdu. They rode an archaic ricksha into the courtyard. A lively and jolly atmosphere prevailed the wedding site where everyone present was brimming over with smiles on their faces. By Chinese tradition, the bride stayed in her "boudoir" dressing herself and waiting. When a party escorted the bridegroom in Chinese-style red gown into the bride's "boudoir" to meet the bride, he was deliberately "obstructed" by many of the bride's relatives. When at last the emcee chanted loudly, "Kowtow to the bride's parents, please," the groom, who did not understand Chinese, foolishly took it as having nothing to do with him and was about to leave. Amid the laughter of the crowd who stopped him, the bride happily kowtowed thrice, presented tea to the bride's parents, and ate *tangyuan* (boiled glutinous rice dumplings). All was going on perfectly by Chinese tradition in the purest sense.

Amid the crowd's excited loud voice and laughter, my mobile phone rang unexpectedly, which helped me to escape just in time the wining and dining at the wedding reception following the ceremony. Danny and I walked out of the hotel gate and I told my American friend who could speak fluent Chinese that he should by all means stay at Jinli Hotel when he came to Chengdu again. He asked, "Where are you?" I answered, "I'm in Jinli," and he shouted in great astonishment, "How on earth did you fall into a well (Jingli)? Do you need any help?" I had such a good laugh that I almost dropped my mobile phone onto the ground. You see, a minimal variation in the pronunciation of Chinese characters can lead to a tremendous difference in meaning.

Not far ahead of Jinli Hotel, an ancient-style handicraft workshop named *Zhuoshang* Silk Workshop was crowded with visitors watching the making of brocades. Brocades are a kind of silk fabric made of thousands of mulberry silkworm cocoons. In ancient China, only emperors and kings, generals and ministers, and the rich were entitled to use brocades. In making silks of the highest quality and brocades as colorful as a rainbow, washing and drying the cocoons in the sun are the most important steps. We saw a wooden cooker with a diameter of about two meters over a stone stove and in it cocoons were piled high above the brim. The workshop keeper steamed the cocoons with burning charcoal till well done, then macerated them in some water, and finally tore apart these finger-sized steamed cocoons. There were several female silk workers in blue homespun garments standing around the wooden bucket. They were tearing apart those cocoons skillfully and then pulling and stretching them out to the length of about one *chi* (a Chinese unit of length, 3 *chi* = 1 meter). Then they would be dried in the sun and separated into silk threads, which, eventually, would be hanged under the beam and dried in the shade. Under the wooden window at the other end of the workshop, a loom was creaking—a female brocade worker was quietly weaving dried-in-the-shade silk threads together. If you do not see for yourself, you will not know how difficult it is to weave silks into brocades. Thousands of silk filaments thinner than a hair were wound over some wooden apparatus and hundreds of threads attached to sticks kept moving up and down. This brocade-weaving task, as I saw it, was accomplished by two workers, with one of them picking filaments up above and the other weaving them together underneath. The division of labor was very clear, allowing of no mistakes. I stood there for half an hour and saw that less than half a centimeter of brocade was weaved. But all the hues of the brocade were perfectly bright and beautiful, every thread of the vivid design was visible, and the pattern and workmanship were definitely nice and exquisite. These silk filaments could be weaved into such gaily-colored brocade! I was so amazed that I could not help thinking that only God could work miracles like this.

Late in the afternoon, the glow of the setting sun wound its way through the window, showering sparks of golden light on the antiquated loom and the female worker's eyelashes that were hanging low which looked as fascinating and as a beautiful oil painting…On the wall behind her hung many silk wall hangings: pine and crane symbolizing eternal youth and longevity, peony standing for wealth and loftiness, God of Longevity presenting a peach, and the like. All these embroidered pictures are unique to China and to Chengdu as well. What an excellent idea it was to establish such a workshop: In buying a silk quilt or a silk wall hanging, you see and appreciate the ancient art of spinning and weaving that has almost vanished.

By the pond in Jinli Street, dozens of tourists gathered around a stand and burst into laughter every now and then. An American man in a red Chinese-style costume and casual jeans was drawing a portrait of a customer: a handsome young man sitting on a stool, first his eyebrows, then his eyes, nose, hair, and ears…Along with the moving of his paintbrush, a cartoonlike portrait appeared vividly before our eyes, quite exaggerated but very much alike. This American man was good at self-marketing, advertising himself as having been given the title "caricaturist" by President Bush in person. Sitting beside him was a typical girl of Chengdu, petite, elegant, and with a light brown hair. She sat there, saying no words except when tourists asked her the price. Her job was to seal her husband's paintings with plastics and receive the fee, $3 per portrait. The painter told us, he had been to many cities and his favorite was Chengdu, where he had settled permanently. "I like Jinli so much," he said with a strong Texan accent.

Beside the cartoonist's stand, there was a stand called *Jiti Chanming* (Crowing Roosters and Chirping Cicadas), with many weaved animals that made Danny linger on and on. These vivid little creatures are made from palm leaves and thin bamboo strips after a special series of steps. The little cicadas and birds can almost pass for genuine. And the straw sandals, which had been serving as laborers' shoes for thousands of years—peasants wore them to go to work in the fields, woodmen in the mountains, and craftsmen in the workshops—have become tourist's souvenirs nowadays.

On Jinli Street, the night watchman constitutes the most comical sight. He wears a turban, a short gown, a pair of riding breeches-like trousers, and straw sandals and carries a lantern and a gong. He is attired in the same way as those night watchmen who made a living by patrolling the streets and announcing the watches over half a century ago, but in the former you cannot discern any of the latter's apparent wretchedness. Nowadays, the night watchman is the most captivating of all the beauties in

Jinli. On hearing the sound of his gong approaching, countless tourists will aim their "long- or short-barreled guns" at him, who has become the most frequently photographed star in Jinli.

As we strolled through the deep alley, our view suddenly cleared up and we stopped in front of an ancient-style stage. The background of the stage was a huge facial make-up of Sichuan opera, which set us thinking of the pride of Sichuan opera: face-changing. In the middle of the stage there were two old-fashioned wooden armchairs. A most beautiful girl was playing *zheng*, an ancient Chinese zither with 25 strings, the melodious music floating in all directions. My train of thoughts ran wild, as if it had returned to the past: opera singers wore long gowns and flicked their sleeves, acting gifted scholars and beautiful ladies, emperors, kings, generals, and ministers… Although I had never watched any performances of Sichuan Opera, I could feel a certain aura that had accumulated for thousands of years spreading out slowly around the stage, merging into the air, and floating everywhere—it was the aura of "The culture of the Three Kingdoms."…This aura reminded me of Lijiang in Yunnan Province and even those alleys in Vienna…As Xintiandi (New World) in Shanghai can be said to be an artificial landscape like new wine in old bottles and a magnificent setting rooted in Shanghai's cosmopolitan culture, so Jinli is a section of Chengdu's historical memory.

At first sight Jinli may strike you as quite similar to Xintiandi, but when you take your time walking through and savoring Jinli, you will discover the deep undercurrent of the culture of the Three Kingdoms. It is exactly where Jinli differs from Xintiandi, and where Lijiang is no match for Jinli. Jinli is a page of annotations in the history textbook of Chengdu, a nostalgic map of Chengdu, and a little street in the "city of paradise" as well.

A leisurely walk through this alluring alley will intoxicate you despite yourself. When you feel tired you may sit down to have a short rest, imagining over a cup of green tea the passers-by's long life. Some of them are dancing amid the bouquet of good wine and coffee; some idling away on wooden benches, their elegant clothes flapping in the wind. It is said that because of Jinli, one will miss Chengdu in specific terms…Jinli seems to be the most beautiful at dusk: The glow of the setting sun is sparkling on roofs; lights have not been turned on; the excited noises made by tourists are dying away; and the distant sky is veiled in dull red, calling to mind what is left of the Tang Dynasty at its heyday…Life is a drama per se, with you and me acting our own parts as time fleets by.

While I was strolling through Jinli Street, the rugged bluestone flagging impressed me as an elder who had experienced ups and downs in society, highs and lows in life, and never failed to watch over his age-old home. Everything seemed to be simple, unsophisticated, and serene, just like this blue sky in spring, so deep and remote that a glance might send you into infinite reverie. I paused and looked up, seeing roofs rolling up and down on both sides; even the flag-signs of various stores—either rich and gaudy, or simple but elegant—hated to be neglected and fluttering in the breeze, they made a splendid view. But these signs had something in common: all were suffused with the interest and charm of an antique taste. I was infatuated with *Sanguo Chayuan* (Tea Garden of the Three Kingdoms), whose charm lay not only in the green tea in dainty cups, but in the natural changes in temperature brought about by the pleasantly warm sunshine and cool breeze. It is composed of a courtyard paved with flagstones and shaded by ancient banyans, where you sit beside the red wall, sipping the fragrant tea in teacups with lid and saucer, and it is said that sometimes you can even be in time for a performance of the Sichuan opera.

The inhabitants here are immensely fortunate, for the mild climate in Sichuan Basin and the altruistic irrigation by Dujiang Weirs for several thousands of years have resulted in this "paradise on earth." They are gentle, cultivated, patient, leisured, and enjoying life at their ease, yet in terms of food, they spare no effort to seek something rare, something unusual, and something special. The biggest restaurant in Jinli Street is *Sanguyuan* (Three Calls Garden) opposite the Tea Garden of the Three Kingdoms. The theme of the restaurant is based on the stories of the Three Kingdoms, to which the employees' outfits, the decorations on the tableware, the design of the menu, and even the names of the dishes all refer. The moment you enter the restaurant, you will see the floor paved with stone slabs, reddish brown small wooden compartments standing in a queue, wooden crossbeams and a gallery stretching overhead, and Chinese palace lanterns of various colors hanging under the gallery. The first course I ordered was cold dishes held in eight square bowls of three *cun*, which were subject to geometric permutations and combinations. The waitress in a costume of the Han Dynasty slightly unsealed her red lips and said: "It is called *baguazhen* (Eight-Diagram tactics)." The other courses followed the development of the stories of the Three Kingdoms: *caochuan jiejian* (borrowing arrows with straw men in boats)—a boat-like vessel with several spicy fingerlings strung together by a bamboo skewer; *kurouji* (the ruse of self-injury)—columns of balsam pears stuffed with ground meat; *dandao fuhui* (keeping an appointment with no company but one broadsword)—a broadsword-like silver carp with the head and tail off and some bok choy arranged as the Chinese character "ding" at one end; and *Kongming mantou* (spongy steamed bread), *sanzu dingli* (tripartite confrontation), *shezhan qunru* (arguing heatedly against a group of scholars), and so on. On hearing those names, my curiosity was immediately aroused and I could not wait to open the "embroidered bag of excellent stratagems" and dive into the mysteries.

Luxin Senlin Shaokao (Green Forest Grill) is a restaurant that has turned the roadside Chengdu snacks into an elegant vogue. The word "grill" may remind most locals of such a sight: at the dimly-lit roadside, pots and pans are laid out on a tricycle, and the chef-keeper is furiously fanning up the flames of the burning coal with a palm-leaf fan till the smoke floats upward to the accompaniment of the frizzling of the grill. Beside the tricycle, the customers are chewing spareribs voraciously, or savoring each morsel of a bunch of somewhat hot potatoes. The food is quite coarse, and not so hygienic, but quite delicious. So *Luxin Senlin Shaokao* has brought such tasty food into Jinli Street and put the vulgar grill into the modern atmosphere of a beautifully decorated restaurant, providing gourmands with a sanitary place where they can eat grill at ease. Seated inside, you will feel enchanted by the wonderful ambiance: decorated with antique taste, the yellow light makes you feel warm, and walking on the squeaking floor, you feel as if entering a pleasant inn. After you have ordered *boboji* (bunches of chicken in an earthen bowl), a plate of aromatic and crisp *kaopaigu* (roast spareribs), and a bowl of *jisitang* (sliced chicken soup), the ancient street outside the window takes on a new appearance: The flagging is reflecting gleams of blue light, and the lanterns on the corner tower are flickering, which look like something permanent in the past and something uproarious in modern times…

Jinli Street highlights the local traits, folkways, the grass roots, and an easy life. Various kinds of snacks all over the street feed your sight, and you can hear hawkers in traditional clothing crying out for customers—as one cry falls, another rises. Every child will be excited to eat sugar paintings which are made as follows: some refined white sugar and brown sugar plus a little maltose in a pannikin are put over a slow fire and simmered gently until the sugar is able to be pulled into filaments; the handicraftsman scoops up some syrup with a small soup ladle and trickles it back and forth over a board covered with edible oil until a painting comes into being. It requires that the handicraftsman should be quick of eye and deft of hand and his hand should move nonstop so that the painting can get done at one go. A moment's pause will result in the solidification of the syrup and one step short of success. After the completion of the painting, the handicraftsman will attach a bamboo bar to it, remove it with a small scoop, wait until it coagulates a bit, and then insert it into a straw bundle for sale. The sugar paintings in Jinli Street deal with a wide range of subjects, including characters in novels and dramas, flowers, birds, insects, fish, and beasts, either two-dimensional or three-dimensional. As the sugar syrup is a trickling liquid, there are no identical paintings even if they treat of the same subject. What an aesthetic pleasure it is to watch the handicraftsman's consummate skill and every variety of sugar paintings! The children hand the money to the hawker and then look closely at the different sugar paintings inserted in the straw bundle; after they have inly chosen their favorites, they spin the bamboo needle on the wheel excitedly and expectantly and stare at the rotating pointer with wide-open eyes…Although it is not easy to direct the pointer at their favorites, they will end in getting a sugar painting anyhow. Then they will stick their tongues out and lick up the sugar painting bit by bit…Such sugar paintings—the locals call the whole thing *zhuantangban'er* (spinning the sugar wheel)—are a kind of snack common in Chengdu's streets and lanes. Like *dandanmian* (Sichuan-style noodles with peppery sauce), *douhua'er* (bean jelly), and *bingfen'er* (a curd made from malaxis bancanoides), they are carried on the shoulder and peddled along streets. Danny dragged me and ran here and there, with a sugar-coated haw on stick in the left hand and a glutinous rice cake in the right. Poor me! While taking pictures along the way, I had to use my hands to carry for him things that are pleasant to eat, to play with, or to look at.

Chengdu snacks, such as *sandapao*, *malachuanchuan* (bunches of food with cayenne pepper cooked in hot pot), and *douhua*, are well-known in China and all of them can be found in Jinli Street. The most distinct one is *zhengzhenggao*—a snack dating back

Jack Quian

to ancient times—sold at the store at the end of the street. It was with much difficulty that we finally pushed our way to the counter and bought several *zhengzhenggao* in order to eat them to our heart's content. *Zhengzhenggao* is a cake made from corn flour plus some sugar, which is put into a very small earthen bowl, steamed for less than half a minute and then wrapped in a lotus leaf. Corn's natural sweetness, wrapped up in the delicately fragrant lotus leaf, tastes of Mother Nature. After having eaten several *zhengzhenggao*, I felt as if I had enjoyed the savor of nostalgia to the full.

Walking inward, we saw flag-signs of various colors hanging all over the street. In front of the wooden counter of a store, there was an earthen jug of good liquor. A man walked over and cried, Good liquor! I turned around and saw right before my eyes a big bearded fellow in a brown gown of the Han Dynasty, with a copper buckle on the waistband and a blackish yellow turban around the head. Carrying a broadsword, he disguised himself as Zhang Fei and shouted out: "Old gentlemen and young, as you're now in Jinli, please have a taste of the genuine beef of the Three Kingdoms era." The selling point of *Zhangfei niurou* (Zhang Fei-style beef) does not lie in the beef but in the story: tradition has it that in 215 of the Three Kingdoms era, Prefect Zhang Fei was locked in a stalemate with the enemy in Bameng Mountain, Sichuan for over fifty days, and then he caught the enemy off guard by a surprise attack from a different path and forced a disastrous defeat on the enemy. When he withdrew his troops back to Chengdu after the victory, he rewarded generals and soldiers alike with his favorite beef. Thus it was called Zhang Fei-style beef when his offspring passed down his way of cooking the beef to later generations.

Lu Zhaolin, a poet in the Tang Dynasty, once described the prosperity of Jinli like this: "A feast of fragrances is held in Jinli, / where orchid is already in full blossom early in the year. / Dense polychromes stretch toward the distant horizon, / and clusters of lighted candles adorn the remote sky." The restoration of Jinli Street not only provides the locals with one more place for rest and recreation at leisure, but more significantly, it induces fantastic reveries as it is imbued with profound historical interest and saturated with infatuating modern appeal. We happened to walk into an ancient-style building, where there was a snow-white screen wall inside the lofty curved gables and we had to walk around the screen wall before entering the house. Under the eaves were hanging many lanterns with Liu Bei, Zhao Yun and some other characters from the Three Kingdoms painted on them. Carved doors and windows, black door planks, a sign-cloth with the Chinese character "*cha* (tea)," tall columns standing on stone plinths, cyan bricks and black tiles, dripping eaves tiles, and the like, all of them gave off a strong antique charm. Midway through the alley, there was a small square paved with foursquare cyan bricks. On one side there was a screen wall, on which was engraved a very big Chinese character "*fu* (good fortune)." Around the square grew ginkgo, small-leaf fig trees and some other formed trees. Then we walked across a small stone arch bridge and saw many carvings in relief on its balustrades; underneath, a streamlet was flowing slowly past. At the end of the streamlet there was a gallery of relievos extolling Shu brocade and depicting the history of the southern Silk Road. Over this gallery there was another relievo about Shu brocade, mainly portraying the scenes of picking mulberry leaves and boiling cocoons. A bit ahead, there was a store selling *danhonggao* (baked egg cakes), a famous Chengdu snack. The pan was as big as a tea saucer, and the stove looked like a toy for playing house. I saw several pretty lean Sichuan girls busying themselves in the kitchen and felt as if they were playing house. Some of them were making baked egg cakes, and others steaming certain beef and glutinous rice cakes with a tiny bamboo steamer. Sometimes they knocked at the thick bamboo tube, and sometimes at the bamboo steamer; rat-a-tat, rat-a-tat, after several such clear and crisp sounds, the beef was done and the cakes ready to be taken out of the steamer. While deftly wrapping the beef inside green reed leaves, they uttered some cries in a clear and melodious voice, which, what a pity, I did not understand.

After who-knows-how-long, we walked past the memorial archway of the Han marketplace and entered the food section where people kept gathering and moving. Here snack bars joined with each other end to end and stretched out so far that you could not see all of them at a glimpse. There were yellow fermented glutinous wine, Juntun *guokui*, Chinese crispy bread with beef, *maojiezifen* (vermicelli made from sweet potato starch with small intestine), *tangyouguozi* (sugar-coated fried glutinous rice balls on skewers), Lezhi *guokui*, beggars' chicken (mud-coated roast chicken), Leshan *boboji* (bunches of chicken in an earthen bowl), mugwort wormwood New Year cake, *sandapao*, juicy beef balls, tortoise tuckahoe jelly, shredded hare meat, *maocai* (bunches of food with cayenne pepper cooked in soup), lotus seed porridge, teppan-yaki, lamb shashlik, glutinous rice slices with peach seed, Tianjin *goubuli* steamed stuffed bun, boiled dumpling, wonton, boiled rice dumpling, special flavor noodles, pickled spareribs, diced hare meat, and what not. I took pictures while walking past every snack bar, carefully dodging the voracious eaters. I had never heard of many of the snacks, and I seated myself and ordered a bowl of Chongzhou buckwheat noodles. This tiny bowl of noodles looked blackish and tasted pleasantly tough; the seasonings were typical of Sichuan style, with just the right kind of spicy flavor, and I felt like another bowl after wolfing it down.

I have been to some places that I forgot the moment I returned from there; meanwhile, I have been to some other places that I had looked forward to visiting before my trip and that I suppose I will never forget all my life. Jinli seems to me to be such a place that I will never be able to forget. Especially when night has fallen, some romantic touch is added to Jinli, where the shadows of lamps are flickering. And how beautiful it is when all the red lanterns are lit at the same time. Perhaps because my eye has already been stricken by all the colors, everywhere seems to be pervaded by a romantic atmosphere; not just the lights are blazing with color, but those half-open eyes wandering under the neon lamps in Jinli are identically multicolored and look like surrealist portraits. A friend of mine said, teahouses in Jinli offer customers a certain indifference to fame or gain, in addition to a pot of fragrant tea to relish a simple life in this world. Bars in Jinli, however, belong in the dim light of night. You may order a drink, miss a certain person, close your eyes, and go to your dreams of the past dynasties. At night, bars are the most dazzling places where you may hold a glass of red wine in the hand, lean on a chaise longue in the open air, take a sip, and listen to the watches approaching from or leaving for the distance...Or, you may sit at the bar counter enveloped in a dense mist of alcohol and start to fancy, to get intoxicated...

When night has fallen, the red lanterns in Jinli are hung high and lit up. Sometimes the delicate fragrance of tea floats over, and sometimes the strong redolence of coffee lingers. Restaurants are alive with a hubbub of voices, and stores are ablaze with lights. One of my friends took Danny away to his home, but I chose to stay in Jinli. Leaning against the window on the second floor of my dwelling in Jinli Hotel, with my eyes half closed, I took a sip of green tea, listened, looked, and mused with concentrated attention...For a moment, I seemed to have gone to a dreamland, maybe real, maybe imaginary, and a feeling of "being unable to tell the present from the past" drowned me all over. Such sudden trance and deep intoxication are exactly how the charm of Jinli works. The red color is an auspicious and joyful color in Chinese culture and my favorite as well. So I walked and melted into all this red...

There are bars of all descriptions in Jinli Street, and although they are modern establishments, they have no difficulty in blending in well with the ancient town. Once in Jinli, every tourist would love to go into a bar and take a seat, so bars are always crowded and jolly inside. Yet it is more agreeable to sit outside of a bar: there are several homely square tables, with two benches opposite each other and a huge red lantern hanging overhead. The bars join with one another end to end, and everyone is enjoying himself or herself to the full. Your ears are swarming with songs—either pop music or folk songs from fortified mountain villages. Everywhere is brimming over with gaiety and merriment, and everything seems so bewitching and melodious. Owing to these bars, you can find all that you want in this short street: wine, music, friends, lovers, reminiscences, and expectations...I cannot help reveling in such a place where everyone can forget all worries and immerse himself or herself in everything around...

Sifangjie (Square Street): It is a Bohemian-style bar in the likeness of an old house in Lijiang's back streets, unpretentious, natural, cleverly partitioned off by curio shelves, highlighting refined and colorful folkways, and displaying abstract historical, national, folk, and religious space-time. The customers can relish drinks and at the same time, appreciate the cultural ambience that the owner has endeavored to create; as the lamplight is waning, they can forget the secular affairs that have been bothering them and set free their unworldly hearts for the moment.

Caoyingba (Cao Cao's Camp): This bar is a combination of the quintessence of traditional Shu culture and neoclassicism's characteristic simplicity, freshness, naturalness, and decency. With a glass of whiskey with ice in the hand, you can stretch and sink yourself into a good-sized sofa under a homely ceiling fan made of palm-leaf fans. You can also let your unbridled thoughts and feelings flow along with the graceful melody while the primitive-looking leather-silhouette lamps and nostalgic CDs keep stirring your sight and sensibility...

Xingxing Shese (Travelers' Traces and Photographers' Colors): It is a bar with a photograph theme, allegedly where backpackers, photographers, car travelers, sightseers have a drink, chat, have reunions, daydream, and shoot the breeze. You can feel at home here whether you are striving hard for success or sparing no money to enjoy yourself, whether you are single or married but unwilling to return home until late into the night. It is both the starting-point and destination of many hikers, and the stopover of many people away on a journey as well. Here customers can have a spree, or take their ease and drink to no excess; they can be lazy or relaxed, quiet or crazy, sober or confused—closest to the root of human nature as it is. Lectures on traveling, movie and television previews, solo exhibitions of photographs, travelers' seminars and the like are often held here.

Chenghuang Julu (Orange-Yellow and Tangerine-Green): A poem reads like this: "The lotus has withered and its large raintight leaves also died back; / the chrysanthemum has faded, but its stalk remains in spite of frost. / Please remember the most beautiful time of the year, / that is, when oranges turn yellow and tangerines are green." Peculiar to autumn, orange-yellow and tangerine-green are the most beautiful colors of the year. The decorations inside match the name of the bar perfectly. Surrounded by a profusion of colors, there are cozy printed high-back sofas and slow nostalgic music…Take a sip of the intoxicating purified liquor, and you will feel its bouquet lingering on your lips and teeth; the smoke of the unquenched cigar in the ashtray is rising slowly, taking along what is occurring to you in a trance. In the shadow of the staircase, a huge engraved mirror hangs from the beam down to the floor. Standing before the mirror and looking around, you will feel as if the legacy of the Three Kingdoms has found its way here…

Zhujiufang (Heated Wine Club): It is inconspicuous, but it makes you feel warm; you can surely find something to your liking from the wooden storied building and tables, earthen bowls and cups, several dishes of assorted spiced and braised meat with peanuts, a goblet of *kaoliang* wine heated on the spot, and the pots and pans in the showcases. There are three bamboo wares on the windowsill—do you know what they are? A kind of measuring vessel made of bamboo and used by the common people to measure all sorts of liquid. The one used for the measuring of wine is called "*Jiutizi* (wine measure)." You walk on the circular wooden stairs up to the second floor and something catches your eye immediately: hanging on the wooden walls are capes, straw strainers, calabashes, and even a bow. Throwing the wooden window open, I enjoyed the beauty of Jinli at night; and in the meantime, I heated the green-plum wine served by the smiling proprietress, drank over a dish of green soy beans, a dish of aniseeds, and a dish of sliced dried bean curds, and felt as if I were replaying the discussion over heated wine about who were heroes in the Three Kingdoms.

The bar opposite the window is *Xifuhui*, with the English name "West Meets East." It adopts the uncomplicated style of European and American bars and offers genuine coffee ground and brewed on the spot, typical western snacks, and a variety of beverages popular in the west. Thus the simplicity and unsophistication of ancient-style Jinli Street melt into Italian-style romantic atmosphere. At a table outside of the bar, several foreigners were chatting cheerfully with several Chinese in vivid illustration of the bar's name. Looking around, I saw one bar standing after another: *Heigen* (Black Root), *Zuisanguo* (Drunk with the Three Kingdoms), and the like. It was probably the most beautiful moment in Jinli. Time elapsed amid the strong bouquet of drinks. After three cups of good wine, I felt my blood boiling, my ambition burning, and even an urge surging inside to eliminate vice and exalt virtue with my pen and voice my opinions on governmental and political affairs.

More than 2,000 years ago, Zhuo Wenjun, who led a life of narrow means after elopement, was drawing water from an age-old well in Chengdu to heat wine, and at her side, Sima Xiangru was brushing up books in preparation for the imperial examinations. Deeply moved by the poem "A Male Phoenix Wooing a Female One" written to her by Sima Xiangru, this beauty from a rich family had made a determined move to elope with the gifted scholar, who had nothing in his house but bare walls, in order to "win the heart of one person and remain with him a devoted couple till the end of our lives." No sound of *qin* (a seven-stringed plucked instrument) can be heard any more by Wenjun Well; instead, a Sichuan opera entitled "A Male Phoenix Wooing a Female One" is often presented here. With the purpose of verifying the love story that has been passed from mouth to mouth, many people come to Chengdu and specifically, to Jinli, to see with their own eyes why on earth that classic saying "it is not good for a young man to go to Sichuan" originated from this place that has nourished such romantic feelings and decadent lifestyles.

Lianhua Fudi (Lotus Mansion) is a bar with a façade peculiar to a rich and influential family, but it relies on a bright lounge to create a lively atmosphere. The transparent glass partitions off the space to a turn without obstructing our sightline. The most remarkable feature is the balcony; full of vitality, the whole green makes you wonder whether you are leaning upon a balustrade outside of a window on the loft of some ancient family, or you have just found a quiet retreat from a life of luxury and dissipation amid a modern city. The moment you open the door, you see a screen wall and then antique-like ornaments interspersed from roof to corner, and everything in sight is pure poetry. Lotus-like candles are put on the water. When a breeze arises, the pink silk curtains begin dancing gently; behind the waving bead door curtain, you can see the shadows of human figures standing up sideways or turning around; when the door curtain is flicked up, appears a girl demurer than a lotus. Walking along a corridor, you will arrive at an open-air place of entertainment. Rockeries pile up without restraint and the heart-shaped pond is covered with lotus flowers, which are in full bloom and therefore look extremely enchanting. Everything in sight seems so beautiful that you may fall into a trance and wonder whether it is a dreamland. Nothing in life is more joyous, since we cannot always remain intoxicated and stay in the dreamland. While you sit inside the bar, everything before your eyes can easily get you into a trance: on the one side the ancient architecture and historical figures are loaded with a strong sense of history, yet on the other, the modern bar stands in the forefront of trends. You cannot keep yourself sober inside such a dreamlike space appealing to your sight…A rather small commercial street as it is, Jinli is pervaded by the strongest grass-roots atmosphere in Chengdu, just like a beautiful Sichuan girl who impresses outsiders as being very indigenous, very warm-hearted, and very hospitable. The green tea, silk quilts, Shu brocades, Shu embroideries, the inexpensive but substantial Chengdu snacks laid out on the stands, the flag-signs and signboards fluttering in the wind, the Chinese red paper-cut pasted on the windows, the bright red lanterns hanging over the door lintel, the hawkers' crying with a strong Sichuan dialect, the endless stream of people, and what not—all of these are indeed "jinli" ("brilliant and beautiful")!

Jinli Street highlights Chinese characteristics and the local color of Chengdu and impresses you as a space-time where reality and history join together. As a matter of fact, urban construction in China is faced with a crisis. That is, an unavoidable set pattern results in such a cruel fact: all cities are covered with steel-and-cement structures, lacking in individuality and looking almost the same as each other. This crisis is even spreading through Europe. We find that during the course of the globalization of urban images, the individuality and cultural characteristics of every city are disappearing imperceptibly. When the McDanold's and the Starbucks land and take root in every corner of the earth, when urban streets differ from each other only in the permutation and combination of the same kinds of stores, we are confronted with another cultural crisis. When such modernization has become something in common, it might be unworthy of the so-called modern beauty in the real sense; instead, it turns into a cultural stereotyping and stagnation. Although Jinli Street cannot represent Chengdu's history and culture to the full, it imparts a positive message: traditions can be beautiful and traditional culture can also have considerable intangible value. When foreign tourists drink the heated samshu at *Zhujiufang*, or pick up some spiced bean curds at *Sanguyuan*, such images actually embody the charm of Chinese culture and the concept of what is Chengdu. Jilin Street organically combines the restoration of Chengdu's traditional architecture and the preservation of the culture of the Three Kingdoms, representing a continuation of Shu culture and holding more intrinsic value than the seemingly magnificent steel-and-cement jungle. Such intrinsic value not only benefits Chengdu's economic development, but also will advantage Chengdu's cultural and historical preservation more greatly. Every place to which people swarm must have something inviting; every place that shows due respect for the past and exploits its unique historical and cultural appeal to outsiders enables people to fully experience harmony and tolerance; and once they come, they are reluctant to go.

It is exactly where Jinli's charm lies. Even if you have just taken a sip of tea, walked through a street, eaten a morsel of *chuanchuanxiang*, and what not, there is an imperceptible sensation that guides your senses, or rather, plays on your heartstring. It feels as if a girl's soft hands hold up your hands slowly and pull you into her soft bosom…

Tips:

Jinli Street
Add: No. 231, Wuhou Temple Street, Chengdu
Phone number: 028-66311313
Website: www.cdjinli.net

Jinli Street is located within the First Ring Road in downtown Chengdu, adjacent to the famous Wuhou Temple Museum. To get there, you can take Buses No. 1, 10, 94, 109, 57, 304, or 306. It is a 30-minute ride from the airport and a 20-minute ride from the railway station. In Jinli Street, there are more than 40 business establishments, such as *Sanguo Chayuan* (Tea Garden of the Three Kingdoms), *Sanguyuan* (Three Calls Garden Restaurant), *Sexiangwei Mingxiaochi* (Famous Snacks with Color, Aroma and Taste All Present), Jinli Hotel, *Lianhua Fudi* Bar (Lotus Mansion Bar), *Zhujiufang* Bar (Heated Wine Club), *Zuisanguo* Bar (Drunk with the Three Kingdoms), *Zhangfei Niuroupu* (Zhang Fei-Style Beef Store), *Zhuge Liannu* Store, *Kaimendafa Zahuopu* (Making-a-Fortune-Upon-Start-Up Variety Store), *Pinyuetang Zhubaoyuqidian* (Moon-Enjoying Jewelry Store), *Yelang Laranfang* (Batik Clothing Store), *Xishenfang* (Happy Gods Workshop), *Jinxiuguan* (Beautiful Brocade Store), *Shuzhongbao Shujindian* (Shu's Treasure Shu Brocade Store), *Zhuoshang Cansifang* (Silk Workshop), *Shutao Chayedian* (Shu's Billows Tea Store), *Jiaozi Yanguan* (Beloved Children Tobacco Store), *Shuijingfang* (Swellfun Liquor Store), *Xinshengyuan Shenronghang* (Ginseng and Young Pilose Antler Store), *Baojingzhai* (Precious Mirror Store), *Baixing Xungen Tang* (Seeking-the-Roots-of-Hundreds-of-Family-Surnames Store), *Tangmabing* (Mr. Tang's Sesame Cake Store), *Jiujiuya* (Spiced Duck's Neck Store), *V Yizhan* (V Dak Snack Bar), Häagen-Dazs Ice Cream Store, *Luxin Senlin Shaokao* (Green Forest Grill), *Qingshanyu* (Cyan Feather Fan Store), *Qingyaxuan* (Elegance Ancient-Looking Painted Pottery Store), *Shuyu* (Indonesian Clothing Store), and *Dongqing Xiyun* (Eastern Charm and Western Appeal Store). You can window-shop or buy something, eat or put up for the night, fully relishing the unique charm of the local traits and folkways of Chengdu.

Hotels:

Jinli Hotel
Jinli Hotel is a three-building complex based on the architectural style of the late Qing Dynasty and the early Republic of China, composed of *Kezhan* (the hotel proper), *Yinlu* (the secluded cottage), and *Furong* (the hibiscus mansion), each with its distinctive features. In the courtyard there are winding corridors and lanes, lesser courtyards, and flower gardens, and in front of or behind the houses rockeries rising aloft, green trees affording umbrage, and streams murmuring, all of which are in perfect and rational arrangement and constitute a tranquil and serene environment. The interior of the hotel is decorated with a simple, classic, and elegant taste, and equipped with whole sets of antique-like mahogany furniture, modern deluxe washrooms, optical network, and central air-conditioning system.

"Who cannot help feeling that our fleeting life is like deliverable mail and an empty dream as well? / So anywhere we can stay may make our home." In front of such a hotel like Jinli Hotel, how could you resist the temptation to come in and stay?

Jack Quian

Phone: 028-66311335
Fax: 86-28-85552516

Food:

Sanguyuan (Three Calls Garden Restaurant)
It is a theme restaurant based on the stories of the Three Kingdoms, to which the employees' outfits, the decorations on the tableware, the design of the menu, and even the names of the dishes all refer. The moment you enter the restaurant, you will see the floor paved with stone slabs, reddish brown small wooden compartments standing in a queue, wooden crossbeams and a gallery stretching overhead, and Chinese palace lanterns of various colors hanging under the gallery.
Phone: 028-85586381

Luxin Senlin Shaokao (Green Forest Grill)
It is a restaurant that has turned the roadside Chengdu snacks into an elegant vogue and put the vulgar grill into the modern atmosphere of a beautifully decorated restaurant. Seated inside, you will feel enchanted by the wonderful ambiance: decorated with antique taste, the yellow light makes you feel warm, and walking on the squeaking floor, you feel as if entering a pleasant inn…
Phone: 028-66311339

A Street for Delicious Food:

Boboji (bunches of chicken in an earthen bowl)
Slices of chicken and chicken giblets strung together by bamboo skewers, steeped in heavy condiments, and dished up in an earthen bowl—probably that is how the dish has got its name. It smells exceedingly aromatic.

Congxiang Tudou (diced potatoes with scallions)
Peel and dice boiled potatoes, then stir-fry them in a frying pan with edible oil, add some condiments, continue stir-frying till they become golden on the surface, sprinkle some cumin and minced scallions, and dish up into little plastic bowls. It is extremely aromatic.

Bing fen
It is made of the juice of a plant called malaxis bancanoides, and looks like a jelly, yet tenderer. Black or brown, served with water ice and brown sugar syrup, it tastes nice and cool, sweet and smooth.

Kaohongshu (baked sweet potato)
Bake sweet potatoes on the wall of a brazier with burning coals in the middle, turning them over several times before they are well done. You can smell the aroma of the baked sweet potatoes from a great distance. Take a bite, and it tastes sweet and glutinous.

Ye'erba (cooked and pounded glutinous rice paste wrapped in leaf)
Put some meat filling or sugar filling in a wrapper made of glutinous rice flour, clothe it all in a vegetable leaf, and then steam till done. The hawker cries like this: "*Ye'erba, Ye'erba…*"

Longtou Xiaochi (dragon-head snacks)
Over a stove there is a copper pot in the shape of a dragon, in which the water is always boiling. As soon as an order is placed, some brake flour will be put into a bowl and steeped in boiling water. White fungus soup is offered in addition.

Suancai Douhua (bean jelly with pickled Chinese cabbage)
A delicious but inexpensive snack that can be subdivided into pure bean jelly with pickled Chinese cabbage, bean jelly with pickled Chinese cabbage and spareribs, bean jelly with pickled Chinese cabbage and aquatic foods, bean jelly with pickled Chinese cabbage and fresh meat, and the like. It is easy to prepare it: Boil bean jelly, pickled Chinese cabbage, bean sprouts, oyster mushroom, sausages, fungus-vegetable, and everything in broth, and eat when it is done. You can eat it while boiling, or boil it while eating. The hawker increases or decreases the amount of ingredients according to the number of customers, for the payment is determined by it. Therefore, you can eat it alone, yet it is jollier to dine in groups.

Suanlafen (hot and sour Chinese vermicelli)
A snack similar to vermicelli in northern China, but tenderer. Mix sweet potato starch with water, put it into a colander, hold the colander tight with one hand and pound it with the other to drop the threadlike vermicelli into boiling water, take the vermicelli out of the water when it is done and cool it in cold water. Seasoned with chilli, vinegar, Sichuan pepper, and the like, it tastes hot and sour. The snack is really a joy to eat and especially to young ladies' liking.

Guokui (scone)
Roll the dough into thin elongated ellipses, spread the filling evenly on them—for different flavors, there are different fillings, which are usually meat seasoned pro rata with soybean flour, sesame, scallion, ginger, refined salt, aroma salt, white sugar, Sichuan pepper, peach kernel, sweet sauce, peanut, black bean sauce, and everything—roll up the elongated elliptic piece into a cylinder, erect the cylinder, flatten it out and roll into a thin piece, sprinkle sesame on both sides, fry it in a frying pan with some sesame oil till both sides turn golden.

The fascination of *guokui* lies not just in its deliciousness but also in its cooking procedure. Seemingly eager to show off, the *guokui*-maker beats the table with the rolling pin in steady rhythm during the intervals of rolling the dough and makes a thunderous noise, which, however, sounds very pleasing to the ear like drumbeat. You can enjoy the buy-one-and-get-one-free preferential treatment; that is, while you buy some *guokui*, you can watch the maker's performance for free.

Stores:

Zhuoshang Cansifang (Silk Workshop)
It is a traditional handicraft workshop that makes silk quilts by a thousand-year-old method. It was originally established in Langzhong, one of China's famous historical and cultural cities and Sichuan's capital of natural silk. Its superfine "China's Pride" silk products are all made of high-quality silkworm cocoons from the mountainous north Sichuan, after a working procedure of macerating, steaming, making cocoon pouches, forming cocoon layers, hanging to dry, pulling, stretching, spreading, ironing, connecting, sewing, and arranging. They are light, soft, comfortable, and of perfect air permeability; moreover, they can protect and improve your health by facilitating sleep, keeping out the cold, the wind and the moisture, relieving rheumatic pains, dispelling mites and bacteria, and maintaining constant temperature. They contain no poisonous or harmful chemicals and are green environmental products. If you would like to show filial piety to your parents, give presents to your relatives and friends, or communicate good opinions and strengthen ties to others, they are a perfect choice.

Yingxiangfang (Reflection Workshop)
T-shirts here are characterized by unique printed designs—Chinese characters, types of facial make-up in opera, head portraits, and the like—so that you can rest assured that nobody in the street wears the same T-shirt as you. This little store is decorated in an exquisitely fine and tasteful style: The wooden floor is conspicuously inlaid with a large iron sheet emitting a soft dull light, on which are branded the carefully-designed name of the store and its logo. The artistically represented name, colorful lanterns, wooden counter, exquisite small portraits hanging on the walls, carefree and leisurely gold fish in the corner, they each makes a view fresh and unusual.

Fucheng Fang (Luck and Prosperity Store)
Gray-brick old walls, lanterns pasted up with paper, an outmoded wheelbarrow in the shape of a cock's head leaning against the window, and yellowish light glowing through the window—could you imagine that a traditional ancient-looking small store like this sells dolls of the Italian Triangel?

Bars:

Lianhua Fudi (Lotus Mansion)
It is a bar characterized by a façade peculiar to a rich and influential family and antique-like ornaments interspersed from roof to corner—everything in sight is pure poetry. Taking a few steps forward, and looking up at the sky, you will discover a transparent glass that partitions off the space to a turn without obstructing your sightline. The distant sky seems as serene as water, while the bar, situated in a bustling street, is as excitingly noisy as fire. The most remarkable feature is the balcony: you open the door and see greens; standing there, you melt into the green. For a moment, you cannot tell whether you are leaning upon a balustrade outside of a window on the loft of some rich family in the ancient Kingdom of Shu, or you have just found a heartwarming and solaceful haven away from a life of luxury and dissipation in a modern city. French food and cocktail are offered here, and you can also place an order of coffee or green tea. Amid the music in the lounge, you can sink yourself into the cozy sofa and relish the flowing melody with a smile at the corners of your mouth. Or you can stand up and swing every cell of your body gracefully and lithely in rhythm, facilitating its purely hedonic chemoreception to alcohol and music,

and amidst the alluring atmosphere floating along with the air, experiencing an irredeemably perfect joy with the theme of romantic and mysterious light of night.
Phone: 028-85537676

Sifangjie (Square Street)
It is a Bohemian-style bar highlighting freedom, unpretentiousness, and naturalness in combination with the appeal of refined and colorful folkways like that of an old-house bar in Lijiang's back streets. Adorned with green plants and cleverly partitioned off by curio shelves, it displays the multiplicity of historical, national, folk, religious, and artistic subjects. The customers can relish drinks and at the same time, appreciate the cultural ambience that the owner has endeavored to create; as the lamplight is waning, the abstract space-time upstairs and the interest and appeal of the superposition of superficial components of several kinds of cultures can make them forget the secular affairs that have been bothering them and set free their unworldly hearts for the moment.
Phone: 028-85569947

Xifuhui (West Meets East)
It is the sister bar of Carlo TOO, which adopts the uncomplicated style of European and American bars. While listening to foreign classic music, you can relish authentic Italian food, genuine coffee ground and brewed on the spot, typical western snacks, and a variety of beverages popular in the west. Surrounded by a casual English-speaking atmosphere, looking at the frolicking crowd outside, you feel as if your thoughts and feelings keep drifting back and forth and permeating among the simple and unsophisticated folkways of ancient-style Jinli Street and an Italian-style romantic ambiance.
Phone: 028-66311308

Caoyingba (Cao Cao's Camp)
This bar is a combination of the quintessence of traditional Shu culture and neoclassicism's characteristic simplicity, freshness, naturalness, and decency. Under a homely ceiling fan made of smaller palm-leaves fans, you can stretch and sink yourself into a good-sized sofa by primitive-looking leather-silhouette lamps and listening to nostalgic CDs, let your unbridled thoughts and feelings flow along with the graceful melody. While you are looking carelessly at the ice thawing slowly inside your whiskey, the thousand-year-old culture of the Three Kingdoms, along with the curling smoke between your fingers, keep stirring your and all posterity's sight and sensibility…
Phone: 028-85550388

Zhujiufang (Heated Wine Club)
"Over heated wine Cao Cao and Liu Bei discussed who were ambitious heroes in the Three Kingdoms while enjoying green plums." How could there be no gulping down flowing bowls since there is already gobbling meat? Here you can find the wooden storied building and tables, earthen bowls and cups, several dishes of assorted spiced and braised meat with peanuts, a goblet of kaoliang wine heated and sold on the spot, and if you like, rice wine, yellow wine, and even fruits and beer can also be heated. You only have to pay 20 or 30 *yuan* for treating your friends here to a drink of wine to their hearts' content. After gulping down three cups of heated wine, you may feel your blood boiling and your ambition burning; looking into the

distance from the window, you may want to follow the examples of the ancients to wave and scold, to drive out evil and usher in good and to voice your opinions on governmental and political affairs.
Phone: 028-85583698

Xingxing Shese (Travelers' Traces and Photographers' Colors)
It is a bar with an outdoor-life theme, where backpackers, photographers, car travelers, sightseers and others have a drink, chat, have reunions, make friends, daydream, and shoot the breeze. You can feel at home here whether you are fond of mistreating yourself by seeking adventures or sparing no money to enjoy yourself, whether you are single or married but unwilling to return home until late into the night. It is both your starting-point and your destination, both your stopover on a journey and your home. Here customers can have a spree, or take their ease and drink to no excess; they can be lazy or relaxed, quiet or crazy, sober or confused—almost being themselves. Here travelers can exchange experiences, get acquainted, and make an appointment to travel in company with each other by holding lectures, forums, and slide shows on special travel routes, movie and television previews, solo exhibitions of photographs, travelers' seminars, and the like.
Phone: 028-66311332

Chenghuang Julu (Orange-Yellow and Tangerine-Green)
"The lotus has withered and its large rain-tight leaves also died back; / The chrysanthemum has faded, but its stalk remains in spite of frost. / Please remember the most beautiful time of the year, / That is, when oranges turn yellow and tangerines are green." The grass is supposed to be thinly scattered and leaves on trees to have fallen down in autumn and winter, but in *Chenghuang Julu*, these two seasons are represented as full of colorful brilliance and vitality. The most beautiful sceneries of the year are illustrated to the full here. There are cozy printed high-back sofas and sweet nostalgic music; take a sip of the intoxicating purified liquor, and you will feel its bouquet lingering on your lips and teeth; the smoke of the unquenched cigar in the ashtray is rising, rising slowly, taking along what is occurring to you in a trance. In the shadow of the staircase, a huge engraved mirror hangs from the beam down to the floor. Standing before the mirror and looking around, you will feel as if the extraordinary movie *2046* is being reproduced here…
Phone: 028-85583698

Zuisanguo (Drunk with the Three Kingdoms)
This bar is a combination of the quintessence of traditional Shu culture and neoclassicism's characteristic simplicity, freshness, naturalness, and decency. With a glass of whiskey with ice in the hand, you can stretch and sink yourself into a good-sized sofa under a homely ceiling fan made of palm-leaf fans. You can let your unbridled thoughts and feelings flow along with the graceful melody while the primitive-looking leather-silhouette lamps and nostalgic CDs keep stirring your sight and sensibility…
Phone: 028-85550388

Heigen·Sifangjie (Black Root ·Square Street)
It is a place where you can indulge an infatuated and muddled state of mind that keeps roaming amid rouge and powder. Every ray of lamplight is filled with temptation, and every *cun* of space is permeated with romance…Under the roof beam of the second floor, there hang peerlessly beautiful bellybands and delicate three-*cun* shoes for Chinese women's bound feet, around

which linger your happiness and sadness, melancholy and yearning, perplexity and expectation, and your past, present and future…You may appreciate them alone, or share them with others to your heart's content. Everything is penetrated by the intoxicating bouquet of wine under the dim light of night.
Phone: 028-85569947

III. A Gourmet City

I have been to many cities in the world and seen a great variety of customs, practices, and sights of these cities. To learn about a city, one should walk with one's own "feet," feel with one's own "heart" and observe with one's own "eyes." Yet for such a special city as Chengdu, one cannot fully appreciate it until one has tasted with one's own "tongue."

During my stay in Chengdu early in the 1980s, salted and dried pig's heads in the shape of a fan were for sale in a store selling non-staple foodstuffs at Yanshikou. The people of Chengdu gave them a genteel-sounding name: butterfly pig's heads. If the pigs in heaven knew about it, they would surely wonder despairingly: Why bother to give us such a beautiful name if you're going to eat us? Later in the United States, I asked several persons from Chengdu about this kind of food, unexpectedly they knew nothing about it, which made me doubt if they truly came from Chengdu…*Dandan* noodles (Sichuan-style noodles with peppery sauce) sold by the cultural palace were my favorite. They cost one *liang* (a unit of weight) grain ticket and nine *fen* Renminbi per bowl. The store was always crowded with customers eating with a whishing sound, their heads wet with sweat and their mouths dripping with sesame oil full of crushed dried red chili pepper. Those who came later had to stand close to those who were eating and keep their eyes on the latter; otherwise, the stools would disappear sideways without a trace the moment the latter stood up to leave. The neighbor of the store selling *dandan* noodles was one selling *fuqi feipian* (husband and wife's sliced pot-stewed entrails of oxen), in front of which there was always a long queue of customers with lunch boxes in the hand…I remember that I ordered a bowl of sliced beef and entrails of oxen soaked in sesame oil with crushed dried red chili pepper. It was so hot that after the first mouthful, my mouth began to burn as if on fire. I asked a waiter for a cup of cold plain boiled water and was given a bowl of steaming soup instead. Well, the moment I gulped down the soup, I burst into tears…

Fuqi feipian is actually pot-stewed entrails of oxen dressed in certain sauce: ox's hearts, tripes, tongues, tendons and other edible offal are sliced after being pot-stewed, and then an elaborate dressing made of chili pepper, Sichuan pepper powder, crushed roast peanuts, roast sesame, and chopped celery is poured on the slices; the dressing looks strikingly red and transparently oily. The dish tastes tongue-numbing, hot, fresh, fragrant, soft, sticky, crisp, smooth and tender. The folk story about *fuqi feipian* goes like this: During the early years of the Republic of China (1912-1949), Guo Zhaohua, a salesman in a beef store, brought home some discarded edible offal and together with his wife, he washed the offal clean, sliced it, mixed the slices with some self-made dressing, and then sold them to some coolies and paupers. Because the dish was conscientiously prepared, delicious, and cheap, it gradually made a name for itself; because the man and his wife always stood side by side in crying out to sell the dish in streets, people began to call it "*fuqi feipian* (husband and wife's sliced pot-stewed waste parts of oxen)," which sounded precise and familiar; and as it became more and more famous, the character "fei (waste)" was replaced by its homophone "fei (lung)."… Many local delicacies in Chengdu have stories similar to that of *fuqi feipian*; while eating, you not only have a taste of the flavor unique to Chengdu but also get to know a culture peculiar to Sichuan cuisine…

Chengdu

There is a widely known saying among the people of China: "When it comes to eating, go to Sichuan; when it comes to tastes, go to Chengdu." Of the four most famous schools of culinary art in China (Beijing cuisine, Sichuan cuisine, Jiangsu cuisine, Guangdong cuisine), Sichuan cuisine boasts tongue-numbing, hot, delicate, and fresh tastes and a variety of flavors, as "each dish has its unique taste and no two dishes have the same flavor." Such special flavors as fish-flavored, *gongbao* (with peanuts), and water-boiled are incomparable at home and abroad, such cooking methods as cooking twice, adding *guoba* (crispy rice), flavoring with *paojiao* (pickled chili pepper) or with *douban* (broad-bean sauce) are well-known worldwide, and Chengdu snacks have built up a reputation of being "the best food of the world." Located in the middle of Sichuan Basin, Chengdu abounds with produce, businessmen and travelers, and writers and scholars; besides, Chengdu has seldom been plagued by the chaos of war in the long history of China and the people have been living in peace and contentment; as a result, the people of Chengdu have been sparing no effort in cooking and eating. They are equipped with sufficient time, energy, and interest by history and life. Numerous in variety, elaborate in preparing and cooking, meticulous in the selecting of ingredients, highly varied in flavor, pleasing in color, aroma, taste, and appearance, Chengdu food contains the best of Sichuan cuisine. Chengdu snacks amount to nearly 200 kinds, including Dragon *Chaoshou* (wonton) in Chunxi Street, the Lais' *Tangyuan* (boiled glutinous rice dumplings) in Zongfu Street, the Zhongs' Dumpling in Litchi Alley, the Mice Hole Zhangs' Duck, *Liangfen* (cold bean jelly) in Dongzikou, *Zhide Xiaolong Zhengniurou* (steamed beef in a tiny bamboo steamer) in Changshun Street. For common people food is everything; if a fastidious culinary culture features largely in a city, then it proves that the inhabitants of this city have a good grasp of the art of living. And this is the case with Chengdu.

When our host in Chengdu banqueted us in Red Apricot Restaurant, I first picked up a genuine slice of twice-cooked pork with my chopsticks. Don't look down at this twice-cooked pork, which is actually "the most aromatic" dish of Sichuan dishes. Our host said, twice-cooked pork originated from sacrificial ceremonies of the folk; that is, cooked pork that had been offered to gods and ghosts in propitiation or to ancestors in reverence

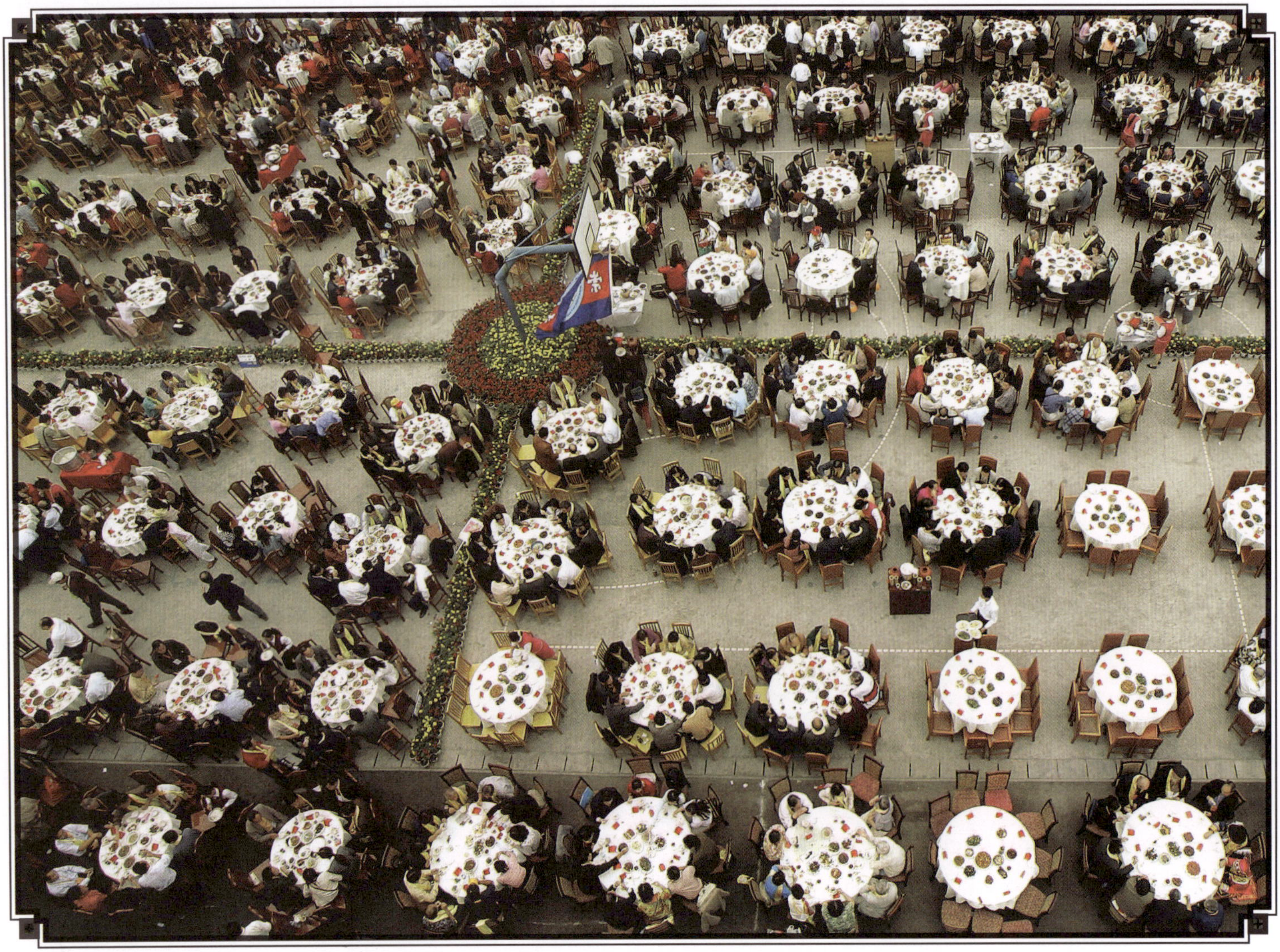

was brought back after the ceremonies to be cooked again and eaten, hence the name "twice-cooked pork." It is a dish that requires meticulous attention to the selecting of ingredients, stewing, slicing, and frying. To cook the dish, it is necessary to select the pork from the tip of a pig's buttocks. It is said by famous chefs of Sichuan cuisine that one pig cannot produce three dishes of twice-cooked pork, which attests to the high standard in selecting the ingredients. The pork cannot be too lean or too fat; half-lean-half-fat pork with skin is the best. The character "twice" in the dish's name "twice-cooked pork" is enough to make clear the characteristics of the cooking procedure: It involves both stewing and frying that comes after stewing. While stewing the whole piece of pork, you should fish it out of the boiling water when it is a little more than half-done and cut it into slices after it cools down a bit. Here "slices" can be replaced by "thick slices," for the pork cannot be cut into too small and too thin slices but ones a bit on the broad and thick side instead. After being stewed and sliced, the pork should be fried in a heated wok and hence it is accurately called "twice-cooked pork." While frying, garlic sprouts should be added and besides soy sauce, you must flavor the pork with broad-bean sauce from Pixian County plus a little sugar—sweet soy sauce will be better. Particular attention should be paid to the duration and degree of frying: The dish is ready when the pork slices curl a bit, which is commonly called "ready when oil-lamp-shaped curls are formed." There is a small town called Lianshan near Chengdu, and Lianshan twice-cooked pork is well-known. Why? Because every slice of pork weighs about two *liang*, as big as a human palm and as thick as a little finger, and it tastes rich but not greasy, deliciously aromatic and spicy…

It is said that cooking on earth started in Chengdu. It may sound exaggerated at first, but as a matter of fact, cooking arose in Chengdu and its neighboring country as early as 5,000 years ago. Historical records and many wares unearthed by archaeologists have proved that by the Sui (581-618) and Tang Dynasties and the Five Dynasties (907-960), there were an even greater variety of Sichuan dishes in Chengdu, which, over the Yuan (1271-1368), Ming, and Qing Dynasties, evolved into a system with a unique style. By the end of the Qing Dynasty and the early years of the Republic of China, the cooking methods of Sichuan cuisine had been almost fully developed, and tongue-numbing and hot, strange-flavored, and many other flavors had matured; Sichuan cuisine finally made a name all over China as a distinctive regional school of China's culinary art.

As Sichuan cuisine has been becoming more and more famous, even foreign people have fallen in love with Szechuan (the spelling of "Sichuan" in American English) delicacies. Earlier Chinese restaurants in foreign countries mostly offered Yue dishes, that is, Guangdong dishes, and in terms of varieties, Sichuan cuisine compared quite unfavorably with its Guangdong counterpart. But in recent years, as a result of reformation and melioration, New Sichuan cuisine has been able to present more and more dishes and a wider variety of cooking methods than Guangdong cuisine. The same kinds of raw materials can be cooked in many different ways and the flavors of the dishes turn out to be more and more refined, which has brought Sichuan food into fashion all over the world. Especially in the USA, there are several or even tens of Chinese restaurants entitled "Szechuan Restaurant" in almost every city. As powerful as a thunderbolt, Sichuan dishes have swept through the gigantic Chinese food service industry in the USA and become the mainstream Chinese food abroad today.

Paul Fleming, an American who traveled to Chengdu earlier in his life, was indelibly impressed by the delicious dishes in Chengdu. As a result, and in order to satisfy his own appetite for Sichuan dishes, he opened a restaurant named "PF Chang's China Bistro" in Scottsdale near Phoenix, USA in 1993. Unexpectedly, it became extremely popular with American gourmands and he had to open a second one, a third one, …And finally, he has established nearly one hundred chain restaurants throughout the USA and his company has even gone on the stock market (NASDAQ: PFCB) as the only one of all the Chinese restaurants in the USA that total more than 40,000. Its stock quote has increased from the initial several dollars per share to today's over 40 dollars per share and its turnover amounted to 0.675 billion dollars in 2005, which surely testifies to the charm of Chengdu food.

Chengdu food, which contains a great variety of dishes, is undergoing continuous melioration and enrichment, and New Sichuan cuisine seems to be blossoming everywhere. The rallying place of New Sichuan dishes is Yangxixian Street for Food and Recreation, where you can find restaurants offering Sichuan dishes, Guangdong dishes, and the others, big hot pot restaurants, and even local snacks such as Shuangliu *Laoma* (Old Mother) Rabbit's Heads. Various traditional and new-fashioned restaurants stand end to end on either side of the street and extend beyond the Third Ring Road Flyover in the west: *Yinxing* (Gingko), *Shengtaosha* (Remarkable Skill in Sifting Gold from Sand), *Nantaiyue* (Moon over the Southern Platform), *Rongxingyuan* (Prosperity Restaurant), *Kuaile Laojia* (Happy Hometown), *Fuwanjia* (Immense Happiness), *Shizilou* (Lion Restaurant), *Daronghe* (the Harmonious Big City of Hibiscus), *Taoranju* (Happy and Carefree Restaurant), *Lijingxuan* (Restaurant with a Beautiful View), and so on. These restaurants of different styles all have trademark dishes of their own, which enable them to establish a firm foothold in Chengdu. Stir-fried field snails with chili pepper, braised chicken with taros, and bunches of rabbit boiled in a hot pot in *Taoranju*, braised pork in soy sauce, strong-smelling preserved bean curds, and steamed fish's head with chopped red pepper in *Maojia Fandian* (the Maos' Restaurant), red apricot chicken and eel with vermicelli made from bean starch in Red Apricot Restaurant, and steamed bighead carp's head with chopped red pepper, *Ronghe* spareribs, and auspicious meatballs with coriander in *Daronghe* are all delicacies that have built up a great reputation long before. *Rongxingyuan, Kuaile Laojia, Fuwanjia, Shizilou,* and *Dabaisha* (Big White Shark) are all time-honored hot pot restaurants, whose unusual merits have been proved by their enduring popularity.

But no matter how greatly New Sichuan cuisine has reformed Sichuan cuisine, there remain several unalterable traditional elements, such as chilies and pickles. The people of Chengdu cannot do without pickles or chilies for their life. There are a wide variety of pickles in Chengdu; every time you dine out, no matter what main courses or delicacies you order, the appetizer must be pickled chilies, or pickled ginger, pickled Chinese cabbages, pickled radishes, and the like. The people of Chengdu pickle all vegetables. The cooking methods of frying, stir-frying, pot-stewing, quick-stir-frying, and frying-after-stewing or vice versa in Sichuan cuisine require flavoring with pickled chilies and pickled ginger. Even vegetable dishes such as stir-fried shreds of pumpkin need pickled chilies. And pickled cowpeas, pickled lotus-shaped cabbages, and pickled radishes play a major role in such homely-flavor dishes as bean jelly with fresh meat, minced meat with pickled cowpeas, minced meat with pickled lotus-shaped cabbages, minced meat with pickled radishes. What's more, pickles can be served independently as casual dishes; pickled cucumbers, pickled Chinese onions, pickled garlic bolts, pickled bamboo shoots, pickled cowpeas, and pickled lotus-shaped cabbages often function as the best appetizers to be eaten together with rice porridge and steam buns for breakfast. Chilies, to be sure, play a more important role in Sichuan cuisine, for Sichuan cuisine highlights the tongue-numbing, hot, fresh, and steaming hot tastes, which can never be done without chilies. Take pockmarked woman's bean curd for example. If the dish only tastes tongue-numbing, fresh, and steaming hot, but not hot enough with chilies, then it is a failure. Indispensable as chilies are, they cannot be misused in cooking, and the proper proportion between chilies and the other ingredients is a great stroke of skill, which constitutes the finest and most ingenious part of Sichuan cuisine. In case of improper proportion, the tempting aroma and extraordinary flavor will by no means come by. The proportion of hot and tongue-numbing condiments to the other ingredients varies with different dishes. Boiled beef must be hot but fresh, tongue-numbing but aromatic; ox's tongues with lettuces must be hot but crisp, tongue-numbing but light…On the whole, the hot flavor should suit one's palate.

To learn about the tasty but inexpensive Chengdu snacks in person, Danny and I went searching for delicious food all over the streets. We often ordered a portion of each snack and shared it with each other. A mouthful for you, then a mouthful for me, we just took a taste and left some space in our stomachs for something new. Once we ate 5 meals in one day, which cost less than 20 dollars:

Breakfast: *Dandan* noodles and chicken soup

We took Bus No. 4 at Tianfu Square in downtown Chengdu and got off at Babao Street, opposite to a movie house. On the left of the movie house there was a time-honored restaurant selling noodles with stewed chicken. We ordered four *liang dandan* noodles and two bowls of chicken soup, both of which were the chef's dishes of this restaurant. The restaurant closes at 1 p.m., so it would be better to go there a bit earlier. The total cost was 10 *yuan* Renminbi.

Lunch: At Pockmarked Woman Chen's Bean Curd Restaurant

We took Bus No. 27 and got off at the Qingyang Temple stop, where we saw a Pockmarked Woman Chen's Bean Curd Restaurant with, allegedly, the longest history of all. We ordered its trademark dish and several other Sichuan dishes to keep it company. We did not finish them all, which cost only 20 *yuan* Renminbi. In authentic time-honored restaurants, we had to eat only those trademark dishes; otherwise, there would be little space in our stomachs for the next meal.

Afternoon refreshment: At Xiao Tan's Bean Jelly Restaurant

We again took Bus No. 4 and got off at Northern Alley bus stop. Small as it was, the restaurant was quite famous and anybody you asked could tell you where was Xiao Tan's Bean Jelly Restaurant. We ordered Xiao Tan's bean jelly and in summer it would be better to ask for iced bean jelly in fermented glutinous wine. We had two bowls, which cost 10 *yuan*.

Supper: At *Huangcheng Laoma* (Old Mother in the Imperial City) Hot Pot Restaurant

You would not know what a hubbub of voices sound like in a restaurant until you come here. This best known hot pot restaurant in Chengdu occupies the whole of a tall building, whose façade is filled with sculptures featuring local residences in west Sichuan and whose pillars make a show of their inner corrugated steel bars on purpose. Its interior decoration looks very modern and tasteful. We ordered a yin yang hot pot, half spicy and hot and half not, and spent 100 *yuan*.

Midnight snack:

Before we returned to our hotel, we bought some *bangbang* chicken (clubbed sliced boiled chicken), *Jiuchi* (name of a town in Pengzhou) pressed salted duck, and the like, which cost fewer than 10 *yuan*.

The dishes in Chengdu are agreeable not just in taste but also in sight. Once I walked into a restaurant named "*Buyi* (clothes made of cloth worn by common people and scholars not in government)," on whose gate was engraved its motto: "Humankind will never perish, and eating will last forever; long live Sichuan cuisine, and long live this restaurant." The stairs were flanked by a stone mill, a windmill, and an old well; the façade of the restaurant looked like an ancient local residence in west Sichuan, and the inside, like a courtyard in the countryside. The restaurant's most competitive dish was sliced boiled chicken, which, instead of being piled in order on the bowl, was soaked in ice-cold soup sprinkled with light yellow pickled chili, gaily-colored pickled carrot, transparent white pickled ginger, and green soy bean; the dish tasted fresh, sweet, and a little sour—quite unique indeed. Crisp intestines with chili, stewed crucian with bean curds, twice-cooked leaf beets and other dishes all tasted tongue-numbing, hot, fresh, and aromatic—typical of Sichuan cuisine. Here I also watched a performance of making *sandapao*: The chef rubbed a cooked glutinous rice paste into round pellets with his hands, then with a flick of his wrist, a pellet was sent hopping, skipping, and jumping over three successively arranged brass plates, and as a result, the white pellet was coated with fragrant and crisp soy bean powder and crushed peanuts and could be eaten after being dipped in melted brown sugar. The customers could enjoy the aromatic and sticky pellets and the chef's acrobatic stunt at once. You could not help but exclaim over the local people's luck to savor delicious food: Why could ordinary raw materials be made into hundreds of delicacies too beautiful to be absorbed all at once?

The people of Chengdu are hospitable and one of the ways to show their hospitality is to invite guests to dinner. Hardly have their out-of-town friends arrived in Chengdu when they take them on a tour of the streets, eating snacks all the way. There are *dandan* noodles, the Hans' steamed stuffed buns, the Tans' bean jelly, the Guos' *tangyuan, ye'erba, fuqi feipian*, pockmarked woman's bean curd, and what not. You will surely get confused by all those names; but in the meantime, you will understand all of a sudden why the people of Chengdu always sniff at the food in the north. About every dish of Sichuan cuisine there is a historical story or a legend, in which consist the roots of both Sichuan culinary culture and the people of Sichuan as a whole. Such is the case with Chengdu snacks, which boast not only a great variety but also relevant stories. The most popular Sichuan dish, pockmarked woman's bean curd is a case in point. As the story goes, the dish was concocted by Mrs. Chen Liu, chef of Chen Xingsheng's Restaurant at Wanfu Bridge in Chengdu during the early years under Emperor Tongzhi's reign in the Qing Dynasty, and it was named after the pockmarks on her face. The bean curd cooked by Mrs. Chen Liu looked brilliantly red and beautiful in appearance; sprinkled with crisp aromatic diced beef, it tasted tongue-numbing, hot, aromatic, crisp, tender, steaming hot and looked in good shape—typical of Sichuan cuisine. Hence the restaurant was entitled "Pockmarked Woman Chen's Bean Curd." Chengdu and Guangzhou are two cities whose inhabitants pay the most attention to eating, and it is why there are two popular sayings: "When it comes to food, go to Guangzhou" and "When it comes to eating, go to Chengdu." But the styles of cooking of the two cities are widely different from each other. To be specific, Guangzhou cuisine emphasizes the importance of raw materials while Chengdu dishes highlight condiments. Most of the raw materials of Chengdu dishes are not rare or expensive, but both the condiments and processing are not in the least coarse or crude. For example, the chefs of Sichuan dishes use nothing other than coarse salt, brown sugar, perennial chilies, broad-bean sauce from Pixian, hot pickled mustard tubers from Fuling, and the "Dahongpao (big red gown)" brand of Sichuan pepper. They cannot be meticulous enough.

My friends in Chengdu said, the food industry in Chengdu was similar to the fashion world: A particular dish might sweep the city of hibiscus like a whirlwind; if it was really unique, it would remain popular after being renamed, and if not, it would disappear without a trace after a while. Every citizen of Chengdu takes part in developing local delicacies and a homely dish with a unique flavor, such as the Xuans' rabbit's heads, Mom's *tihua*, Zhao Laosi's duck's intestines, may become widespread. In Chengdu, many men of letters are keen on doing researches on food and true delicacies always come from the common folk. Those famous time-honored restaurants often rely on mass production and standardized but stereotyped management, so there is not much to be said for the tastes of their snacks. If you happen to dine in a small restaurant in some back lane, you will possibly come across a dish that you will never forget for your life. Therefore, it is often in those inconspicuous small restaurants that a pleasant surprise is waiting for you. You had better go to explore those ordinary alleys in order to truly excite your taste buds.

I especially liked *maocai* (hat dish) on the roadside. The cook put all kinds of materials such as bean sprouts, sliced lotus roots, bean curds, and pakchoi into a bamboo-weaved "hat," placed the "hat" into a pot of overcooked hot soup to boil the materials till they are done, and then added some condiments. Now the customers could start to eat them with relish. I think this kind of "small restaurant not without flies" can be said to be the pith and marrow of a city's food industry; there travelers can always get to know warm-hearted and hospitable local people and eat top-grade authentic local delicacies at a fair price. The local delicacies there cannot be matched by those sets of snacks offered in famous snack restaurants, for the latter cannot satisfy the fastidious appetite of the people of Chengdu.

Once, I walked with a native friend into a small restaurant specializing in *tihua*. The waiter seemed to know my friend quite well and shouted at once: "Two excellent forepaws…" My friend turned up four fingers and said, "Four!" The waiter teased smilingly, "Elder brother seems to have gained much in force…" Laughter rose from all directions in the hall. It was the first time that I had eaten *tihua*, which is actually what the northeasterners call pig's feet. While the northeasterners mainly smoke or pot-stew pig's feet with spices, the people of Sichuan stew them without seasoning. With a bowl of fresh soup without seasoning and a small plate of dipping, the stewed pig's feet with snow peas are rich yet not greasy, tender, and ready to melt deliciously in the mouth and leave a lingering aftertaste.

Allegedly, *tihua* is capable of beautifying one's face and rejuvenating one's skin and is therefore to the liking of many beauties in Chengdu. Perhaps it is why the girls of Chengdu boast a fair skin?

Nine Big Bowls, which refer to the nine main courses served at weddings and funerals in the neighboring country of Chengdu, are representative of the dishes that have spread from countryside to city. For those people who were born in the countryside during the 1960s and 1970s, "Nine Big Bowls" is a phase that implies immense happiness. Till now, Nine Big Bowls have remained the main courses of wedding receptions in the neighboring country of Chengdu. There, a wedding reception usually lasts for three days: the wedding day, the day before that, and the day after that, respectively named the wedding feasts, the Sichuan pepper feasts, and the thank-you feasts. For three days, meals will be served to guests at any time they arrive. But only on the wedding day, Nine Big Bowls are available. Various dishes are piled high in five plates, nine bowls, and six basins, extraordinarily aromatic, delicious and refreshing, displaying to the full the dry-stewed, dry-braised, fish-flavored, peanut-flavored, tongue-numbing and hot, strange-flavored, spiced with Sichuan pepper and chili, and hot with boiled spiced oil flavors—the eight typical flavors of Sichuan cuisine. The wedding feasts highlight "*sanzheng* (three bowl-steamed dishes)" (steamed glutinous rice, sweet steamed streaky pork, and salty steamed streaky pork), "*jiukou* (nine pot-steamed dishes)" (steamed whole chicken, steamed whole duck, steamed pig's upper leg, steamed pig's joint, steamed whole fish, crisp pork, steamed layers of egg and pork, chopped entrails of pigs, and choice seafood) plus four cold dishes (cold chicken, cold pig's stomach, cold pig's head or cold pot-stewed meat, cold roast peanuts or cold cucumber) and four fried dishes (fried shredded meat with hot pepper, fried shredded meat with garlic bolts, fried shredded meat with hotbed tuber onions, fried sliced meat with dried slices of tender bamboo shoots, or fried sliced meat with lettuce, fried peas with shortening, and the like). The sour soup with shredded meat and hotbed tuber onions is insuperably tasty. I was so amazed at the flavor of a local dish called "*danyuanzi* (egg rolls)" that after a taste, I went directly to the kitchen to watch the chef cooking it: Stir and mix shelled eggs, pour the fluid into a heated wok with edible oil, get the excess out of the wok, and a thin golden egg wrapper is seen covering the bottom of the wok; mix shredded meat a bit on the lean side with the seed powder of Gordon euryale and egg paste, add ginger extract, salt, thick broad-bean sauce, and other condiments, put all of them into the egg wrapper, roll them up into a cylinder with the diameter of a cup, put the cylinder-shaped egg roll in a steamer, slice up the steamed egg roll, stuff the slices with potatoes, lean meat, and

the like, put them back to the steamer, and add some chopped scallions and sesame oil after they are taken out of the steamer. While watching all this, I cannot help behaving like a voracious eater.

A discussion of peasants' food cannot leave out Juntun *guokui*, which, very popular in Chengdu, can be said to be pizzas with the characteristics of the neighboring country of Chengdu. It was drizzling that day and we went to a small town called Juntun near Chengdu. There are only several narrow and short streets in the town and after you have walked slowly from south to north and then back, or from east to west through the whole town, smoking a cigarette all the way, you will find that there is still a segment left of the cigarette. It is the simplest small town near Chengdu, with no famous beauty spots or historical sites. Without *guokui*, Juntun Town might remain as unknown as the other small towns around Chengdu. Why is it called Juntun? And why is it *guokui* that has made Juntun famous? Tradition has it that Zhuge Liang stationed troops here, so it was named "Juntun (a place to station troops)." While marching and fighting a war, the troops must bring solid food with them as there was no enough time to cook food, and the homemade *guokui* in Juntun, which was delicious and easy to carry and had a long shelf life, met the needs of the troops. Now nearly a thousand years have passed, and *guokui* has turned from a kind of "military food" into "popular food."

The most famous *guokui* store in Juntun Town is called "Liuguangmao's Crisp Juntun *Guokui* with Fresh Meat Stuffings of a Thousand Flavors," a name too long to be remembered by everyone. But the *guokui* sold here is really tasty and it attracts so many customers that more than 20 chefs working together cannot meet the demand and there is always a queue waiting. Besides this store, every ten meters or so in the town there is a *guokui* store, and the total may come to at least over ten. It is estimated that more than 1000 locals sell *guokui* outside the town, mostly in Chengdu. If an investor takes the lead in unifying the signs, centralizing the management, specifying the standards, and regulating the manufacturing process, can't all the more than 1000 *guokui* stores be integrated into a *guokui* store chain? As Pizza Hut, which is insignificant in the USA, can open chain stores in China, why can't the people of Chengdu go to sell Juntun *guokui* in the USA?…

It is most enjoyable to watch the whole process of making *guokui*. An oven, a kneading board, and a cupboard with sliding glasses make up the storekeeper's entire outfit of equipment. The first step is to knead *guokui*. Attention please, the show has begun. The storekeeper is knocking at the kneading board with a rolling pin in the right hand and, rat-a-tat, rat-a-tat, making melodious sounds that are long or short, quick or slow by turns. Then his left hand begins to toss the dough onto the kneading board with a bang, which is repeated again and again. Then, in between the knockings of the rolling pin on the board, he rolls the dough into thin elongated ellipses, spreads the filling evenly on them, and then rolls up every elongated elliptic piece into a cylinder, erects the cylinder, flattens it out and rolls into a thin piece, and finally sprinkles some sesame on both sides. The second step is to fry *guokui* in a frying pan with some sesame oil and keep turning it over till both sides get golden. The third step is to bake. Remove the frying pan, and underneath there is a baking oven, with a blazing fire in the middle and a clean wall around. Put *guokui* into the oven and recline it on the wall, and then put the frying pan back on the oven. After a while, remove the frying pan again. A tempting aroma is floating out and customers cannot help swallowing their saliva. *Guokui* must be made by knocking and tossing; seemingly eager to show off, the storekeeper knocks at the kneading board with the rolling pin in steady rhythm during the intervals of rolling the dough and makes a thunderous noise, which, however, sounds very pleasing to the ear like drumbeat.

Jack Quian

A certain bean jelly with pickled Chinese cabbage has prevailed in Chengdu in recent years. It is actually a kind of small hot pot without seasoning, including pure bean jelly with pickled Chinese cabbage, bean jelly with pickled Chinese cabbage and spareribs, bean jelly with pickled Chinese cabbage and aquatic foods, bean jelly with pickled Chinese cabbage and fresh meat, and other varieties. The cheapest one costs three or four *yuan* Renminbi per portion, delicious but inexpensive. More importantly, you can ask more portions of bean jelly free of charge till you are full up. It is easy to prepare bean jelly with pickled Chinese cabbage: Boil bean jelly, pickled Chinese cabbage, bean sprouts, oyster mushrooms, sausages, fungus-vegetable, and everything in broth, and eat when they are done. You can eat them while boiling, or boil them while eating. Now if you place an order of Chinese vermicelli with pig's large intestines, you will feel thoroughly satisfied.

The pig's large intestines look like the charcuterie in French cooking, and the vermicelli is similar to noodles made from bean or sweet potato starch in north China, but thinner. Mix sweet potato starch with pea starch, potato starch, and water, put the mixture into a colander, hold the colander tight with one hand and pound it with the other to drop the threadlike vermicelli into boiling water, take the vermicelli out of the water when it is done and cool it in cold water. Now, the storekeeper standing in the steam throws you a word in "Mandarin Chinese with Sichuan characteristics": "A big bowl or a small bowl?" Then the storekeeper snatches a handful of shiny vermicelli from the cold water, puts it into a little bamboo basket, adds a few pea sprouts, quick-boils them in a pot of soup stewed with pig's large intestines and young pig's lungs and then pours them into a bowl, and finally sprinkles some vinegar, chili oil and chopped scallions on them. Now a bowl of steaming Chinese vermicelli with pig's large intestines is served to you; you stir it several times and the soup is immediately dyed red by the chili oil. They look so colorful: red soup, darkish sweet potato vermicelli, green chopped scallions, and milky white pig's large intestines. The air seems to have a sour and hot taste and reminds you of Cao Cao, the first King of Wei during the Three Kingdoms who quenched his thirst by thinking of plums. The vermicelli is deliciously sticky and soft; with a lingering aroma in your mouth, you feel agreeably light and fresh between your lips and teeth; the hot taste scurries back and forth inside your throat and the aromatic flavor charges at your palate; the velvety vermicelli sets off the sour, aromatic, tongue-numbing, and hot tastes, which fill to the full all the internal organs of your body. Heavily or gently, slowly or quickly, different flavors massage your sense of taste in an orderly way. As such, Chengdu snacks lay a strong emphasis on the coordination of color, aroma, and taste. Generally speaking, there is a bottle of vinegar on the table; if you prefer a sourer taste, you can add vinegar to your liking. *Guokui* is available in stores selling Chinese vermicelli with pig's large intestines; some are stuffed with meat, some sweet, some sprinkled with spiced salt, and even some made of nothing other than flour. To go with Chinese vermicelli with pig's large intestines, you had better buy a *guokui* made of flour and nothing else. You may take a bite of *guokui*, a mouthful of vermicelli, and a drink of soup, then pick up a slice of pig's large intestine and chew it slowly until it melts into a stream of oily juice and spreads all over your mouth; by the time you have finished the soup, you are already dripping wet with sweat.

Now it is time to place an order of *bingfen*. To make *bingfen*, some seeds of a certain plant are wrapped up in some gauze, put into some clean water and rubbed nonstop with the hands; during the rubbing, the seeds produce some sticky liquid, which is mixed with the water and a little peppermint, and soon, the mixture becomes a transparent and light brown jelly, temptingly shiny and quivery. The jelly quivers in the spoon, as if a flick of the wrist will drop it down to the ground into pieces; carefully it is put in a bowl with ice cubes, and some roast peanut powder and melted brown sugar are added. You may stir everything in the bowl with the small spoon, then put a spoonful into your mouth, and you are sure to get overwhelmed by the aroma of peanuts, the sweetness of melted brown sugar, and the coolness of peppermint…The tender *bingfen* flees here and there inside your mouth and at the moment it must occur to you: What's the use of foreign jelly?

The day when we returned to Chengdu from Mount E'mei, we had dinner at "*Shunxing* Old Teahouse." We were treated to Chengdu snacks, and altogether more than 20 varieties were piled before each of us: the Zhongs' dumplings, dragon wonton, *dandan* noodles, the Lais' *tangyuan*, *danhonggao* (baked egg cakes), pearl-shaped *yuanzi* (boiled rice dumplings), north Sichuan-style *liangfen*, and what not. I said to Danny, "Since you rarely come here, have a taste of every variety." But there were more than 20 varieties! Although all of them were nice to palate, he had a limited stomach and could not go on after the first more than 10 varieties.

It is said that ever since the Zhong's Dumpling was established by its founder, Zhong Shaobai in 1931, it has been swarmed with customers. The main difference between the Zhongs' dumplings and those in north China lies in the fact that the former have a thin wrapper and are stuffed with minced pork and no vegetables. When they are served, certain special boiled spiced oil is poured on them and they are slightly sweet, salty, and hot—quite unique in flavor. Dragon wonton makes a feature of thin wrappers, tender stuffing, and fresh soup: the half transparent wonton wrapper is made of superfine flour with a little seasoning, which is kneaded slowly and rolled with a rolling pin; the pork stuffing is fine, tender, smooth, aromatic, and agreeable to the taste; the soup is cooked by deep-stewing meat from some parts of a chicken, duck and pig on a hot fire and then a low fire…And the name of the snack has its origin in the idiom "Together dragon and phoenix bring luck and prosperity."

In Chengdu, if you ask the natives, which is the tallest building here? They may not necessarily know the answer. But if you ask, which restaurant offers the most delicious food? They are sure to list over ten restaurants in one breath. Everyone that has been to Chengdu cannot help but exclaim over the natives' attitude toward food. The inhabitants of this "land of abundance" seem to have an exceptional interest in eating. They are fond of eating, good at eating, and adept at eating; it is safe to say that their eating has yielded taste, culture, wealth, and a standard of choice food. The saying "For common people food is everything" can be most revealingly illustrated in Chengdu. Essentially, the Chengdu branch of Sichuan cuisine was created by the people of Chengdu in eating and playing with food. While playing with food, variety and constant change are needed to have more fun and as a result, Chengdu food has developed into a system richer and more colorful than ever with inexhaustible tastes and flavors. Reportedly, there are more than 30,000 restaurants and snack bars in the high streets and back lanes of Chengdu; even at dead of night, if you want to dine out, there is always somewhere to go. In the downtown area, several streets for food and recreation line up like a fan from west to east: Yangxixian Street for Food and Recreation, the Hot Pot Street in the New Fu-Nan District, the Food and Recreation Zone around Du Fu's Thatched Cottage, Shuangnan Food Zone in Wuhou Temple Street, Yulin Food Zone, Kehua Street and Lingshiguan Street for Food and Recreation, Nanyanxian Street for Food and Recreation, Wangping Street for Food and Recreation, and the like.

Yangxixian Street for Food and Recreation is a key spot recommended by all travelers' guides to Chengdu. In this ten-kilometer-long street are gathered most of the glories of the food industry in Chengdu and stands one well-known restaurant after another: *Lijingxuan, Nantaiyue, Fuwanjia, Rongxingyuan, Shizilou, Daronghe, Taoranju, Baguyuan* (Ba's Grains), *Maojia Fandian*, and so on.

Jack Quian

While chatting with some friends in Chengdu, I saw they often felt at a loss for what to eat for the next time, which reminded me of the Italian people and the French people: for them eating was one of the most important things in life. As a result of paying much attention to food, the people of Milan has cultivated a keen interest in fashion design; and likewise, thanks to the inhabitants' love of dainty food, Paris has become the world capital of fashion. Chengdu does not lag behind Milan and Paris in pursuing the latest fashion, but in terms of the pace of change of popular food, it even surpasses the other two cities, which is no exaggeration at all. Out-of-towners think to eat hot pots is the right thing to do in Chengdu, but they do not know that the hot pot here is subject to constant change, which has resulted in many new varieties, for example, the stewed rooster hot pot, the beer-flavored duck hot pot, the rabbit hot pot, the hot pot cooked on an earthen oven, the fish's head hot pot, the goose's intestines hot pot, and the fish's head hot pot with sour radish. Many variations of the hot pot have also emerged, such as the Lian pot, the Shao pot, the soup pot, and the cold pot.

Autumn in Chengdu is very short, and winter seems ready to clasp the hands of summer at any time. Having just said goodbye to nighttime beers and snacks, the people of Chengdu, who are good at, fond of, and adept at eating, begin to welcome the season of soup pots, hot pots, and *chuanchuangxiang*. What is a hot pot? As long as there is a pot over a fire, then a hot pot can be cooked. Then what kind of pots and fuel are used? They have undergone many and varied changes since ancient times. Hot pots can be seen everywhere in Chengdu, and instead of looking around, you can actually smell out a hot pot restaurant: Floating in the air is a tempting aroma, which probably sets you thinking of a pot of red boiling soup, various food swirling around in the soup, and the tongue-numbing and hot tastes lingering on the tip of tongue. If you are a stranger in the city, there are two ways for you to arrive at the destination, a hot pot restaurant: If you are very confident of your sense of smell, you can try to follow the floating aroma to a hot pot restaurant; if you do not have any unique requirements, you may as well choose a hot pot restaurant overcrowded with customers.

Why are hot pots so popular? As a matter of fact, there is every reason for any tongue-numbing and hot food a bit on the special side to get popular in Chengdu, whose inhabitants ardently love tongue-numbing and hot tastes. Owing to the sincere cooperation between diners and restauranteurs in repeated experiments and technical innovations, hot pots have now become a kind of dishes that highlight the tongue-numbing and hot tastes with the five flavors (sour, bitter, sweet, pungent, and salty) in harmonious proportion, hot but not dry, tongue-numbing but not pungent, and with a mild aftertaste; much emphasis is put on the freshness and tenderness of raw materials, the appearance, quality, and variety of dishes, the diversity of wares, the adeptness of cutting and slicing skills, the beauty of designs and patterns, and the simultaneous satisfaction of the senses of sight, smell, and taste. Eating hot pots is different from eating Sichuan dishes; the latter's levels of color, aroma, taste, and appearance can be ascertained by diners upon the first bite, and as they completely depend on chefs' level of skill, diners can do nothing but passively accept everything served to them. However, it is not the case with hot pots, which involve diners to a great extent. That is, the taste of hot pots depends on whether diners are experienced or not, whether they can rightly control the duration and degree of instant-boiling the materials different in kind so that crisp food will not taste soft and tender food can melt instantly in the mouth. Therefore, while eating hot pots, every diner has to take part in the cooking and test his or her own level of cooking. The hot pot was originally invented by the people of Chongqing, but the people of Chengdu combined it with shish kebabs of Xinjiang Uygur Autonomous Region and created *chuanchuanxiang*, a snack unique to Chengdu: String slices of meat and vegetables together by bamboo skewers, instant-boil them in brightly red boiling soup, then dip them in a small plate of oil or crushed dried red chili pepper, and put them into your mouth; inside your mouth, they produce three strong tastes—tongue-numbing, hot, and steaming hot—and make you feel utterly pleased. Nobody could have imagined that this kind tongue-numbing, hot, fresh, and steaming hot food, which originated from an alteration of hot pots, should become *chuanchuanxiang* which, till now, has remained popular for more than ten years.

Walking in the high streets and back lanes of Chengdu, you will see big or small snack bars selling *chuanchuanxiang* everywhere; those low tables and stools painted in red, steaming pots of boiled spiced soup, and bunches of bamboo skewers constitute a special sight of Chengdu. When you go to fetch the materials to be boiled, there are almost a hundred kinds on the shelves like those in a supermarket; thin slices of meat and fresh vegetables are strung together by thin bamboo skewers and customers mostly snatch up many a bunch and go back to their seats. Although it costs only one *jiao* Renminbi per bunch, you can demand whatever services are available there during the eating: now you shout, "More tea!" And after a while you shout again, "More soup!"…The meal costs only a bit over ten or twenty *yuan* Renminbi, but the waitress may possibly get exhausted in running errands for you; and when you are ready to pay the bill after finishing the meal, you can still shout, "Count the skewers!" Upon leaving, you may hear the pleasant "Mandarin Chinese with Sichuan characteristics": "Come and eat the delicious *chuanchuanxiang* again!" "Boss, go slowly, and come again!"

My native friends told me, everywhere in Chengdu, you could at any time easily find a snack bar that sold tasty food at cheap prices. There are several tips that will help you judge which snack bar offers good food and services: there is a long queue of customers waiting; many of the customers are pretty women; neither the proprietor nor the waiters or waitresses look cold, or irritated, or angry. If a snack bar can meet these requirements, then it should almost be the one you are looking for. The most reliable advertisement, to be sure, is passed from mouth to mouth. If some "pioneers" have been to that snack bar, then it cannot be possibly wrong for you to have a try. On the third evening, I found a snack bar according to the above "principles." Before I went in, a couplet on the gate took me by surprise: the first line was "Long live the People's Republic of China," the second line was "How hospitable the people of Sichuan are," and the horizontal scroll read "Eat and drink to your heart's content." Hardly had I walked across the entrance than a young man in charge of greeting customers shouted at the top of his voice: "Two heroes, one private room!" The moment I sat down, the young man came over and asked, "How about two 'handsome young men'?" I nodded doubtfully and realized when the dish was served that he had actually recommended two "pot-stewed spiced rabbit's heads." The dishes that customers had ordered were renamed by this young man in a poetically beautiful way: stir-fried shredded potato was replaced by "working for the interest of an opposing group at the expense of one's own"; *gongbao* chicken wings, by "spreading the wings and flying high"; dry-braised duck's feet, by "traveling throughout the world"; and pot-stewed spiced pig's tongues, by "honeyed words."…

Lengdanbei, which opens at night, makes up another part of Chengdu's culinary culture. Around nightfall, you can see the sign "*Lengdanbei*" at the entrance to almost every restaurant, big and small; in front of the restaurant, there are a row of tables, which is a grand sight itself; the tables are crowded with plates of all sizes, which are filled with various kinds of cold food, including meat and vegetables—too many to be taken in all at once. "*Lengdanbei*" means drinking beer while eating nighttime snacks. The people of Chengdu do not like drinking beer at home or in a bar; they like doing so on a square. From May to October, from dusk till late into the night, there are several places in Chengdu where huge crowds of people drink beer together: Beer Square at Chengdu International Exhibition and Convention Center, the open ground in front of Sichuan Province Athletics Center,

Jack Quian

the square inside Sichuan Normal University, the Charming Campus food and recreation zone inside Southwest Jiaotong University, the southern lawn by Nanyanxian Road, the Xiti Olympic Center at Yingmenkou Toad and so on. Beers and beverages of all brands are available in these places, in addition to various kinds of snacks, grills, cold pots, and *chuanchuanxiang*. Chefs with superb skills are cooking on the spot; you see knives and ladles glinting, fire blazing and shining, woks and frying slices shaking and jerking, and in a while the food you have ordered is ready. Looking for diced meat and seafood amid dried chili pepper, chopped scallions and garlic, the diners say "It's great!" again and again, huffing and puffing all the while because of the hot taste. After the meat has been eaten, there remain half a pot of condiments; "Ok, little sister, light the fire, add some vegetables to the pot and give me a bowl of cooked rice," the diners say. And then bean curds, lactuca angustana, and konjak start boiling away inside the pot. There are more empty bottles and dishes, and the diners' faces begin to blush. With delicious food, refreshing drinks, and pretty girls, the people of Chengdu lighten the mood of their city.

In the summertime of Chengdu, *lengdanbei* brings together the lasting appeal and special particularities of the marketplace, which are described as mild and moderate, slow-paced and leisurely. *Lengdanbei* is the night salon in downtown streets, where all customers, whether white-collar workers and gentlewomen or small tradesmen and potters, can enjoy themselves. It is impossible to define the customers there by social classes: Rich people? White-collar workers? Wage-earners? By the side of *lengdanbei*, there are Benz and BMW, Xiali and Alto, as well as bicycles and tricycles; such a sight can be rarely seen in other cities. *Lengdanbei* can make male customers, rich or poor, big cheeses or small potatoes, feel so relaxed that they take off their coats, show a lean or fat upper part of the body, and sit justly and confidently on a public occasion in the streets. Those who come *to lengdanbei* are mostly belly-gods, who order bean curds from Xiba, spicy small fish from Xinjin, bitter bamboo shoots from Changning, rabbit's heads from Shuangliu, and even chilies are divided into two-gold-bar ones, millet-shaped ones, and bullet-shaped ones…If they do not place the right order, they will be laughed at for being "disqualified."…

Perhaps Chengdu is not the only city on earth that requires you to appreciate it with your "tongue," but if you want to figure out everything about Chengdu, both its leisureliness and its rich experience, you must learn to taste it with your "tongue." Recalling the food in Chengdu after my return to Phoenix, USA has been a cruel torture for me; I have to swallow saliva again and again until my throat becomes dry and coarse like a parched and tearless riverbed. Both rabbit's heads and bean jelly, both Chinese vermicelli with pig's large intestines and *chuanchuanxiang*, come to my mind time and again. As a matter of fact, everyone who has been to Chengdu finds it impossible not to like this city. Even though your ears are filled with Chengdu dialect that sounds like a foreign language, even though you cannot avoid dripping wet with sweat as if taking a sauna every time you go out, even though hot chilies and tongue-numbing Sichuan pepper make you show your teeth and grimace in pain again and again, even though it is not so easy to find traditional flavors, you cannot help but get close to and like this city once you come to Chengdu. Like floating dandelion, Sichuan cuisine has been sowing seeds all over China and swaying with charm amidst the wind of improvement and innovation. Both hot pots and fried dishes, both *malatang* (bunches of food with chili pepper cooked in hot pots) and *dandan* noodles, have been fascinating people with their unique flavors to such a degree that they do not want to leave or yearn to come day and night…No doubt Yong Tao, a poet in the late period of the Tang Dynasty, extolled Chengdu like this: "The rich bouquet of liquor has been floating around since my arrival in Chengdu, and I do not want to go to work as an official in the imperial court in Chang'an again."

Tips:

Chengdu Snacks:

Dandan Noodles:
Dandan noodles are a famous Chengdu snack made of flour. To prepare the snack, you should first roll a flour paste with a rolling pin into noodles, then boil the noodles till well done, and finally sprinkle some stir-fried minced pork on them. The slender noodles plus the crisp and aromatic thick gravy are fresh, slightly salty and hot, and very tasty, filling your nostrils with a rich fragrance. Widespread in Sichuan, this snack is often used as part of dim sum in a banquet. Its name originated from the fact that at the very beginning, it was sold by peddlers carrying a *danzi* (two baskets) with a shoulder pole. The ingredients total more than ten, including dark soy sauce, melted lard, sesame oil, sesame paste, mashed garlic, chopped scallions, chili oil, Sichuan pepper powder, vinegar, bean sprouts, and gourmet powder.
Add: No. 41, Tidu Street, Chengdu
Phone: 028-86744134

Fuqi Feipian (husband and wife's sliced pot-stewed entails of oxen)
It is a famous local dish well known throughout China. Beef, ox's tongues, hearts, and scalps are sliced after being pot-stewed, and then an elaborate dressing made of top-quality brine, chili oil, coriander, celery, and scallions is mixed and stirred with the slices. The slices are blended with the dressing right before the dish, which is delicate, aromatic, and agreeable to the tastes, is served.
Add: No. 23, Zongfu Street, Chengdu
Phone: 028-86617171

Pockmarked Woman Chen's Bean Curd:
Established in 1862, the restaurant offers Pockmarked Woman Chen's bean curd, which looks brilliantly red and in good shape; sprinkled with crisp aromatic diced beef, it tastes tongue-numbing, hot, fragrant, crisp, tender, steaming hot—typical of Sichuan cuisine. Tradition has it that the dish was playfully named after the pockmarks on the proprietress Mrs. Chen's face.
Add: No. 197, West Yulong Street, Chendu
Phone: 028-86627005

The Zhongs' Dumpling:
Founded by the three brothers of the Zhong family, the restaurant offers dumplings with chili oil and dumplings in light soup, which are celebrated for their thin wrappers, choice ingredients, tender filling, and fresh taste. The main difference between the Zhongs' dumplings and those in north China lies in the fact that the former is stuffed with minced pork and no vegetables. When they are served, certain special boiled spiced oil is poured on them and they are slightly sweet, salty, and hot—quite unique in flavor.

Add: No. 7, Tidu Street, Chengdu
Phone: 028-86753402

The Hans' Steamed Stuffed Bun:
This restaurant offers steamed stuffed buns characterized by thin wrappers, much filling, and a spongy and tender taste. To make such buns, you leaven the dough and knead it evenly with a little refined white sugar and melted lard, making it tender and spongy. The meat filling must be chopped ham butt pork with 40% fat and 60% lean, to which are added shelled and minced fresh shrimps, soy sauce, pepper powder, Sichuan pepper powder, chicken soup, and so on. A hot fire must be used to steam the buns till the wrappers purse up and feel springy, which means the buns are ready to be served.
Add: No. 116, Section 4, Hongxing Road, Chengdu
Phone: 028-86667191

The Lais' Tangyuan (boiled rice dumplings):
Established in 1894, the restaurant offers *tangyuan* with thin, fine, smooth, and moist wrappers and more than ten kinds of filling such as black sesame, white sesame, shelled peanut, shelled walnut, clementine, and sweetened bean paste. Named after the surname of the proprietor, the Lais' *tangyuan* tastes fragrant, sweet, and palatable.
Add: No. 27, Zongfu Street, Chengdu
Phone: 028-86629034

Dragon Wonton:
Set up in the 1940s, Dragon Wonton makes a feature of thin wrappers, tender stuffing, and fresh soup. The half transparent wrapper is made of superfine flour with a little seasoning, which is kneaded slowly and rolled with a rolling pin into something "as thin as a piece of paper and as fine as silk." The pork stuffing is fine, tender, smooth, aromatic, and agreeable to the taste. The soup is cooked by deep-stewing meat from some parts of a chicken, duck, and pig on a hot fire and then a low fire.
Add: No. 8, the South Section, Chunxi Street, Chengdu
Phone: 028-86666947

Pearl *Yuanzi* (boiled glutinous rice dumplings)
It is a kind of dim sum made of glutinous rice; embedded with a cherry, it looks like a colored pearl and hence comes the name "pearl *yuanzi*." There are a variety of filling, including sweetened bean paste, fresh meat, and black sesame. It tastes moist, fragrant, moderately sweet, and not sticky at all.
Add: No. 73, Daci Temple Road, Chengdu
Phone: 028-86626180

***Yumei Chuanchuanxiang* (bunches of food cooked in a hot pot)**
String slices of meat or vegetables together by bamboo skewers, and instant-boil them in a big hot pot till they are cooked and served. Previously *Yumei Chuanchuanxiang* in Huaxing Street was the most famous. Nowadays, *Chuanchuanxiang* restaurants can be found everywhere in the high streets and back lanes of Chengdu: those low tables and stools painted in red, steaming

pots of boiled spiced soup, and bunches of bamboo skewers constitute a special sight of Chengdu. A bunch of food usually costs several *jiao* Renminbi and after all the skewers are counted, a meal turns out to cost only a bit over ten *yuan* Renminbi per person.
Add: Nos. 169-177, Sanyou Road, Chengdu
Phone: 028-88017243

Notable restaurants in Chengdu:

Thrice *Daoguai Shaocai* Restaurant:
Thrice *Daoguai* (turning left or right at the end of the road) *Shaocai* (stewed-after-frying or fried-after-stewing dishes) Restaurant actually offers home cooking: rice steamed in old-fashioned clay bowls, a variety of cold dishes dressed with sauce, stewed dishes, stewed-after-frying or fried-after-stewing dishes, steamed dishes, and fried dishes. There are no big portions of food and the prices are not high, so the customers can order more different dishes at a time. My favorite dishes include stir-fried heartleaf houttuynia with broad beans, boiled seasonal vegetables, steamed streaky pork with bean sprouts, spareribs stewed with potatoes after being fried, and steamed eggs. The restaurant looks clean and neat, neither unattractive nor luxurious, and the customers will surely feel at home here. If your friends in Chengdu invite you to dinner at Thrice *Daoguai*, it means they already regard you as one of them.
Add: No. 58, Haijiaoshi Street, Jinjiang District, Chengdu
Phone: 028-84522022

Mom's *Tihua* Restaurant:
It is a small restaurant where the customers often have to queue up. *Tihua* (scalloped pig's feet) is quite cheap, eight *yuan* Renminbi for each. It is said that *tihua* can beautify one's face and rejuvenate one's skin and many pretty Chengdu girls are fond of *tihua* soup; perhaps it is why Chengdu girls boast a white skin and a fair complexion. But at the same time, they are afraid of *tihua* soup, for *tihua* is very nutritious and equivalent to a fattening agent. Therefore, pretty Chengdu girls are always subject to mental conflict, ambivalence, and hesitation, but at last, they always decide to eat at all risks!
Add: No. 36, Jule Road, Chengdu
Phone: 028-87010635

The Bais' *Feichangfen* Restaurant:
Feichangfen restaurants can be found everywhere in Chengdu, but it would be best to go to the Bais', which sells the most delicious *feichangfen* (Chinese vermicelli with pig's large intestines) at two *yuan* Renminbi per bowl. The vermicelli in Chengdu is made from sweet potato starch. Mix sweet potato starch with water, put the mixture into a colander, hold the colander tight with one hand and pound it with the other to drop the threadlike vermicelli into boiling water, take the vermicelli out of the water when it is done and cool it in cold water. There are usually two flavors: sour and hot Chinese vermicelli and Chinese vermicelli with pig's large intestines. Chinese vermicelli with pig's large intestines usually goes with *guokui*, so it would be best to find a *Feichangfen* restaurant with a sign that reads "Juntun *Guokui*." A bowl of Chinese vermicelli with pig's large intestines and a *guokui* are ideal partners.

Add: No. 35, North Qingshiqiao Street, Chengdu
Phone: 028-86655716

The Zhengs' Lian-Pot Restaurant:
The Zhengs' Lian-pots are plain-water hot pots, and according to raw materials, they can be divided into sparerib hot pots, black-bone chicken hot pots, duck hot pots, and the like. The Zhengs' sparerib hot pots feature top-quality raw material and condiments such as bell pepper, coriander, and thick aromatic chili sauce. After the spareribs are finished, the diners can add to the hot pot radishes, *yuanzi*, anchovies, and other foodstuffs, which, after being boiled for a while, taste delicate, fragrant, palatable, and refreshing. A hot pot suffices four diners and the prices vary from 48 to 188 *yuan* Renminbi.
Add: Attached Building No. 21, No. 1, North Zhixin Street, Shuangnan Neighborhood, Chengdu
Phone: 028-85088124

Bamboo Sea Specialty Restaurant:
Most of the dishes here relate to bamboos, such as rice steamed in bamboo tubes, braised beef with bamboo shoots, fried bamboo funguses (a kind of edible funguses found in bamboo groves), and bamboo sea cured meat. No diners will fail to place an order of rice steamed in bamboo tubes, which has a unique flavor. To cook it, you should put peas, cured meat, and rice into bamboo tubes and then steam them till done. The rice tastes delicate, fragrant, fresh, and slightly salty. It is said that all raw materials used in the restaurant come from the countryside and are natural green products.
Add: No. 14, Shenglong Street, Chengdu
Phone: 028-85245224

Red Apricot Restaurant:
Representative of New Sichuan Cuisine, Red Apricot Restaurant is a fit place for diners with a desire for not too hot dishes. Recommendable dishes include red apricot chicken, eel with vermicelli made from bean starch, and steamed catfish with thick broad-bean sauce. You had better get there for dinner before six; otherwise, you will have to wait for vacancies together with another 100 diners.
Add: No. 289, Shuhan Road, Chengdu
Phone: 028-87526846

Huangcheng Laoma Restaurant:
Huangcheng Laoma Restaurant is the most famous hot pot restaurant in Chengdu, which, reportedly, has opened chain restaurants in the USA. The interior decoration of the big five-storied building looks quite cool. There is a hall for self-service hot pot on the first floor, where a singer with a folk guitar sings English songs. On the top floor there is a teahouse with a transparent patio, where nostalgic black-and-white movies will be shown every Wednesday and Sunday.
Add: No. 90, Qintai Road, Chengdu
Phone: 028-86257671

Jack Quian

Mantingfang Restaurant:
Mantingfang (Fragrance All Over the Courtyard) Restaurant is a top-grade restaurant that offers Sichuan dishes. Furnished and decorated in a style with both Chinese and western characteristics, the restaurant looks magnificent, graceful, and poised. It mainly offers Sichuan cooking plus edible birds' nest, abalone, shark's fin, and other slap-up food and serves as a perfect place for business luncheons or dinners and gatherings of friends.
Add: No. 15, South Section 3, the Second Ring Road, Chengdu
Phone: 028-85193111

Chuanjiang Haozi Restaurant:
Chuanjiang Haozi (Boatmen's Work Song) Restaurant has a reputation for offering "cool hot pots," that is, unconventional hot pots. The so-called hot pot of "Two Peerless Peppers" is an invention unique to the restaurant. The fresh Sichuan pepper looks green and limpid and tastes delicately fragrant and tongue-numbing while the grounded fried hot pepper looks red and bright and tastes fragrant, hot, and really pungent. In addition, quite a few condiments are mixed and fried with vegetable oil and look bright and shining in color, without any turbid coagulated particles. The hot pot is tongue-numbing, hot, fresh, fragrant, light, and tasty.
Add: No. 1, Huazi Road, West Fangcao Street, Chengdu
Phone: 028-85533111

Grandma's Home Restaurant:
In Grandma's Home Restaurant, there is a big jar for stewing dishes in traditional ways, which, known as "the first jar in west Sichuan," takes several people to hold it in their arms. Inside the jar, which is made of firebricks, there is some charcoal. After being stewed for five or six hours by burning charcoal, such dishes as cade chicken with pea flour cake and edible fungus with green beans savor of the original raw materials and are extraordinarily delicious. Grandma's Home Restaurant also features rice cooked in a covered pot over an earthen oven with burning firewood and presents the diners with a cooking style peculiar to the countryside that they have not seen for a long time. Rice cooked with burning charcoal has an unusual flavor. There is an open-air tea bar in the dooryard of this traditional-style three-line compound, where the customers can have tea, play cards, and drink homemade beer to their heart's content…
Add: 7 kilometers south of South People's Road Flyover, Chengdu
Phone: 028-81234567

Baguo Buyi Restaurant:
With homely raw materials, *Baguo Buyi* (Common folk of the Ba Kingdom) Restaurant concocts innovative dishes with an unusual flavor and contributes to the improvement and betterment of Sichuan cuisine on the basis of unique flavors. It is a good place for entertaining out-of-town guests at dinner, where the dishes are inexpensive but delicious and the interior decoration is pretty pleasant. The proprietor has established a school of culinary art and published several books on Sichuan cuisine. The restaurant's characteristic dish is sliced boiled chicken, which is soaked in ice-cold soup sprinkled with light yellow pickled chili, gaily-colored pickled carrot, transparent pickled ginger, and green soy bean—so beautiful and pleasing to both the eye! The chicken is tender, the skin smooth, the bones crisp, and all tastes fresh, sweet, slightly sour and hot. The other dishes worthy

of recommendation include stewed soft-shelled turtle with taros, stewed eel with bamboo funguses and heartleaf houttuynia herb, and stewed crucian with bean curd.
Add: No. 20, Section 4, South People's Road, Chengdu
Phone: 028-85511888

Qinshanzhai Restaurant:

Qinshazhai (Virtue-Admiring) Restaurant specializes in food cooked with medicinal herbs. It is an ancient-style antique-flavor restaurant with top-grade services located in a three-storied building, which is complete with an artificial hill, brook, pavilion, terrace, tower, and famous calligraphies and paintings of old. All dishes use medicinal materials with a strong emphasis on nutritional value and food therapy and therefore belong to a new style of medicinal cooking. The dishes to be recommended are stewed chicken with gingko nuts and stewed fish with gastrodia tubers.
Add: No. 247, Wuhou Temple Street, Chengdu
Phone: 028-85053333

Old Chengdu Mansion Cuisine Restaurant:

Mansion cuisine refers to dishes cooked for family feasts held by officials, businessmen, and other social celebrities in Chengdu during the 1930s or 1940s. It combines the characteristics of Beijing cuisine, Sichuan cuisine, Guangdong cuisine, and Jiangsu cuisine. Built in the style of the Ming and Qing Dynasties and furnished and decorated with a luxurious and refined taste, Old Chengdu Mansion Cuisine Restaurant serves as a good choice for customers who want to entertain important guests at dinner. The dishes to be recommended include stewed duck with oranges and Chinese caterpillar fungus, beggars' fish, and fried glutinous rice, sesame, and black soybean paste.
Add; No. 37, Qinghua Road, Chengdu
Phone: 028-87328947

China's Club Restaurant:

It is one of the most expensive restaurants in Chengdu, with majestic furnishings and a high-ceilinged hall in the style of Sichuan local residences. The services there are exceedingly thorough and solicitous, but no dishes have impressed me except shark's fin.
Add: China's Liquor City Building, West Southern Railway Station Road, Chengdu
Phone: 028-85199620

The Zhongs' *Juyuanshan* Roast Duck Restaurant:

Established in 1886, the restaurant is built in the style of west Sichuan neatly arranged local residences, with cyan brick walls and black tiles that have accumulated dust of old. I like the sunny private rooms most! Can you imagine anything more satisfying than enjoying delicious food in the sunshine in late autumn?
Add: No. 38, Fuxing Street, Chengdu
Phone: 028-86752927

And more—

The Tans' Fish's Head Restaurant:
Add: Attached Building No. 1, No. 225, Qingshangshang Street, Chengdu
Phone: 028-87777789

Binjiang Restaurant:
Add: No. 16, Central Binjiang Road, Chengdu
Phone: 028-86664198

***Lifeng* (Great Profit) Restaurant:**
Add: No. 235, West Dashi Road, Chengdu
Phone: 028-87027766

Aromatic Sichuan Flavor Restaurant:
Add: No. 9, South Section 3, the First Ring Road, Chengdu
Phone: 028-85598899

***Huixian* (Meeting Immortals) Bean Jelly Restaurant:**
Add: No. 5, Lime Street, Chengdu
Phone: 028-87764612

Old-Line Aromatic Sichuan Flavor Restaurant:
Add: No. 9, South Section 3, the First Ring Road, Chengdu
Phone: 028-85531388

Eight Trees Restaurant:
Add: No. 1, Ping'an Alley, Chengdu
Phone: 028-86277777

West Sichuan Plain Restaurant:
Add: NO. 123, Wusha Road, Chengdu
Phone: 028-86911672

IV. A Tea City

"The teahouses in Sichuan top the world, and those in Chengdu top Sichuan." This widespread saying not only points out the status of Chengdu's teahouses but also the inseverable ties between Chengdu culture and tea. Like bars in Paris and cafés in Vienna, teahouses add a touch of refinement and leisureliness to Chengdu, an ancient yet modern metropolis. The practice of drinking tea prevailed in Sichuan as early as prior to the Qin and Han Dynasties. In 59 B.C., Wang Bao wrote in *Tong Yue* (An Indentured-Servant's Contract) about how the people of Chengdu made tea. It is the earliest record of the practice of drinking tea in China; that is to say, the Chinese practice of drinking tea originated in Chengdu.

Teahouses started to become popular in Chengdu during the Tang Dynasty; by the Song Dynasty, they flourished. During the last years of the Qing Dynasty and the early days of the Republic of China, teahouses rose to the height of prosperity in Chengdu. According to *An Overview of Chengdu*, there were 516 streets and alleys and 454 teahouses in Chengdu in the Qing Dynasty; that is, there was almost one teahouse for each street or alley. By 1935, teahouses in Chengdu amounted to 600 and received over 100,000 customers each day, though the city had a population of below 600,000. Barring women and children who rarely went to teahouses, the rate of teahouse frequenters was surprisingly high. With so many teahouses and tea drinkers, Chengdu surely deserved the title, "The Capital of Tea."

The people of Chengdu are fond of drinking tea and going to teahouses, for a long time ago, teahouses performed important social functions in Chengdu. Various kinds of information were exchanged there and in some trades, deals were made there; in many ways, teahouses were like cafés where the Austrians enjoyed their social life. Later, along with the diversification of the means of information dissemination and the places for social intercourse, such functions of teahouses became insignificant. But the position that teahouses had held in everyday life did not weaken and by now, they have become one of the characteristics of life and culture in Chengdu.

As a matter of fact, even today, teahouses in Chengdu possibly still top Sichuan and China as well as the world. In Chengdu, there are teahouses in downtown streets, tea stands in narrow alleys, tea booths in parks, tea gardens in universities—tea can be found everywhere. Especially in those ancient streets or alleys, every three or five steps appears a teahouse, whose business is unbelievably good as it is usually packed with customers with no empty seats left. To account for this phenomenon, you can find two reasons: First, in Chengdu, countless people visit teahouses; second, customers always spend half a day in a teahouse. As such, teahouses are certainly overcrowded with tea drinkers. No wonder it is said not without exaggeration that about half of the population of Chengdu live in teahouses.

As the people of Chengdu put it, going to teahouses is "paochaguan (enjoying oneself in a teahouse)." As typical of Chinese characters, the word "pao" signifies manifold activities: In Chengdu's teahouses, customers can drink tea, chat with each other, watch Sichuan opera, listen to *Qingyin* (a folk art popular in Sichuan), walk around with their caged birds, take a nap, read some light book, or have their ears cleaned; shoeblacks and fortune tellers wander among the customers, and everybody seems to be leisurely and carefree, enjoying themselves to the full. Inside such an environment, you will be deeply impressed by the easy-going character of Chengdu's society and the strong local flavor of Chengdu's teahouses.

While strolling along the downtown streets, Danny and I chanced upon a two-storied teahouse, where we got an eyeful of cyan walls and green bamboos rising high onto the roof in between a few old-fashioned small tables and felt as if walking into old time. We sat at a wooden window, drank a cup of tea over a plate of cooked sunflower seeds, listened to the lento light music of ancient *zheng*, and felt so serene and free of any thought. Representative of Chengdu's tea culture are actually those tea booths in parks or on riversides: there you sit on an old-fashioned bamboo chair or stool and drink a cup of *gaiwan* tea (tea served in a cup with lid and saucer), while a waiter or waitress adds boiled water to your cup every now and then; you may sit there as if in a trance, or listen to your mp3 player, or look the passers-by up and down without scruple. Such is the "bashi" of the people of Chengdu. This word in Chengdu dialect is more appropriate and more precise than "leisureliness." Generations after generations of locals have been pursuing this "bashi," which has also gradually affected every life that flowed into this city; hence, Chengdu has become a paradise in real life.

Why are there so many teahouses in Chengdu? Located in the subtropical monsoon climate zone, Chengdu Plain is warm and moist all the year around, and as a result, the people of Chengdu have cultivated a great liking for tongue-numbing and hot food. Yet too much tongue-numbing and hot food will cause dryness-heat, which can be tempered with fresh and light tea; besides, Sichuan abounds with tea products and accordingly, tea has become a drink popular with the common people. As *Shen Nong's Pharmacopoeia*, China's earliest book on drugs said, "With a bitter taste, tea can stimulate one's mind, keep one awake, reduce one's weight, and brighten one's eyes." According to the existing research findings, a tea leaf contains numerous chemical substances among which there are more than 450 organic compounds such as: phosphorus, potassium, sulfur, magnesium, fluorine, calcium, iron, copper and many other minerals, as well as protein, amino acid, and alkaloid. Along with the advancement of society and the development of science and technology, a lot of so-called "civilized diseases" have emerged. Modern people's diets include so many fishes, meats, liquors, wines, candies, and deserts that more and more of them have developed an acid habitus liable to acidosis, whose symptoms, with variations in degree, are as follows: fatigue, irritability, flatulency, wind colic, dyspepsia, rapid breathing, mental decline, and so on; an acid habitus also tends to induce myopia, decayed teeth, rickets, neurasthenia, excessive hydrochloric acid in gastric juice, arteriosclerosis, fatty liver, adiposity, hypertension, diabetes, coronary heart disease, and other diseases. But tea, which abounds in caffeine, theophylline, theobromine, xanthine and other substances, is a typical alkaline drink. Tea can be quickly absorbed and oxidized inside one's body, producing high densities of alkaline metabolized substances, which can neutralize in time the acid metabolized wastes in the blood as a consequence of eating too much acid food, maintain the acid-base balance in the blood and a normal alkalescent condition in bodily tissues and fluids, and keep the organism in normal working order. In addition, tea is rich in catechins, which contains tea polyphenols that can effectively lighten and remove chloasma and visibly clear pigmentation on adults' faces. In one word, tea is capable of facilitating digestion, decreasing blood lipids, reducing weight, brightening eyes, lowering blood pressure, beautifying looks, and so on. Drinking a reasonable amount of tea will be of great benefit to middle-aged and old people, especially brainworkers.

On the wall of a teahouse, I saw a notice that specifies the reasons for drinking four cups of tea every day:

1. A cup of Green Bamboo Leaf (a kind of green tea) in the morning: Green tea contains very effective antioxidant and vitamin C, which can not only eliminate free radicals inside one's body, but also help to produce hormone against tension and pressure. The little bit of caffeine contained in green tea can stimulate one's central nervous system and raise one's spirits.
2. A cup of Chrysanthemum Tea in the afternoon: Chrysanthemum can brighten one's eyes and soothe irritability. A cup of chrysanthemum tea with dried Chinese wolfberries or honey can be of great help to dispel melancholy.
3. A cup of *Kuding* Tea (a beverage prepared from leaf of Ilex latifolia) when tired: *Kuding* tea abounds with vitamin B1, vitamin C, calcium, and iron and can nourish one's liver and kidneys and brighten one's eyes.

4. A cup of Black Tea in the evening: Black tea is capable of clearing away heat, brightening one's eyes, nourishing one's encephala, soothing irritability, and strengthening one's bones and muscles.

It might be safe to say that Chengdu is a city steeped in tea. In Chengdu, tea is not used to relieve summer heat and quench thirst but for drinkers to take pleasure in. In an open-air tea garden by the Fu-Nan River, you sit back cross-legged on a beach chair, poising one foot in the air, and feel more than 100 percent leisurely and carefree; time seems to be riding on the rising steam of tea and slowly drifting away, never to return. It is said that to experience the state of ease and leisureliness in Chengdu, you had better start from the morning. You may pick at random a teahouse in an alley or a street or on the riverside, place an order of *gaiwan* tea, half lean back on a bamboo chair, and let the fragrance of tea float from between your fingers, taking the remote time along with your thoughts and feelings…It is hard to imagine what a Chengdu without tea would be like. A local friend told me that in Chengdu, going to teahouses was not a means of consumption but an attitude toward life.

In Chengdu, almost everyone who likes drinking tea has been to the Wenshu Temple. On a sunny day, there are no empty seats in the open-air teahouse in the Wenshu Temple and latecomers have to wait for a vacancy by the side. It was not until we went in that we got to know its inside was much more commodious than it appeared at the entrance. Located at the northwestern corner of Chengdu, the Wenshu Temple is the best-preserved Buddhist temple in the city of Chengdu and one of the most famous Buddhist temples in China as well. Initially established in the Sui Dynasty (581-618), the present Wenshu Temple was rebuilt during the Qing Dynasty after being damaged and rebuilt for a few times in between. There are a great many of famous or ancient trees in the temple, which seems to be very tranquil. While drinking tea there, you may as well burn joss sticks to worship Buddha; in doing so you may find some solace, even if it is worthless for all practical purposes. There are many fortune-tellers at the entrance to the temple who all claim to have a wonderful foresight; you may spend several *yuan* having your fortune told, but don't take it seriously.

As soon as we sat down at a table, a performance of tea ceremony began. We saw an old man in a light gray gown with the white cuffs folded in an ancient style, with a silvery hair, a broad shining forehead, and a pair of deep eyes under a pair of dense brows. We were impressed by his natural and elegant bearing, which revealed his whole-hearted devotion to tea culture. With a sweet smile on the face and a serving tray in the hand, a tall and slim girl in a light green cheongsam inlaid with tens of snow-white jasmine flowers walked to the old man gracefully. The old man started to make tea to the accompaniment of the melodious ancient *qin*: He gently took the lid off each cup, poured some boiled water into it, wash it, and warm it up; then he held up a teaspoon with the left hand, scooped up less than half a spoonful of tea, put it into each cup, stood up, poured some boiled water from the teapot into each cup until it was almost half full, put the lid back on each cup, wait for about half a minute, and stood up again to see if he could smell the fragrance of tea that might already be floating around; when he stood up one more time to fill each cup to the full, tea was finally made.

Now, the girl put all the cups of *gaiwan* tea onto the serving tray and still with a sweet smile on her face, walked to the customers, beckoning them to have a try. The moment we took off the lids, a refreshing fragrance drifted into our nostrils. Danny took such a fancy to the tea that while exclaiming with admiration, he kept flicking the shutter of the camera all the time. I looked at the bottom of the cup and saw a green "pond" with several snow-white jasmine petals floating on the surface. I savored a sip of tea and the aftertaste of jasmine flowers and *Maojian* tea (a kind of green tea) lingered.

Danny had never drunk tea before he came to China, but in Chengdu he asked for tea every day. The day we came down from Mount E'mei and drove for nearly a hundred *li* (a Chinese unit of length, 2 *li* = 1 kilometer) back to Chengdu, Danny wanted to drink tea and our driver suggested that we should go to a "classic teahouse of meticulous construction and representative of Ba-Shu tea culture, which draws from the styles of the teahouses in Chengdu in past dynasties and brings together the architecture of the Ming and Qing Dynasties, mural sculptures, furniture, tea sets, clothing, and tea ceremony into an organic whole."

As we walked into this teahouse named "Shunxing (Success and Prosperity)" and stepped on the floor paved with bluestone slabs, our eyes were caught by all sorts of complicated and puzzling images with antique flavors which came in a continuous stream, and I felt at a loss for where we were as if a drastic change of space-time had taken place. Striding over the tall threshold at the gate over which hung bright red lanterns, I immediately saw a board engraved with Chinese characters, which stated the reasons for starting *Shunxing* Old Teahouse: "…Time elapses quickly, yet who have been trying to evoke our feelings for our old hometown and looking for old walls? Not long ago, Sichuan snacks enabled customers to experience all joys and sorrows that tasted sour, sweet, bitter and hot and brass teapots and teacups with lids and saucers helped them understand many bleak ways of the world…*Shunxing* Old Teahouse was established to fully develop folk delicacies, revive the art of drinking tea in cups with lids and saucers, and make traditional operas and free acrobatic fighting prosper…" Walking along the antique cyan brick walls, I felt as if stepping inside an eventful history: under the dim light there were nine relievos about Old Chengdu lining the "space-time tunnel," which accurately presented an ancient riverside town, a downtown compound, an old-time teahouse and other folk customs and practices in west Sichuan and enabled us to see vivid marketplaces and merchants, blocks and folk residences, pavilions, terraces and towers in Old Chengdu. These relievos were sculpted by a famous sculptor, Mr. Zhu Cheng, whom we had met, with all his heart over half a year; they could be called "a modern *Riverside Scene on the Qing Ming Festival*" in west Sichuan. Most surprisingly, every brick and every stone paved there had been collected at all costs from thousands of households in and around Chengdu. They were not duplicates made of armored concrete but authentic antique bricks and stones that had experienced the swift changes of the world. There was even a brook of clear water, over which there was a bridge, and several big white geese were playing on the water, evoking onlookers' endless reverie of country roads and shepherd boys. I looked at the grove of tall and erect bamboos and the bridal sedan chair, the wheelbarrow in the shape of a cock's head, the windmill, the plow and plowshare, the coir raincoat, the bamboo hat and what not under the wooden window and straw curtain, and could not help but stretch out my hand to touch them, as if touching a period of history that we had never seen before.

If we open China's history of 5000 years, we can smell the fragrance of tea on almost every page; and *qin*, chess, painting, calligraphy, poetry, wine, and tea are vehicles of traditional Chinese culture and arts. The origin of the Chinese character "tea" was first mentioned in *Shen Nong's Pharmacopoeia*, the earliest book on drugs in the world. According to relevant experts' research, this book was written sometime between 221 B.C. to 5 B.C. Around the year 758 during the Tang Dynasty, Lu Yu completed the earliest book on tea in the world—*Book on Tea*, which discusses the ways and experiences of planting tea, preparing tea, drinking tea, and appraising tea systematically and comprehensively. It is said that there are many men of letters in the city of brocade and many tea drinkers in Sichuan. Now in Chengdu, the teahouses total over 4000, but there is a social hierarchy among tea drinkers. The rich people go to first-class teahouses, use tea sets custom-tailored by renowned chinaware kilns, and drink top-grade tea such as *Xueya* (Snow Buds), *Gongcha* (Palace Tea), *Yuqian* (Before Raining), *Yuhou* (After Raining); common people go to common teahouses, use metal tea sets to drink newly-picked tender tea; laborers usually sit on a bench at the roadside and use a big bowl to drink tea made from tea stalks, scrap tea, scissor-cut tea and *Kuding* tea. Lan Moshui, a famous journalist in Chengdu, said, to the people of Chengdu, drinking tea is a way of rest and recreation, a means of social intercourse, as well as a delight in life. The people of Chengdu think of teahouses as places for all kinds of activities and stay there for a whole day; they not just spend their leisure time or have fun there, but in doing so they get their work done, make money, and acquire information. A scholar even claimed with a deep feeling, "Teahouses in Chengdu are a key to an understanding of Chengdu."

Whenever the weather is fine or it is a certain holiday, the teahouses in Chengdu will be crowded. "Whether in first-class teahouses with sofas and cane chairs or small ones in a narrow alley with bamboo chairs and wooden tables, whether in parks or beauty spots with luxuriant flowers and ancient trees, or in farmhouses or courtyards with plentiful bamboos and exuberant grass…it is never difficult for tea lovers to find friends with the same hobby or even intimate friends."

The people of Chengdu say, "When the water boils and the tea smells fragrant, you may chance upon an old acquaintance that you have not met for years; when you taste tea and discuss topics of importance in depth, you may get to know a new friend that you regret not to have known before." …When you have formed the habit of drinking tea and observing the world for a long time, you will gradually realize that life is like tea and drinking tea is like experiencing life. A tealeaf looks so slim, so fragile, and so insignificant, but in truth, it is so subtle and so miraculous. When it is put in a cup and blended with water, it will set free everything it has. At that moment, what is tasted and appreciated is no longer the tea leaf but the water in the cup. Isn't that the case with one's life? Such feeling can be experienced especially when you taste the light flavor of a cup of weak tea. In Chengdu, tea is not simply a beverage but the embodiment of culture, of values, and an indication of one's attitude toward feelings and life; hence it contains a higher level of spirituality. A celebrity once said, "In times of prosperity, people like drinking tea, but in troubled times, people turn to wine". Tea is a gentle and cultured beverage which can only be tasted at leisure and appreciated in times of peace and prosperity. The character of the people of Chengdu is surely like tea: they can always take a sober and rational attitude toward life, not humble nor arrogant, steadfast and persistent, mutually helpful and dependent, and in harmonious unity. I especially like the feint fragrance in Chengdu's teahouses, which permeates the air, lingers between lips and teeth, unfolds in cups, and floats in my heart…It often reminds me of a song:

The feint fragrance is like a spring breeze, blowing a reverie into my mind;

The feint fragrance is like a summer spring, flowing coolness into my heart;

The feint fragrance is like an autumn red leaf, sending a sense of attachment into my nose;

The feint fragrance is like a winter sun, flooding my bosom with warmth.

…

It is said, "Tea is destined to lead us into a tranquil and peaceful state of life." Sitting in a teahouse, you will experience a state of manifold interests in addition to tranquility and peacefulness. Look, on chairs, at tables, in front of pavilions, or amid corridors, throngs of tea drinkers present a splendid sight: there are drivers, beverage dealers, doctors, teachers, travelers, and the like. They are laughing, joking, talking about everything, refined or popular, cultured or vulgar, and exchanging ample and miscellaneous information with each other; speakers are talking with great relish, and listeners are listening with great pleasure, smiling and then laughing off. To fully experience what tea can bring us, you had better go to an old teahouse in Chengdu. Mostly located in a narrow alley or even an ancient and damaged small courtyard, an old teahouse is usually filled with a hubbub of voices: old women are playing mahjong, and old men are chatting with each other or playing Chinese chess; waiters are carrying a steaming teapot to whoever asks for boiled water, and if they are tired of doing it, they may leave a thermos bottle with you. In an old teahouse, there are low tables whose original color is no longer visible, blackish yellow bamboo chairs soiled with grease, tiger-shaped ovens with hot coal and dark cinders inside, shining red short-mouthed copper teapots, and sets of tea cups with lids and saucers that are made of white china with cyan designs and often have harmless cracks as a consequence of longtime regular use. An old teahouse does not necessarily sell top-quality tea; generally it offers *Sanhua* (Three Kinds of Flowers) and *Maofeng* (a kind of green tea), mostly jasmine tea produced in Qionglai, Dayi, Pengshan, and other places around Chengdu, but the tea there can truly give off a fragrance the moment boiled water is poured into the cup. You will like old teahouses from the bottom of your heart as well as the sense of great freedom in mixing well among drivers and beverage dealers. In a sense, in Chengdu today, tea is not just a drink to satisfy one's bodily and sensory needs, it has also acquired a certain social significance and cultural meaning. It might even be safe to say that to the people of Chengdu, tea has become one of the outlets for feelings and emotions.

The practice of drinking tea has benefited from the spread of Buddhism in China. Buddhism insists on staying even-tempered and good-humored and molding one's temperament and advocates sitting in meditation. While chanting scriptures and praying to Buddha as early as the bell rings in the morning and as late as the drum is beaten in the evening, monks will inevitably feel sleepy or tired; and as tea can enable drinkers to have peace of mind, refresh themselves, and keep themselves awake, it has naturally become a mate to Buddhist ceremonies or services. In this way, Buddhism and tea have been brought together by lot and over thousands of years, a whole set of tea ceremonies and tea culture concerning the planting, making, preparing, and appraising of tea have been developed. As a result, with the special instrumentality of tea, monks in Buddhist temples can communicate with outsiders, receive almsgivers, talk of anything under the sun, and explain and preach scriptures.

It is said that the character of the Chinese people is quite like tea: They can always take a sober and rational attitude toward the world, neither humble nor arrogant, but steadfast and persistent, mutually helpful and dependent, and they put much emphasis on making progress together in a friendly and harmonious atmosphere. It is well grounded. On the surface, Confucianism, Taoism, and Buddhism all have their own school of tea ceremony and tea culture, which is not quite similar to one another in form as well as in values. The Buddhist tea ceremony is attended by tranquil solitude under a green oil lamp, aimed at purging one's spirit of desires and ambitions and attaining peace of mind; the Taoist tea ceremony is a means to quest for freedom, naturalness, emptiness, and quiet, and to retire from and rise above this world; the Confucian tea ceremony is meant to rouse oneself for vigorous efforts to fulfill one's aspirations, lubricate interpersonal relationships, and play an active role in society. For all these superficial differences, the three schools of tea culture share a significant common characteristic; that is, they all highlight harmony and peace of mind and actually support the golden mean of Confucianism.

The Chinese people attach great importance to social order, mutual dependence and support, friendship and understanding in human life. In terms of humankind's relationship with nature, the Chinese people advocate the correspondence between humankind and universe, the harmony between the five elements of metal, wood, water, fire, and earth; humankind can ask for everything from nature, but should by all means abstain from upsetting the ecological balance by ceaseless demand. Water and fire are opposites, but under certain circumstances, they can be mutually compatible and supportive. All these thoughts and values have been introduced into the Confucian school of Chinese tea culture, which maintains that in drinking tea, we should try to communicate with each other, create a harmonious atmosphere, and strengthen good-fellowship. In drinking tea, we should hold communion with ourselves and examine ourselves so that we can see both ourselves and others soberly and clearly. Self-examination on both sides can result in the enhancement of mutual understanding; treating a guest to a cup of fragrant tea is a show of friendliness and respect. Such a harmonious spirit in tea culture arises from the golden mean of Confucianism.

My friends in Chengdu told me, that over the course of ten years, teahouses have been emerging like bamboo shoots after a spring rain in high streets and back lanes in Chengdu. What is different from the past, however, is that today's teahouse proprietors attach more importance to service, individualized consumption, and a decoration of top grade and distinctive style. In Chengdu, to try to strike a deal with your business partners, you should go to *Shengtaosha* (Remarkable Skill in Sifting Gold from Sand) Teahouse where many important and influential commercial events in Chengdu have taken place. If you want to have a look at teahouses of a primitively simple style typical of Old Chengdu, you should come to this *Shunxing* Old Teahouse.

Danny looked around in pleasant surprise, for everything there was much too novel to him. There were *baxian* tables (old-fashioned square tables for eight persons) and *taishi* chairs (old-fashioned wooden armchairs), among which waiters in Chinese-style jackets with buttons down the front and waitresses in Chinese dresses were shuttling back and forth, bringing teacups, hot towels, and melon seeds; at the table beside us, with a teapot in the right hand, the waiter performed an acrobatic move, thrust the teapot mouth of several *chi* long with the scalding tongue-like water under the customer's nose, and filled the cup with bubbling water quickly and adroitly. After we were seated at an old *baxian* table, a waiter in a yellow mandarin jacket carried over a teapot with a scalding mouth of almost one meter long in the right hand and several sets of teacups with lids and saucers in the left; he first placed the clinking saucers on the table, then the lids at their sides, and at last, the cups with tealeaves in on the saucers; all of a sudden, he lifted the teapot onto his head, bent his head a bit, and the boiled water drew a beautiful curve and headed directly for the cup; then, he tossed the brass teapot behind, pressed the long and thin mouth of pot closely to his back, leaned forward with the pot, and poured the water rapidly from behind his back; the cup was filled exactly to the full and no drop of water was splashed on the table, which was amazing! I drank tea in a cup with lid and saucer, which was made with Chengdu characteristics, and at ease, I glimpsed a passage on the wall: "The buds are tender and the leaves are fragrant…Red yarns are weaved into gauze and white jade is carved and ground; a *chen* (a measure of weight) of tealeaves are put in a teapot and boiled until they become as yellow as pistil. We drink tea early in the morning, facing the rosy clouds of dawn and late into the night, accompanied by the bright moon. We chat over tea until we are intoxicated, but nobody feels tired as the past and the present seem to be purified by tea, which evoked a special feeling in my heart.

Gaiwan is a tea set peculiar to Chengdu, including a lid, a teacup and a saucer, allegedly invented in Chengdu by the daughter of a west Sichuan governor during the Tang Dynasty. Because without an underlay the earlier teacup often scalded one's hand, the girl began to put a wooden plate under it. To prevent the teacup from tipping over, she managed to put a ring of wax around the center of the wooden plate to fix it. Her invention was developed into teacups of various novel shapes and patterns by later generations. Such kind of teacups are wide at the mouth and narrow at the bottom, with a moderate volume, and the tealeaves can roll over and over fully and be stirred evenly; the lid that does not cover the cup tightly can preserve heat on the one hand and admit fresh air on the other and it can also be used to stir the tea inside the cup to mix it evenly; then with the saucer, you hold up the teacup, which is obliquely or half covered by the lid, and take a sip of tea from between the teacup and the lid, and your mouth is immediately filled with fragrance. The drinking posture unique to *gaiwan* tea not only can prevent the tealeaves from flowing into your mouth, but also looks quite graceful and relaxed. *Gaiwan* tea can be said to have made the drinking of tea into an art, which highlights the leisurely and quietly agreeable style of Chengdu tea culture. The practice of drinking tea in Chengdu is well-known all over China and it can even be said that "Teahouses in Chengdu top the world."

While drinking tea, the people of Chengdu put great emphasis on coziness and taste. The chairs in teahouses are mostly bamboo chairs with backrests, steady and going along with your body; you will not feel tired whether sitting on it or leaning against the backrest, nor will you fall down to the ground while closing your eyes to seek repose. There are teahouses in beauty spots, ancient temples, high streets, riversides, and the depth of back alleys in Chengdu. In some teahouses, you can sing Sichuan opera while drinking tea, which is called "Bai Wei Gu" in Chengdu dialect; that is, tea drinkers play musical instruments and sing for themselves. Reportedly, the repertoire of *Shunxing* Old Teahouse includes the highlights from Sichuan opera, the performance of tea ceremonies as well as Shu music by serial bells. Sichuan opera is a "lowbrow" art in Chinese popular culture, which has sprung up from fields and plots, spread from mouth to mouth, and developed and prevailed in big and small teahouses in Chengdu. The performing art of Sichuan opera boasts a set of highly signifying conventions and rich appeals of life, which are distinguished by great delicacy and variety. Take the expressions of the eyes for example. They can be subdivided into 24 kinds: shock, surprise, dread, fear, joy, anger, sorrow, doubt, worry, hatred, shyness, seductiveness, love, jealousy, drunkenness, sickness, expectation, hope, pride, scorn, craziness, evil, infatuation, and affection.

The list of plays regularly performed on stage amount to several hundred; complete with the four elements of singing, gesticulating, elocution, and acrobatics, each play features a stream of witticism that runs from beginning to end, set off by instrumental music and vocal accompaniment, apart from the consummate skills of face-changing, fire-spitting, water sleeves-swinging that fly their own colors and the signifying conventions of gestures and actions that imply endless subtleties. Face-changing is one of the programs that every tourist must watch in Chengdu. As a very unique way of representing the inner world of a character—that is, the changing of grotesque and ferocious faces signifies the indescribable goings-on in a character's mind—face-changing adds much to the expressive power of Sichuan opera. Every time a famous actor performs face-changing, the theatre is in danger of being overcrowded. Face-changing, which was regarded by actors as a secret unique skill in the past, is actually carried out as follows: Draw types of facial make-up on thin silks, cut away the useless parts, attach a silk thread to each facial pattern, arrange all facial patterns in order according to their sizes, and paste them together; the silk threads are usually conveniently tied to an inconspicuous spot in the costume; when the mood has reached a crucial juncture, the actor, under the "camouflage" of dance movements, pulls off the facial patterns one by one, very quick and neat, without any flaw. The more "faces" he has pulled off, the more skillful he is. There are two difficult points: First, the right amount of bond should be used to paste the facial patterns together, or the actor will feel greatly embarrassed when he pulls off all of them at once or fail to pull off one of them; second, the actor must be very quick and efficient in concealing his true movement from the audience by pretending to do otherwise…

In Chengdu, there are quite a few opera companies shuttling back and forth between stages in big and small teahouses all the time. At nightfall, you will hear the rhythmical clanging of gongs and drums in Sichuan opera; in addition to humorous and witty highlights from Sichuan opera, there are pleasant performances of *Qingyin* (a folk singing art popular in Sichuan that mainly uses *pi-pa*, a plucked string instrument with a fretted fingerboard as an accompaniment), *Tanxi* (Sichuan-style *bangzi* opera), *Jinqianban* (Sichuan-style *kuaiban'er*), and *Yangqin* (a folk singing art popular in Sichuan that mainly uses dulcimer as an accompaniment); even passers-by in the streets will stand still and listen attentively. On many a summer night as such, histories, lives, legends, and myths, which span 5000 years and tens of thousands of miles, flow from storytellers' eloquent mouths into our minds to the accompaniment of a rhythmical and forceful wooden block. I always think of teahouses in Chengdu as a medium of Sichuan opera. To those traditional people of Chengdu, teahouses are living rooms while Sichuan opera is the most important show to which guests are treated. On the stage of Sichuan opera we see the continuation, performance, and cautionary representation of many impromptu comic gestures and remarks in real life, humorous slang expressions in streets and marketplaces, as well as gifted scholars and beautiful ladies in legends. We all know that wine has the power to intoxicate, but we do not know that tea also has the power to intoxicate and Sichuan opera has even the more power to do so until we come to Chengdu.

In the early 1980s, the first time I came to Chengdu, the people of Chengdu liked drinking *Sanhua* tea then, which cost one *jiao* Renminbi per cup. Because I was not used to siesta, I often went to an old teahouse after lunch to drink tea and read books. Hidden from view by the verdant vine, there were over ten square tables of west Sichuan style and six or seven bamboo chairs: simple and casual. The bamboo chairs, made of slim slips, looked as if going to fall apart, but after you sat down and the squeaking sound was over, you would discover that they were actually a splendid achievement in human engineering that had developed over thousands of years: the bamboo armchair allowed the human joints to bend or stretch fully and meanwhile, it did not make you sleepy as the sofa or couch did, and you would not feel tired after sitting on it comfortably for a whole day. The warm afternoon sun leaked through the thick branches and leaves and shone on me, calling forth in me certain thoughts, certain sense of sereneness and of ease and contentment. Tired with reading, I would look up at the sky and then look down at the green tealeaves floating on the surface of water inside the cup; I would watch them slowly descending to the bottom of the cup and hanging there, and I felt as quiet as that then. Everything seemed clean and clear, and the white clouds helped relax my mind. Drinking tea at that moment, you felt as if your feeling would last forever, or just for a moment, and such words as "carefree," "crystal-clear," and "vivid" kept occurring to me…I cherish the memory of that era and that natural atmosphere; nowadays it feels so different when you sit in an extravagantly-decorated teahouse and have to put on a cultured and refined air. Lin Yutang, a famous writer, once said, "As long as a Chinese person has a pot of tea to drink, he or she will feel happy." A couplet that is often seen in teahouses in Chengdu aptly describes such a lifestyle: "Busy in seeking fame, busy in seeking wealth, snatch a little leisure from a busy life and have a cup of tea; hard to earn food, hard to earn clothing, try to find some happiness in a hard life and buy a bottle of wine." A cup of green tea is capable of getting both scholars and common people into ecstasies of delight and being regarded by them as both a reflection and a booster of natural disposition and intelligence, which surely attests to its wonderful taste.

We had barley returned from *Shunxing* Old Teahouse to our hotel and sat down when I received a call from a CEO of an IT company. He invited me to drink tea and I almost blurted it out that my stomach had already been filled with tea to the full; but on thinking of our friendship, his good will and the characteristics of Chengdu's tea culture, I could do nothing but accept his invitation. We went to a teahouse in a place called Liulangwan by the Fu River in Chengdu. There we saw low red brick walls, a wooden porch, comfortable cane chairs everywhere, and many pots of gaily-colored and lively flowers in full bloom hung under the porch and on the flower stands, which looked so rich and gaudy that their colors seemed ready to drip. This castle-shaped two-storied building was covered by wooden grids, on which Boston ivies were climbing at will in all directions. There was a peninsula-shaped garden in the front courtyard, which functioned as an open-air bar. Along the riverbank were placed many beach umbrellas of various colors as well as white, blue, and dune-colored wooden tables and chairs and the bar counter was a big thatched cottage. We felt as if able to smell a great variety of bright-colored and strong-flavored tropical fruits—it was indeed quite like a beach by the sea. There was another bar in the backyard that looked quite like this one. A corridor with a thatched roof wound its way around an umbrella-like big tree and it was very cool there.

My friend said, "If we are going to choose the best teahouse in Chengdu through public appraisal, this one in Liulangwan may be able to make its way into the top ten." The second floor where we were seated was designed like a cabin and even the floorboard looked like the deck of a ship; surely the customers would feel as if drinking tea on a ship. The tables and chairs were not those in an ordinary teahouse but light red sofas with wooden armrests and high backrests, extraordinarily comfortable. The music of ancient *zheng* was floating around in the hall and a wood-framed couplet was very eye-catching: "We do not know what is sweetness and bitterness until we drink tea; we do not recognize an upright and unbending heart until we appreciate bamboo." The waitress adroitly flushed the cups with boiled water, put the lid on the teapot, flushed it and put on the lid again and then, poured the water into a glass; with a tiny teaspoon she spread out the tealeaves in the teapot, poured some boiled water into it, then poured the water into the cups, put on the lids, shook the cups several times, poured out the water, then poured new boiled water into the teapot, steeped the tealeaves for about ten seconds, hence a pot of tea was made; finally, the girl took out the tea-strainer from the teapot with a pair of tweezers, lifted the teapot high and poured the tea down into the cups. The tea was poured down from above the shoulder and made a gurgling sound, just like a spring rain after a long drought. My friend told me, it is the third step of the tea ceremony: "Timely rainfall in many places." While drinking this strong yet not sour Sichuan tea with a lingering fragrance, I felt as if my soul was being stirred. There were many old photos on the walls of this teahouse and even in the water closets you could see paintings about the people and customs of Old Chengdu. The furniture in this teahouse was of a casual style and porcelains and potteries were casually put on the wooden curio shelves; every piece seemed so natural. There was a very big platform in the hall, on which a girl was playing ancient *zheng*, and the intoxicating musical notes rode on the fragrance of the tea and blew on my face; I saw a dense emerald mist floating around the brim of the teacup and the bright green tealeaves gave off a flavor similar to that of frankincense. Inside my mouth, the tea tasted delicately fragrant and deliciously sweet, the flavor lingering on my tongue also spread quickly to my arms, legs and bones, and I felt relaxed and happy all over my body. My friend said, "Besides tea, there were many other beverages made of plants' roots, leaves, flowers and fruits: tuberose, violet, ageratum leaves, aloe, heartleaf houttuynia herb, citronella roots, and what not, as if the customers were the legendary god of farming". In the eyes of the people of Chengdu, drinking tea is life per se as well as one's career and love; it is also the past and the future. It is probably how each time a youth runs into somebody, falls in love with him or her, and then gets crossed in love; it is also probably an old or middle-aged person's entire memory about his or her younger days.

My friend told me that the citizens of Chengdu had been discussing how to define their city for many years, and such titles as "a multicolored city", "a city of success", and "a city of science and technology" had been proposed to confer upon Chengdu. Yet after much discussion, they finally realized that the people of Chengdu could do without anything but teahouses and delicious food. Chengdu is a city steeped in water: "There is a big world inside a small teacup; there is a long history inside a cup of tea." In Chengdu, many a business deals have been made in such a leisurely and relaxed atmosphere in teahouses. Instead of saying Chengdu is a lazy city with the sole emphasis on the pursuit of comforts, I would say that the people of Chengdu know the art of living and working; only the people of Chengdu can contrive such a leisurely, easeful, nourishing, and work-in-leisure way of life. To work with pleasure is an important part of Chengdu culture.

Tips:

Shunxing Old Teahouse:
Located on the third floor of California Garden Hotel, it is an ancient-style teahouse where out-of-towners can watch face-changing, fire-spitting, lamp-blowing, and other unique skills in Sichuan opera and best appreciate the tea culture of Chengdu.
Add: The 3rd Floor, Chengdu International Exhibition and Convention Center, No. 258, Shawan Street, Chengdu
Phone: 028-87649999

Heming (The Crying of Cranes) Teahouse:
This teahouse has been scrupulously abiding by the tradition of Old Chengdu teahouses and many old people of Chengdu still have the habit of coming here for morning tea and a walk with their caged birds. Here, you can watch the performance of *gaiwan* tea ceremony and, once in a while, of quite a few folk practices in west Sichuan of old, such as ears-cleaning, *zhuantangban'er* (spinning the sugar wheel), and vaudeville. The area surrounding the People's Park, in which *Heming* Teahouse is located, was called "the small city" in the past, where the people of "Eight Banners" (military-administrative organizations of the Man nationality in the Qing Dynasty) resided. Therefore, *Heming* Teahouse has preserved more or less of their customs; the gate in the style of a memorial gateway, the waterside pavilion, the winding corridor, the *gaiwan* tea sets, and everything are permeated by a leisurely charm.
Add: The People's Park, Citang Street, Chengdu
Phone: none

Yuelai (Coming with Pleasure) Teahouse:
Located near Jinjiang Theater in Huaxingzheng Street next to Zongfu Street, the commercial center of Chengdu, *Yuelai* Teahouse is nicknamed "the center of Sichuan opera." Every Tuesday and Saturday afternoon there is a show of Sichuan opera and every Wednesday afternoon, the amateur actors and actresses of Sichuan opera get together in this teahouse. While drinking tea here, you can watch Sichuan opera for free. It is the right place to learn about traditional culture in Chengdu.
Add: Near Jinjiang Theater, Huaxingzheng Street, Chengdu
Phone: 028-86782057

The Wenshu Temple Teahouse:
Located inside the Wenshu Temple near Central People's Road and frequented by Buddhist devotees and pilgrims, this teahouse distinguishes itself by its low prices and customers that come in a steady stream. A waiter offers traditional services with a long-mouthed copper teapot.
Add: The Wenshu Temple, No. 15, Wenshuyuan Street, Chengdu
Phone: 028-86952830

Yiyuan (the Book of Changes) Tea Garden:
The name "Yiyuan" comes from *The Book of Changes*, a representative work of traditional Chinese culture, from which many philosophical concepts such as the harmony between humankind and universe, the two opposing principles of yin and yang have derived themselves. *Yiyuan* Teahouse occupies an area of 120 *mu* (a Chinese unit of area, one *mu* is about one fifteenth of a hectare). Inside, there are ancient trees and famous flowers of all shaped and colors; a pavilion, a tower, and terraces set off each other; a brook is flowing between and under artificial rockeries and arch bridges of a unique design. It is very relaxing to drink tea here, but the prices are a bit high. Keep this in mind when you are going to pay the bill.
Add: No. 8, Jinquan Road, Chengdu
Phone: 028-87512222

Ziyun Pavilion Teahouse:
Ziyun Pavilion is the former residence of Yang Xiong (he was also called Ziyun), a great literary master during the Western Han Dynasty (206 B.C.-24 A.D.). Everything in it savors of Sichuan of old: cane chairs, cane stools, cane tea tables, bamboo chairs, and wooden bookshelves. An ancient *zheng* is placed in the hall and visitors may feel free to pluck it. The teahouse offers tea produced by its own tea plantation. Made of even-colored big leaves and fresh buds, the tea, once steeped in boiled water, gives off a sweet fragrance and the water turns bright and light green; it tastes fresh, mellow, refreshing, neither bitter nor astringent. The various kinds of tea are named beautifully: "The notice on who is Number One Scholar," "as fragrant as plum blossom," "buds with morning dew," "floating fragrance in Ziyun Pavilion," and so on. In the teahouse you can receive and dispatch faxes and log onto the Internet.
Add: The 1st Floor, Hongcheng Commercial Center, No. 3, Shenglong Street, Lingshiguan Road, Chengdu
Phone: 028-85233388

Yalange (Elegant Orchid) Teahouse:
This teahouse offers tea, chesses, cards, and feet-bathing services. Red lanterns are hanging under the porch and in the corridor, implying luck and good wishes. Inside there is a gurgling brook and flourishing green potted plants are placed here and there to a turn, adding much vitality to the surroundings and making it extremely refreshing to drink tea here. There are private rooms of various sizes, which surely afford a best choice for gatherings of friends and acquaintances and such entertainments as chesses and cards. In feet-bathing rooms, your tiredness can be soothed after a whole day's work.
Add: The 4th Floor, Yulin Living Plaza, No. 15, South Yulin Road, Chengdu
Phone: 028-85599978

Wenxuan (Cultured) Teahouse:
Located in a fashionable neighborhood, it offers cosmetic and health care services, chesses and cards, food and beverages in an elegant and dignified environment. On the second floor, there is a gigantic fish jar of two meters long, where beautiful goldfishes are swimming to and fro happily. Two styles of massages are available here, the Thai style and the Chinese style. The former consists of simple but practical movements and no pressing of acupoints, while the latter features the pressing of acupoints and a variety of movements: By patting, slapping, rubbing, and pinching certain points on the body surface for tens of minutes, you will be made to feel relaxed and comfortable from the epidermis to the bones. Highly recommendable is the

Lovers' Rose tea offered here; it is a blend of rose petals, megranate juice, and tea, whose color is temptingly pink; it tastes light and fresh and can moisten one's throat and beautify one's looks.
Add: No. 9, Hongwa Temple Street, Chengdu
Phone: 028-85234998

Mingpin (A Great Variety of Tea) Teahouse:
Located in the famous "computer street" in Chengdu, it has an elegant façade that seems very eye-catching to the busy stream of passengers. The teahouse makes use of potted plants and rockeries typical of the landscape gardens in Suzhou and Hangzhou and the green plants are full of vitality and very relaxing. The tables and chairs are white European-style steel products, but fitted with cushions for leaning on, they feel warm and intimate. The floor is covered with a deep blue carpet that feels soft and thick. The *Huamaofeng* tea offered in this teahouse, which is made of *Maofeng*, a top-quality special product in Mount E'mei, is especially worthy of recommendation. To make a cup of *Huamaofeng* tea, a *gaiwan* tea set must be used, and the boiled water must be poured from high above till the cup is about half full; then you should cover the cup with the lid, wait for a few moments till most tea leaves have sunk to the bottom, and add more lukewarm water to the cup; and now, a refreshing fragrance is slowly floating into your nostrils and going to intoxicate you.
Add: Attached Building No. 1, No. 8, North Kehua Road, Chengdu
Phone: 028-85240470

Bamboo Grove Teahouse in Wangjianglou Park:
Situated in Jiuyan (Nine Openings) Bridge, east of Chengdu, next door to Sichuan University, it is a teahouse set off by a bamboo grove. Very popular with the inhabitants of Chengdu who seek recreation and entertainment, it offers mahjong and other disports apart from various kinds of snacks. Wangjianglou Park is the former residence of Xue Tao, where the woman poet has left many traces.
Add: Wangjianglou Park, No. 30, Wangjiang Road, Chengdu
Phone: 028-85210673

The Daci Temple Teahouse:
Located inside the City Museum of Chengdu in the downtown area, the teahouse boasts a long history and an ancient architecture, which can be called its "gold-lettered signboard." Men of letters and scholars often get together here with their friends and acquaintances. Antiques, calligraphies, and paintings are often bought and sold here.
Add: The City Museum of Chengdu, East Wind Road, Shu's Capital Street, Chengdu
Phone: 028-86659321

Shengtaosha (Remarkable Skill in Sifting Gold from Sand) Teahouse:
It is one of the first-rate teahouses in Chengdu, where businessmen try to strike a deal with their partners and rich people indulge themselves in luxurious merrymaking. Inside the building there are units in the style of the 18th-century British royal palace and 13 VIP halls. The teahouse offers coffee of the highest grade, tableware of a unique style, cigars of the best brands, and everything that one may expect to find here. In addition, authentic Western-style food and European-style black tea are

Jack Quian

available here. As *Shunxing* Old Teahouse, which is quite near, stands for the best of Chinese-style teahouses, *Shengtaosha* is the apotheosis of Western-style teahouses. They have something in common with each other; that is, everything offered in these two teahouses is rather expensive.
Add: No. 175, West Fuqin Road, Chengdu
Phone: 028-87744535

V. A Historic City

For many foreign people, Chinese history is the hardest nut to crack, for it is too long, 5000 years! There are too many events, too frequent changes of dynasties, and names too difficult to understand and remember…Once you are in Chengdu, however, you cannot afford to miss its historic relics, for this city is inseparable from its history: It is quite unlikely to find another city with a history of almost 3000 years and a name that has remained the same since its founding!

A friend of mine suggested that an understanding of Chengdu's history should start with the so-called "ninth world wonder," Sanxingdui Ruins, for everything about Chengdu has their origin there. We drove for forty minutes over a distance that took the ancient people of Chengdu nearly 3000 years to cover; thirty kilometers to the northwest of Chengdu, I saw the Chinese characters "Sanxingdui Ruins Museum" on an odd building that looked like a space vehicle.

Sanxingdui Ruins is a cultural relic of the ancient Shu civilization, which dates back to about 3000 to 5000 years ago. With an area of 12 square kilometers, Sanxingdui Ruins is one of the important archaeological discoveries in the 20th century. Inside Sanxingdui Ruins Museum, I fully appreciated the mystery and charm of Bronze Culture. Of the numerous bronze statues, we were amazed beyond words to see three famous fantastic "clairvoyants and clairaudients," who have a gigantic figure, eyeballs bulging noticeably from the eye sockets, ears of a size that cannot be more exaggerated, and a big mouth stretched till the ear roots. The bronze divine tree unearthed in Sanxingdui Ruins can be said to be a most intriguing object and the only one of its kind on earth. It is arranged in three tiers, with nine divine birds perching on its branches, apparently a representation of "the divine Fusang Tree (a divine tree in the East, from where the sun rises)" with "nine suns resting on its branches." Visitors will surely marvel at the luxuriant branches, fruits and flowers, and the divine dragon climbing head over heels down the divine tree, and cannot help asking a question: Of what use is this miraculous and imaginative divine tree, which was made by the ancient Shu people with superb bronze casting and molding technology and craftsmanship? Regarding Sanxingdui Ruins and the unearthed relics, there are a great many mysteries, which have caused a lasting debate among worldwide archaeologists for over half a century. Yet so many of the age-old mysteries remain unsolved till today that quite a few foreign media have reckoned Sanxingdui Ruins as the remains of an "extraterrestrial civilization."

After we got out of Sanxingdui Ruins Museum, we drove south to Jinsha Ruins, which can be traced back to Sanxingdui Civilization. Chanced upon by an excavator at the beginning of the 21st century, Jinsha Ruins is called by world archaeologists "the most important and incredible archaeological discovery in China." As Jinsha Ruins had not been open to the public, we were granted the privilege of entering the site of the Ruins and the storehouse of unearthed relics and looking closely at those invaluable and significant antiques. The receptionist told us, Jinsha Ruins, which is located in Jinsha Village, Supo County, Chengdu, was discovered while digging a street work site. The unearthed invaluable relics amount to over one thousand, including gold ware, jade ware, bronze ware, stoneware, ivory ware, and earthenware, and the ivory ware weighs nearly one ton. They are unparalleled in the world both in scope and in quantity. Most of the relics date back to the late period of the

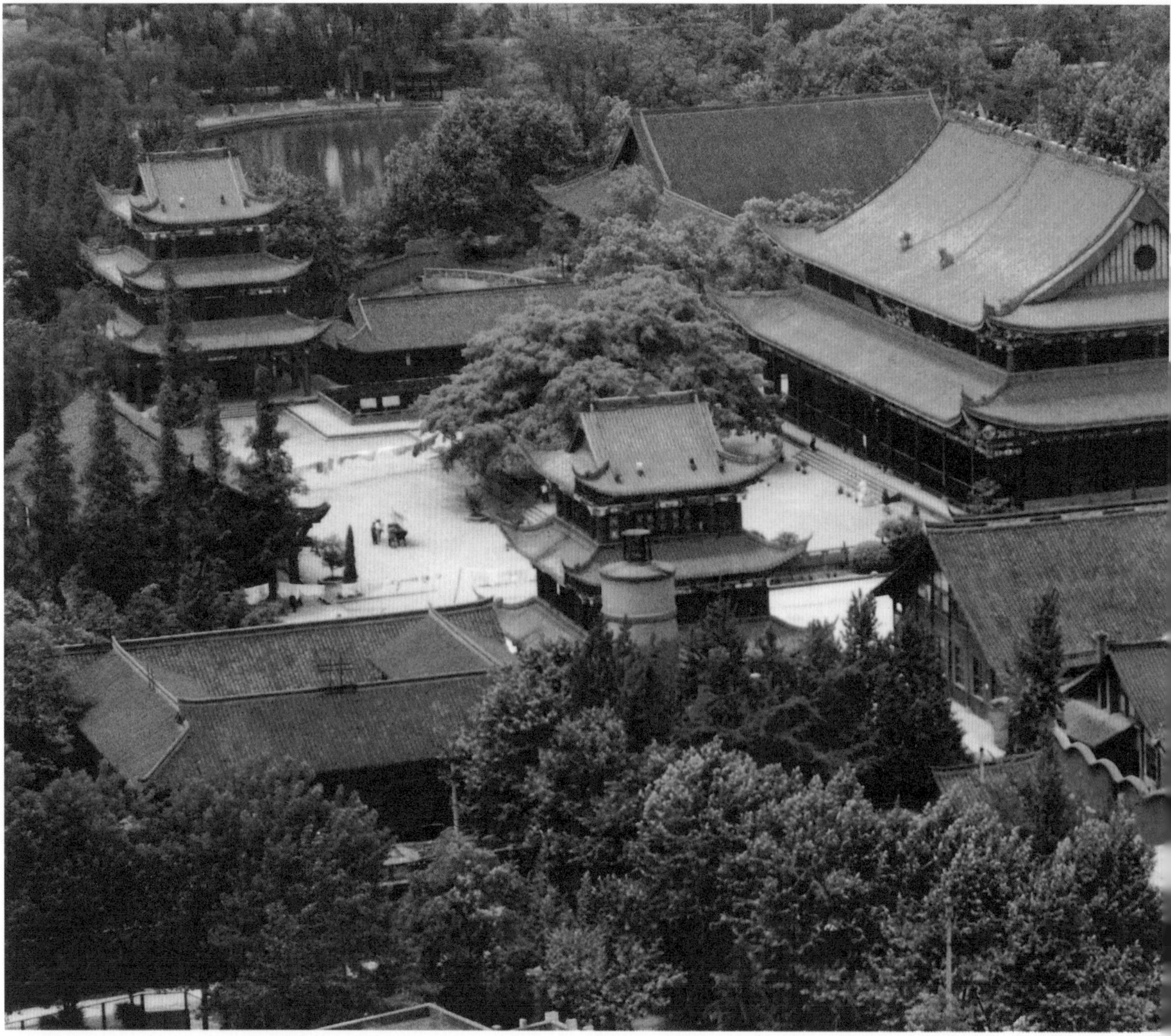

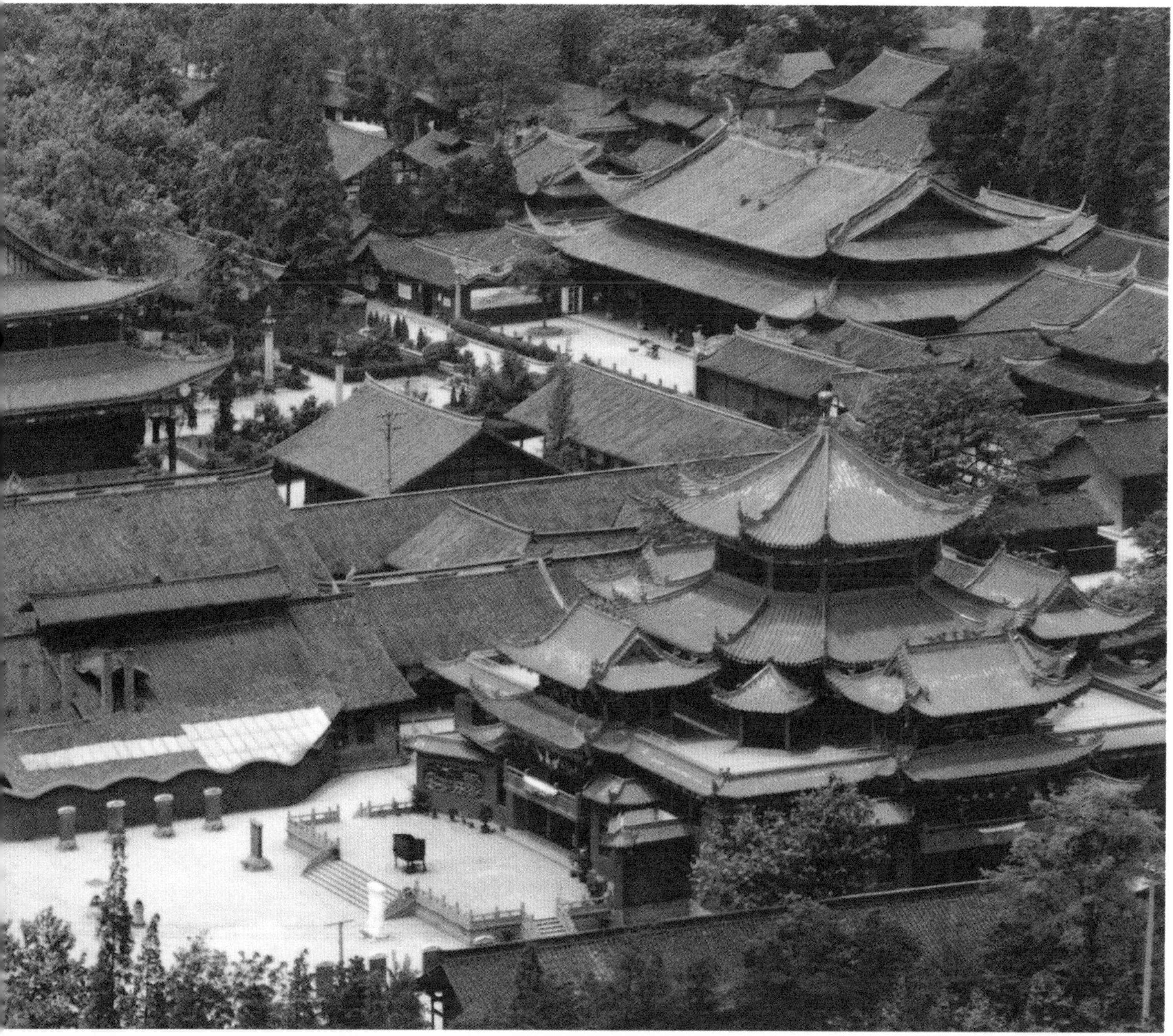

Shang Dynasty (the 17th-11th century B.C.) and the early years of the Zhou Dynasty (the 11th century-771 B.C.) and a small part back to the Spring and Autumn Period (770-476 B.C.). Inside the storehouse under close guard, we looked one by one at the unearthed ivories, wild boars' tusks, ebonies, jade pieces, and various fine and ingenious gold articles. In face of these almost inaccessible treasures, Danny, who had never "come into close contact with" unearthed cultural relics before, could not help but exclaim with awe.

I was made an exception by being allowed to take a photo of rows of ivories sealed up with silica gel in the storehouse and later I hung this priceless photo in the study of my home in the USA. The receptionist said that they had been extremely careful and scrupulous as if performing a surgical operation when digging up these ivories, which would have crumbled to dust if they had not looked out. The silica gel used to seal up one ivory cost over 10,000 *yuan* Renminbi. Among the unearthed gold ware, there are over 30 gold masks, gold belts, round gold articles, and bell-like gold articles; in design and style the gold masks are identical with the bronze ones unearthed in Sanxingdui Ruins in Guanghan, but all the other gold articles are unique to Jinsha Ruins. The jade ware is very fine and of all shapes and colors. The biggest article is a rectangular jade with round holes, about 22 centimeters high, emerald green, and very delicate in carving. When the receptionist put on a pair of gloves and carefully held up this jade article before our eyes, we could clearly see the hair-thin miniature carvings and a human figure on the surface and exclaimed in wonder. Several hundred of bronze articles are mostly small in size, including a bronze statue of a standing man, big-hole bronze articles, bronze dagger-axes, bronze bells, and so on; the bronze statue looks almost the same as the bronze statue of a standing man unearthed in Sanxingdui Ruins. There are over 100 stone articles, including stone men, stone tigers, stone snakes, and stone tortoises, and the like; they are the earliest and finest stone ware that has been discovered in Sichuan up to now. The statues of a man sitting on bended knees look quite lifelike and experts believe they were very likely slaves or captives of a nobleman at that time, which shows that the Kingdom of Shu was already quite strong then.

I felt most excited when I saw the gold foil of divine sunbirds within my reach, glistening and vivid. The pierced patterns of the round gold foil look like a well-proportioned and symmetrical paper-cut. Both the composition of the patterns and the niceties of the design are dealt with meticulously. The inside of the design is composed of a hollowed-out circle at the center and 12 equidistant ivory-like arch-shaped rotary edges around it; these sharp edges, which look like ivories or elongated tusks, are arranged like a gear wheel that has the tendency to rotate clockwise. The outside of the design consists of four divine birds flying counter clockwise, with their necks and legs stretched out, their wings spread out, and their heads and feet joined with each other end to end; surrounding the inside of the design, these birds are arranged in a well-proportioned and symmetrical way. The whole pattern looks like a magic whirlpool, or a rotating cloudy haze, or the resplendent sun in the sky, which is carried on the backs of the four divine birds to fly about in universe…The receptionist said, the gold foil of divine sunbirds has already become the best symbol of Chengdu; as one of the treasures of the ancient Shu civilization, it boasts a uniqueness, peculiarity and identifiability that cannot be replaced by any other cultural relic. The ancient Shu people was one of the earliest tribes to mine for and make use of gold. The gold masks, gold hats and belts, frog-shaped gold foils, bell-shaped gold articles, gold boxes, and the like that we saw are already enough to exhibit the excellent gold-processing technique of the ancient Shu people. Yet the gold foil of divine sunbirds is more cunning in design and more fanciful in style; with simple but vivid images, it reveals the Shu people's myth of the sun, registers the prevailing sun worship in the ancient Kingdom of Shu during the

Shang and Zhou (the 11th century-256 B.C.) Dynasties, and provides us with very important information about the spiritual life of the ancient Shu people and some of the important sacrificial ceremonies at that time.

After I had left Jinsha Ruins, for a long time I could not remove those fine unearthed relics from my mind; I imagined the glories created by the ancient Shu people on this land 3000 years ago and pondered the receptionist's passionate words: The ritual articles unearthed in Jinsha Ruins such as jade dagger-axes and jade tomahawks are obviously identical with those contemporaneous relics in the central plains, which points to the profound intrinsic relation between Jinsha culture and that of the central plains; meanwhile, the rectangular jade with round holes and the pointed tablet of jade unearthed in Jinsha Ruins were not "indigenous" to this land but transported along the Yangtze River—a golden waterway through the ages—from the lower reaches to the upper reaches. The frequent exchange between Jinsha culture and that of the central plains and the lower reaches of the Yangtze River speaks volumes for the fact that the ancient Shu culture was not isolated at that time but an important part of the ancient Chinese civilization. It also reconfirms the "organic whole of many entities" theory about the ancient Chinese civilization: The cultures of different regions have been interactional and interdependent. The wares of the central plains culture were transmitted to the ancient Kingdom of Shu by way of the Yangtze River, which proves that external relations and trade were carried out on a very frequent base in Chengdu; Sichuan was not an uncivilized region that, according to literature, "knew no written languages, or rites or morality;" and Jinsha was already the most important political, economic, and cultural center in the southwest at that time.

The above conclusion has been confirmed by the boat-shaped coffins of the Warring States Period (403-221) recently discovered in the Commercial Street in Chengdu. These 14 boat-shaped coffins with the remains of husband and wife in were unearthed from a 600-square-meter cemetery of the ancient Kingdom of Shu dating back to about 2500 years ago. All of them were carved from entire nanmu wood, the largest being 18 meters long. The cemetery, where most of the coffins were kept well, was the family cemetery of some royal kinsman or nobleman during the reign of King Kaiming in ancient Shu Kingdom. Experts believe that there must have been more than 30 coffins in the cemetery before it was damaged. Because the cemetery had been steeped in water for a long time, the corpses inside the coffins were reduced to skeletons, but the earthen and wooden relics remained bright-colored. According to the receptionist, although no gold or silver or jewelry was unearthed there, the unrefined copper ware, earthenware, lacquer ware, bamboo and wooden articles, and other important cultural relics amount to hundreds. Among them, the lacquer articles, which are dazzlingly gay in color, gorgeous in design, and numerous in variety, are the only finest works of art in lacquer ware of the Warring States Period in Sichuan that has been discovered so far. In the cemetery, there are still two well-preserved coffins waiting to be opened to examine the corpses, which may present important discoveries. At present, the preservation of the cemetery is still under discussion. Relevant experts hope that a museum can be built on the site to preserve the cemetery properly.

My visit to the three grand cultural sites has enabled me to gain a basic understanding of ancient Shu civilization during the important periods ruled by Yufu, Duyu, Kaiming, and the other kings. Through the resplendent and unique culture, I have perceived the mystery and strangeness peculiar to ancient Shu civilization and have come to revere the rich and profound history of Chengdu.

About Chengdu, Du Fu, a great poet in the Tang Dynasty, wrote two lines of verse: "Thinking back to the formerly-visited place, I feel like having had a dream; under the city of hibiscus there was an endless flow of water." As described by Du Fu, Chengdu at that time was a city where water and sky merged in one, hibiscus was in full bloom, and everywhere brimmed over with poetic and picturesque interest and charm. During the Five Dynasties (907-960) and Ten Kingdoms (902-979), it was not the kings or civil officials or generals but Lady Pistil who had made a name in the annals of history. Tradition has it that in order to insinuate himself into the good graces of Lady Pistil, his beloved concubine, King Meng Chang of the Late Shu Kingdom ordered his subjects to plant hibiscus everywhere in Chengdu; when they came into bloom, the whole city looked like a beautiful brocade of forty *li* long; hence Chengdu has been called the city of hibiscus since then. Beautiful and charming, the hibiscus flowers can bear comparison with the national beauty of peony; in addition, they have a lofty and unyielding character in spite of frost and snow; they prove to be a worthy emblem of the rich and beautiful city of Chengdu. Today's Chengdu is actually a city in which various cultural groups coexist harmoniously with each other and it combines the characteristics of many other big cities. For example, the people of Chengdu pay no less attention to politics than those of Beijing, the commercial atmosphere in the streets is no less strong than that in Shanghai, and there are many modernistic artists, underground rock and roll bands, enthusiastic football fans, mahjong master-hands, and the like in Chengdu. But Chengdu is also a city with a profound sense of history and culture; deeply rooted in their minds, this sense derives from a concept of tranquil but not silent history and culture and underlies the existence and aspiration of the people of Chengdu.

As a result, outstanding men of letters whose life and career were anchored here emerged one generation after another through the ages. The long gallery of historical figures in Chengdu has been nearly fully occupied by men of letters. And then, the people of Chengdu kept well the Wuhou Temple, the Daci Temple and Wang Jian's Mausoleum and rebuilt Du Fu's Thatched Cottage, the Wenshu Temple, the Qingyang Temple, and so on. Chengdu reminded me of the hibiscus flowers that have been bathed in morning dew for about 3000 years: bright-colored and indomitable, charming but not lacking in individuality; especially the dewdrops on their petals, like sparkling and crystal-clear pearls, carefully embrace rays of sunlight and then send them out gently…Thousands of years of wind and rain plus the poetic and picturesque creations of literators and scholars have nourished this miraculous city and nurtured its cultural profundity.

I remember the first time I came to the Qingyang Temple early in the 1980s, I was caught in a heavy rain; while standing under the dilapidated and ruined eaves to keep away from rain, I heard a fit of whining sounds of *xiao* (a vertical bamboo flute); a blind man selling *xiao* was playing an ancient tune with which I was unfamiliar; it sounded melodious, sentimental and exceedingly plangent amidst the rain. Listening to the whining sounds, I felt lost behind the curtain of ancient raindrops, which, like tears of ancestors, were quietly dropping down from the age-old eaves and washing away the light travel fatigue in my young soul. I stood silently behind the falling rain and stretched out my palm. The cold raindrops fell on my palm, splashed about like crystal-like flowers and then dropped down to the ground in pieces, as if telling me the ruthlessness of time. I walked to the blind man, bought two *xiao*, and put some money in his box. I still remember the whining sounds and I have kept one of the *xiao* and brought it to the USA. Now more than twenty years have passed, and where is the man selling *xiao*?

During my stay in Chengdu, I had not scheduled a visit to the Qingyang Temple, but because the plangent sounds of *xiao* had been resounding in my heart for over twenty years and could not be forgotten, I decided to spare some time from my tight schedule and go to visit the Qingyang Temple on Section Two of the West First Ring Road in Chengdu. The Qingyang Temple is a well-known ancient Taoist temple in China. It was first built in the Zhou Dynasty, flourished during the Tang Dynasty, and underwent destruction and reconstruction quite a few times. Taoism was founded in the Eastern Han Dynasty (25-200), regarding Lao-tzu as its founder and his *The Book of Tao and Its Virtue* as its classical scripture. Chengdu was one of the cradles of Taoism. A flower festival was held here every year on the 15th day of February in Chinese lunar calendar, which was said to be Lao-tzu's birthday. The Qingyang Temple turns out to be worthy of its laudatory title, "the first Taoist temple in west Sichuan." It covers an area of tens of *mu*, and the hall buildings stand one after another and look grand and majestic. Its entrance gate had been renovated and appeared antique, grand, and solemn, and three golden big Chinese characters "Qingyang Temple" were shining dazzlingly in the sun. I got to know from the guide's introduction that the three characters were written by An

Hongde, magistrate of Huangyang County in Chengdu during Emperor Qianlong's reign in the Qing Dynasty and could be said to be an important cultural relic in the Qingyang Temple. The entrance gate was flanked by two stately-looking stone lions. Walking inside, I saw crowds of people moving in front of and behind the halls, some of them strolling, some worshipping on bent knees, and some praying. The air was permeated with a strong scent typical of licenses and candles, the license-burner was overflowing with tears of red candles, and countless pieces of yellow paper were on fire in the bronze tripod caldron. Paper ashes were swept along by the heated air and danced back and forth in the sky, just like snowflakes that floated down in a movie's artificial setting. The fronts of the pious pilgrims' coats and their shoulders were covered with "snow-like pear flowers." I had not imagined that there were so many pilgrims here in the Qingyang Temple; many of them, who streamed by my side with a yellow bag on the back, obviously came from afar.

Before the Ming Dynasty, there had been endless streams of pilgrims to the Qingyang Temple, which, however, was destroyed in chaos caused by war late in the Ming Dynasty. Most of the existent architectures have been rebuilt successively since the Qing Dynasty. Among them, the Eight Trigrams Pavilion was rebuilt sometime between the reign of Emperor Tongzhi and that of Emperor Guangxu during the Qing Dynasty. The foundations of the pavilion are divided into three layers: the upper layer is round in shape, the middle one, octagon, and the lower, square. And the main body of the pavilion is round. The Eight Diagrams of sky, earth, thunder, wind, water, fire, mountain, and marsh command one direction respectively and the whole pavilion embodies the traditional Chinese belief that heaven is round while earth is square. The whole pavilion is made from wood and stone, surrounded by no walls but woodcarvings with tortoise-cloud patterns, and linked together closely by neither bolts nor wedges, but by square woods and square rafters with square holes dug in them. There are sixteen pillars in the pavilion, including eight outer ones with eight vivid winding golden dragons on each. It is said that all together there are eighty-one dragons in the entire pavilion, which symbolize Lao-tzu's eighty-one transformations.

The quiet path led to the Original Chaos Hall, where I suddenly heard fits of dimly discernible and melodious music. I looked around and saw a band of Taoist priests in Taoist priest's robes playing Taoist music. The music made me feel extraordinarily relaxed and happy and touched my dream-seeking heart like sounds of nature…

At the Scripture Printing Press to the right of the Hall of the Three Pristine Ones, I saw *The Selections from the Taoist Canon*, a collection of the main canonical scriptures of Taoism. The collection was composed of 245 volumes of books and printed under Emperor Kangxi's reign during the Qing Dynasty. Reportedly, the carving of the printing blocks took 15 years and resulted in more than 14000 blocks carved on both sides in pear wood. The tranquil surroundings, the majestic statues, the melodious music, the fragrant tea, and the tasty vegetarian diet, and everything informed me of the profundity and breadth of Taoist culture.

Actually, during my stay in Chengdu, I had been touched by the profundity and breadth of history from beginning till end. In my flight to Chengdu, I wrote in my notebook: In the depths of the basin there is a thatched cottage, and there once lived the "Sage of Poetry" who has touched my heart during my childhood—who would miss Du Fu's Thatched Cottage in Chengdu?

It was in the afternoon of the fourth day that we came to visit Du Fu's Thatched Cottage with reverence. Walking into this beautiful landscape garden, we were surrounded by a dense umbrage, fresh air, and the chirping of birds, which enabled us not only to meditate on the ancient times but also to enjoy the romantic atmosphere of nature. No wonder right here the poet could have created beautiful lines of verse that would endure forever! This Thatched Cottage had been rebuilt by later generations and I could see no dilapidated sight as described like this: "In August a high autumn wind angrily howls, and sweeps three layers of thatch off my cottage." Although the former residence of the "Sage of Poetry" is lacking in antiquity and dreariness, I still recorded it with my digital video recorder. Du Fu was born in Gong County, Henan Province and died in Hunan Province. Without a permanent home, he spent his lifetime moving from west to east and traveled through almost half of China. In 759, afflicted with an official career of no promise, poverty as well as illness, he led his family on a trip to Sichuan. Perhaps the poet had no other choice then, but it proved to be a right and wise move, for his life, which had remained miserable from cold and hunger for a long time, changed for the better in Chengdu. With the financial support of his good friends, Du Fu built a thatched cottage in the western outskirts of Chengdu and lived there for four years. During this period of time, he created over 240 poems, many of which were very popular. The relatively rich and quiet life in Sichuan, its simple and honest customs and morals, and the evergreen and brightly beautiful idyllic scenery, all helped to greatly relieve the poet's melancholy state of mind; besides, they added much freshness and brightness to his poetic mood, which had always been depressed and gloomy. In 765, owing to the successive deaths of his good friends, Du Fu lost his important support in Chengdu and had to move his family out of Sichuan by water. In 770, he died of illness in a boat on the Xiangjiang River at the age of 59.

This thatched cottage built by Du Fu has not only been regarded as a sacred place in the history of Chinese literature, but also become a historical site in which the people of Chengdu take an indescribable pride. Today, Du Fu's Thatched Cottage is actually a beautiful landscape garden, a combination of the "thatched cottage" with the ancient Fan'an Temple on the east, with a total area of over 300 *mu*. The two characters "Thatched Cottage" inscribed on the board that hangs on the entrance gate was written by one of Emperor Kangxi's sons in the Qing Dynasty. From the entrance gate to the rockeries in the rear garden, there are four hall buildings in succession, which are linked with each other by ancient paths in the middle and corridors on

Jack Quian

both sides. In between, there are pavilions that face one another, terraces that stand high or low, luxurious trees, and gurgling water, which are characterized by a refined style: deep and serene, simple but elegant.

Du Fu was one of the greatest poets in Chinese history. The comprehensive mind of the people of Chengdu inspired the poet to compose many a poem that enjoyed great popularity and will leave a good name to posterity; meanwhile, the poet's thatched cottage has not only built up a reputation for Chengdu that will last forever, but also has become a monument in Chengdu that will endure for all time…Walking out of Du Fu's Thatched Cottage, I thought of two lines of verse written by Du Fu: "Where can be found the Prime Minister's temple? Amid dense growths of cypresses, outside the city of brocade." So we found our way to the well-known Wuhou Temple…

Chengdu

Built during the Tang Dynasty, the Wuhou Temple consists of five main buildings: the entrance gate, the second gate, Liu Bei's hall, a corridor, and Zhuge Liang's hall, which lie regularly from south to north on the central axis. Beyond the entrance gate stand six stone tablets under a dense shade and an age-old cypress tree whose trunk is several armfuls in perimeter, allegedly planted by Zhuge Kongming (another name of Zhuge Liang) himself. Beyond the second gate, there is a spacious grand hall, where Liu Bei's gilded statue sits in the middle of the main shrine, accompanied by those of Guan Yu and Zhang Fei respectively to the east and west of the main shrine. In China, everyone knows the story of how these three men became sworn brothers and accomplished great historic feats during the Three Kingdoms. Walking out of Liu Bei's hall and across a courtyard with a horizontal board hanging on its entrance that reads "Wuhou Temple," we arrived at Zhuge Liang's hall. In the altar sits a gilded clay statue of Zhuge Liang, who looks cultured and composed. An intelligent and resourceful prime minister in the history of China, Zhuge Liang has been regarded as a model official loyal to his sovereign by the Chinese people.

Over the past several thousand years, a Chinese sometimes had to make a lamentable choice, for example, between politics and literature, between being a government official and being a human being. Whether in the past or in the present, the choices have always been politics and being a government official, for they are too tempting, but the majority of people believe that history usually chooses literature that will endure forever instead of politics that aims at quick success and instant benefits. In Chengdu, I have discovered a converse way of thinking: The people of Chengdu not only cherish the memory of those men and women of letters and sages, but also those government officials who have made contributions to this land in history, and a page of historical memory or a monument has been dedicated to each of them. Valuing human ties of love, friendship, comradeship and so on is one of the characteristics of the folkways in Chengdu. Wherever a government official in history came from, as long as he had brought benefits to the local people, the natives of Chengdu would feel deeply grateful to him, build a temple in memory of him and remember him till the end of day. Both the Wuhou Temple and Dujiang Weirs enable us to see the reward for being a "good government official." As long as the government officials worked for the interests of the local people in earnest and brought them benefits, the natives of Chengdu would never forget them; and among them were Li Bing and Zhuge Liang…

Jack Quian

In Chengdu's bustling and prosperous downtown area, there are two sites typical of "Old Chengdu". They are like a loose leaf of history, informing visitors of the lifestyle, interests and taste of the natives in Chengdu. They also serve as the best-known visiting card of Chengdu: the Wide Alley and the Narrow Alley. Under the blazing sun, I walked into this picture scroll of history: The Wide Alley was not wide at all; it was actually an uneven road, narrow and meandering. The Chinese parasol trees on both sides were casting their shadows, dim or not, on the road, the sunlight penetrating in between the leaves, and the walls and pillars whose paint had peeled off silently voicing the stories of generations after generations. The sun was baking the narrow driveway inside the alley and cicadas crying tirelessly in the branches. Walking in the alley, I felt as if my train of thoughts was pulled into a certain whirlpool in the long river of history and time seemed to slacken its speed; the mottled gray walls and cyan tiles had shut the urban hub-bub out and the post-meridian alley was unexpectedly quiet. Looking ahead, I saw a winding zigzag alley of great depth and it seemed if I walked a few steps further, I would be reluctant to leave…Several children were reading books quietly on the roadside. An amiable-looking old man was sitting on a bamboo chair at a door, half drunk and half asleep; now and then he held up the cup of tea to his mouth and then fell into a state of isolation again, as if he were recalling the past years that had vanished like running water. A gentle breeze was brushing past and I smelled whiffs of the trees' scent; the leaves were swaying in the breeze and specks of light were scattered on the ground. At the intersection of history and reality, everything seemed to blur and become more and more remote…Over 200 years ago, in 1718, the central government of the Qing Dynasty sent 3000 troops to suppress an armed rebellion in the border area, and then over 1000 troops were stationed in Chengdu, where barracks were built to help the officers and soldiers of the "Eight Banners" and their families settle down. The civil officials and military officers lived in the Wide Alley and the lower-rank officers and soldiers in the Narrow Alley. Since then the two ancient alleys have been kept well. Now what we see are the courtyards and houses with tile roofs built in the Qing Dynasty. All the cyan tiles, gray walls, red doors and eaves, and hitching posts at the door tell visitors that rich and important families once lived inside. The tall door lintels and patterned wainscots combine the characteristics of common residents' homes in west Sichuan and the cultural traits of the Manchu and Mongolian nationalities in the north.

While walking in the Wide and Narrow Alleys, it would be best if you pause somewhere, close your eyes, take a deep breath, and smell the flavor of the primitively simple and uneventful everyday life of the people of Old Chengdu. Or you may as well sit on a stool on the roadside, buy a newspaper, read some news about the local life, and listen to an old man whose family has been living there for generations telling true or untrue stories.

In the Wide Alley, there is a famous hotel called "Longtang (Dragon Hall) Hotel," which is actually a compound with houses around a small square courtyard. Many domestic or foreign tourists often come to stay in this hotel, for it is cheap and convenient, and more importantly, they can saunter in the Wide Alley at any time. The proprietor himself is an experienced backpacker. People of different colors keep coming in and out of the hotel, making it the "United Nations" in miniature. There is another hotel called "Xiaoguanyuan (A Small Garden with a Grand View)." It is also a compound with wooden houses around a square courtyard that feels deep and serene with many ancient trees. The proprietor is a painter in the traditional Chinese style, with whom tourists interested in traditional Chinese painting can exchange views and learn from each other.

In the eyes of the people of Chengdu, the Wide and Narrow Alleys represent less a period of history than certain reminiscence, certain remembrance, and certain spiritual anchorage. The climbing vines that hung down from the eaves seemed about to lead you into the depth of history. Open or closed gates were spotted with dust; the mascots carved in the door lintels were already peeling off; on the roof ridges, kylins with bare fangs and brandish claws and uptilting roof corners were musical notes in perfect harmony, singing the songlike history of the Wide and Narrow Alleys. I felt as if time had turned back for many years. I lingered among these door lintels with carved patterns and cyan bricks and tiles, paused for some time and then moved on, trying to comb out the historical and cultural texture of this city. I ran into an office building, which was actually a richly ornamented compound with houses around a square courtyard paved with cyan bricks…I felt as if walking into the days of old, or into a prince's secluded residence. I imagined that one day I could sit at the window and drank tea in a cup with lid and saucer over a dish of melon seeds; the surroundings were so tranquil that I could concentrate on feeling the lasting appeal of seclusion and serenity. Walking out of the compound, I saw gray walls, gray earthen tiles, gray courtyards, exquisite black tiles with carved patterns, mosses that resulted from years of rain, and green thatch grass that spelled desolation…All of them had witnessed the swift changes of the world and a resulting tranquility that seemed remote but very near; hence the alley got colors and a voice of its own. Pushing open one of the gates whose paint had peeled off, I could vaguely make out the grand view of old from the dignified façade that barely existed, and inside the majority of the compounds, there were few residents, dilapidated houses and clusters of weeds. I was suddenly seized with a sense of loss that I had never experienced before and I looked up at the sky over the alley, which seemed near at hand; at the end of the alley stood the years past and an ancient lifestyle was fading away…Although I knew that many historical relics would vanish in the course of urban construction, I was still anxious about the possibility that many years later, people might not remember these old houses marked with the evanescence of worldly affairs as they shuttled back and forth in this city, crossing through hundreds of years of wind and cloud, through shining spears and armored horses in those days as well as a faded prosperity…

That evening when I met Mr. Hao Kangli, a friend of mine who is a former deputy mayor of Chengdu and currently holds the post of standing member of CPC Chengdu municipal committee, I told him about my worries and impressions. Mr. Hao, who is well versed in photography, smiled and said, "We have the same worries and fears as you do, so when we are trying to develop and build a New Chengdu, we attach great importance to the preservation and development of Chengdu's historical and cultural heritage. You can rest assured that Chengdu does not pursue a modernization based on blind expansion but a balanced development of economy, politics, culture, and society as well as a harmonious coexistence between traditional culture and modern civilization."

He said, "As you know, Chengdu's latitude is 30 degrees north and on both sides of this latitude there have appeared a series of world wonders or inexplicable phenomena, such as the pyramids of Egypt, the Sahara Desert in North Africa, the Suez Straits, Mount Everest, the Three Gorges (Qutang Gorge, Wu Gorge and Xiling Gorge) of the Yangtze River, the entrances into the sea of the Yangtze River and the Mississippi River, the Bermuda Triangle. And more amazingly, the five religions—Christianity, Islam, Judaism, Buddhism, and Taoism—all originated on either side of this mysterious latitude! We're not just puzzled by such unsolved mysteries, which, however, lend us a motivation, a power based on self-confidence, and lead us to understand and build Chengdu from a historical point of view…"

The night in Chengdu was very lovely. Standing at the window in my hotel room, I looked at the streams of people in the streets and the dazzling neon lights, listened to the crying of the tricycle drivers and the rolling noises of the wheels, and saw all of them flowing to and converging in one of the roads in this city. Standing amid such a surrounding, I felt as if returning to a certain moment in my prelife. As such, Chengdu is an ancient capital city that has been bathed in the ceaseless river of history for over 3000 years and in its high streets and back lanes there are too many stories and romances. Both the cyan tiles with poetic flavors in Du Fu's Thatched Cottage and the gray walls with marks of years past in the Qingyang Temple have been telling us the long history of Chengdu. Even when you walk in the streets, the raindrops and falling leaves that keep brushing your face are imbued with a sense of history…

Tips:

Sanxingdui Ruins Museum:
Located by the site of Sanxingdui Ruins, 30 kilometers away from Chengdu, the museum occupies an area of 200 *mu* and comprises buildings of 14,000 square meters. The exhibition is divided into four parts: "Three Stars Accompanying the Moon—The Resplendent Ancient Shu Civilization," "The Kingdom of All Gods—The Mysterious Primitive Religion," "Shu's Soul of a Thousand Years—Fantastic Selected Cultural Relics," and "Three Stars Shining Forever—The Excavation of and Research into Sanxingdui Ruins." From the discovery of Sanxingdui Ruins in the 1930s to the excavation of two sacrificial pits in 1986, worldwide attention had been attracted to and focused upon the long history, fine cultural relics, unique culture, and mysterious flavor of Sanxingdui Ruins. Dating back to about 4,000 to 5,000 years ago, Sanxingdui Ruins was the center of ancient Shu Kingdom with the longest history in Chengdu. Many important academic questions concerning Sanxingdui Ruins and its unearthed cultural relics have remained unresolved mysteries till today.
Add: Sanxingdui Ruins, Guanghan, Sichuan
Phone: 0838-5500349
Website: www.sxd.cn

Jinsha Ruins Museum:
Situated in Jinsha Village, Supo County, the western outskirts of Chengdu, Jinsha Ruins is one of the most important archaeological discoveries since Sanxingdui Ruins was unearthed in Sichuan Province. The excavation of Jinsha Ruins is of great importance to the research into the history and culture of ancient Shu kingdom. It has produced precious materials lacking in previous literature, which will surely lead to the rewriting of the ancient history of Chengdu and of Sichuan as well. More than 1000 invaluable cultural relics were unearthed in the site, including over 30 gold articles, over 400 jade wares, over 400 copper wares, 170 stone articles, over 40 ivory articles, and ivories with the total weight of nearly one ton. There is also plenty of earthenware. Further excavation will possibly result in more important discoveries.
Add: Jinsha Ruins, Supo County, Chengdu
Phone: 028-66270171
Website: none

Du Fu's Thatched Cottage:
With the total area of 300 *mu*, it is the former residence of Du Fu, one of the famous poets in the Tang Dynasty during his stay in Chengdu away from his hometown. You can see small bridges, flowing water, plum gardens, and bamboo groves interspersed here and there and you can appreciate plum flowers in spring, lotuses in summer, chrysanthemums in autumn, and orchids in winter. Walking inside, you may not only meditate on the ancient times but also enjoy the romantic atmosphere of nature. The main buildings include Da Xie (the Office Hall), the History in Poetry Hall, the Firewood Gate, and the Gongbu Temple. On display are an introduction to Du Fu's life, editions of Du Fu's works printed since the Song Dynasty, and various translated versions.
Add: Thatched Cottage Road, Chengdu
Phone: 028-87319258
Website: www.dumuseum.org.cn

Jack Quian

The Wuhou Temple:
In memory of Zhuge Liang, premier of the Shu Han Kingdom (221-263), the Wuhou Temple is an important tourist site in the city of Chengdu. Inside the temple, you can see Liu Bei's hall, Zhuge Liang's hall, Liu Bei's mausoleum, and Zhuge Liang's gilded statue. On exhibition are replicas of unearthed cultural relics of the Shu Han Kingdom and pictures about the history of the Three Kingdoms. There are also numerous calligraphies, paintings, and couplets.
Add: No. 231, Wuhou Temple Street, Chengdu
Phone: 028-85559027
Website: www.wuhouci.net.cn

The Qingyang Temple:
Located inside the First Ring Road, the New West Gate, Chengdu, the Qingyang Temple is the Taoist temple with the longest history and the largest dimensions in the city of Chengdu. The existing buildings were rebuilt during the Qing Dynasty, including the *Sanqing* Hall (the Hall of the Three Pristine Ones), the *Doumu* (Big Dipper) Hall, the *Hunyuan* (Original Chaos) Hall, the *Lingzu* (Numinous Patriarch) Hall, the *Zijin* (Purple Gold) Platform, and the *Bagua* (Eight Trigrams) Pavilion. In the temple, you can also see *The Selections from the Taoist Canon*, a woodcut collection of the main canonical scriptures of Taoism, the stone statue of Lu Dongbin, a famous Taoist priest in the Tang Dynasty, and the like.
Add: No. 9, Section 2, West First Ring Road, Chengdu
Phone: 028-87766584
Website: www.grtc.cn

The Wenshu Temple:
With more than 300 Buddhist statues, the Wenshu Temple is the best-preserved Buddhist temple in the city of Chengdu and the seat of both Sichuan Buddhist Association and Chengdu Buddhist Association. Facing south, the temple occupies an area of 6 hectares and beyond the entrance gate, one after another, stand the Hall of Heavenly Kings, the Mahavira Hall, the Hall of Kwan-yin, Manjusri and Samantabhadra, the Dharma Lecture Hall, and the Buddhist Scripture Tower. The Bell Tower and the Drum Tower sit opposite to each other in the east and west wings, so do the dining room and the guest room. All the halls and towers are linked together by long corridors and dense pillars. The temple contains more than 190 rooms and covers over 20,000 square meters. The windows of the halls and towers boast a great variety of pierced carvings of fine and exquisite design, which are invaluable specimens for the research into ancient Chinese architectural carving. Nearly 10,000 volumes of Buddhist scriptures are stowed here.
Add: No. 15, Wenshu Temple Street, Chengdu
Phone: 028-86952830
Website: www.konglin.org

Yongling Mausoleum:
Located in East Fuqin Road, Fanhua Street, the Central District, Chengdu, Yongling Museum is also called Wang Jian's Mausoleum, that is, the mausoleum of Wang Jian, one of the emperors of the Early Shu Dynasty during the Five Dynasties. The Mausoleum is 15 meters in height, 80 meters in diameter, and 225 meters in circumference. Supported by 14 double stone

archways, the mausoleum is divided into the front, middle and back chambers, with the total length of 23.6 meters. Wang Jian's coffin is placed in the middle chamber, and there are carvings on the east, south, and west of the stone bed. One group of carvings depicts 12 Hercules uplifting and supporting the coffin; unique and strange in design, they look different from each other.
Add: No. 5, Yongling Road, Chengdu
Phone: 028-87760688
Website: www.ylmuseum.com

Wangjianglou Park:
In memory of Xue Tao, a famous woman poet in the Tang Dynasty, Wangjianglou (Tower Overlooking the Jinjiang River) Park sits among a dense growth of trees and bamboos by the Jinjiang River in Chengdu, with the total area of 170 *mu*. Inside the park, weeping willows brush stone balustrades, shining waves reflect Wangjiang Tower, green bamboos flank winding paths, and pavilions and towers set off each other. Chongli (Admiring Beauty) Pavilion, Zhuojin (Washing Brocades) Tower, and Yinshi (Composing Poetry) Tower stand side by side along the Jinjiang River; Wuyunxian (Five Cloud Immortals) House, Quanxiang (Fragrant Spring) Pavilion, Pipamen (Loquat Door) Alley, Qingwan (Fresh and Graceful) Chamber, Huanjian (Washing Paper) Pavilion and the other memorial buildings are arranged artfully and tastefully, with numerous plaques, couplets, and inscribed tablets. Xue Tao loved bamboos all life long and to commemorate her, later generations have planted over 150 kinds of indigenous and exotic bamboos in the park.
Add: No. 30, Wangjiang Road, Chengdu
Phone: 028-85249305
Website: www.wangjianglou.com

VI. A Water City

Chengdu boasts giant pandas, numerous historical sites, and a rich dietary culture, but there are more charming things to the city. The people of Chengdu also take deep pride in a simple and natural life, happy time that is extremely easy to obtain, and inexpensive but satisfactory enjoyments.

On the map of China, Chengdu is like a transfer station that links the prosperous central plains and the wild frontier plateaus. Its airlines, railways, highways, and the southern "Silk Road" that has been lost for hundreds of years lead to the relatively developed coastal areas in southeast China at one end, and to the mysterious and beautiful Qinghai-Tibet Plateau at the other. Chengdu is not only richly endowed by nature, but also immensely favored by its forebearers. In west China where water is always in short supply, Chengdu is a city embraced by water.

Like the Seine River in Paris and the Danube River in Budapest, the Fu-Nan River flows through Chengdu, nourishing the city and nurturing its millions of inhabitants and all vegetation. And the water is not just natural but also historic and volitional. It seems to be the soul of Chengdu; without it, Chengdu could not be Chengdu and it would lose its energy and vitality entirely, and as a soulless city, its richness, populousness, beauty, prosperity, and everything else seem to be forced and unnatural. No other city in China can compare with Chengdu, which stands right on the middle ground between fantasy and reality.

Some people say Chengdu is a historic city in China; some say Chengdu is the most leisurely city in China; and others say Chengdu is a city nourished by water. The latter turned out to be true, for on the second day hardly had I opened my eyes when I heard the rustle of falling rain outside my window; I pulled open the curtain and saw the entire Chengdu city enveloped in a misty rain. I remembered an essay on the Internet, which claimed that water was one of the most important reasons why Chengdu remained intact for thousands of years. "The two rivers that flow through the city have been incessantly irrigating Chengdu and cultivating in her people the wisdom in face of time and the composure and self-confidence that an ancient city is supposed to possess in face of the evanescence of worldly affairs. The running water of wisdom passes through the city quietly, immersing men and women, old and young, transfusing gentle gene into the marrow of the city, and planting a ripple of talent into its bones' organic matrix." Standing at the window, I could truly feel Chengdu in terms water: The watercourses thickly lining her body were her winding blood vessels, the drizzle dancing wildly in the sky was the source of her gentle dense mist, and the continuous Jinjiang River moistened this poetic yet dreamlike city and provided its soul with comfort and solace. Looking at the city of Chengdu that was wrapped in the boundless rain curtain, I imagined a scene like this: In the Tang Dynasty about a thousand years ago, it was also June and it was also raining in this city of brocade; the blue, clear water of Huanhua (Bathing Flowers) Brook was quietly rising, the fragrant wild flowers on the banks were swaying in the rain, and the sweet-smelling camphor and cypress trees in Du Fu's Thatched Cottage were embraced by the elves of rain. As such, they kissed this city night after night, moistened the poet's dreamland, and inspired him to write such beautiful lines of verse: "A good rain knows the timing / And in spring she comes. / Quietly she arrives with the wind at night / And moistens everything without making any noise…" (Du Fu).

I am always fond of the tranquility set off by rain by contrast, for only under such circumstances can the eyes of life see my soul and examine its transparency, peacefulness, and contentment at the moment…The city of Chengdu, thanks to the Creator, has absorbed the most of supernatural talents indigenous to the land of Ba-Shu and converged all the rivers in the plain in west Sichuan; It hides the profundity of the Shu culture among the landscape and vegetation and like water, preserves a life force that can penetrate time and space.

Right then I decided to go on a tour of the streets by car. Our car was driving slowly, the rain outside the window was like a theatre curtain, and behind the curtain there were rows of indistinct tall buildings…Suddenly, I saw an antique roofed bridge with black tiles and red walls "floating" on the surface of the water, flickering like a mirage over the glistening waves…

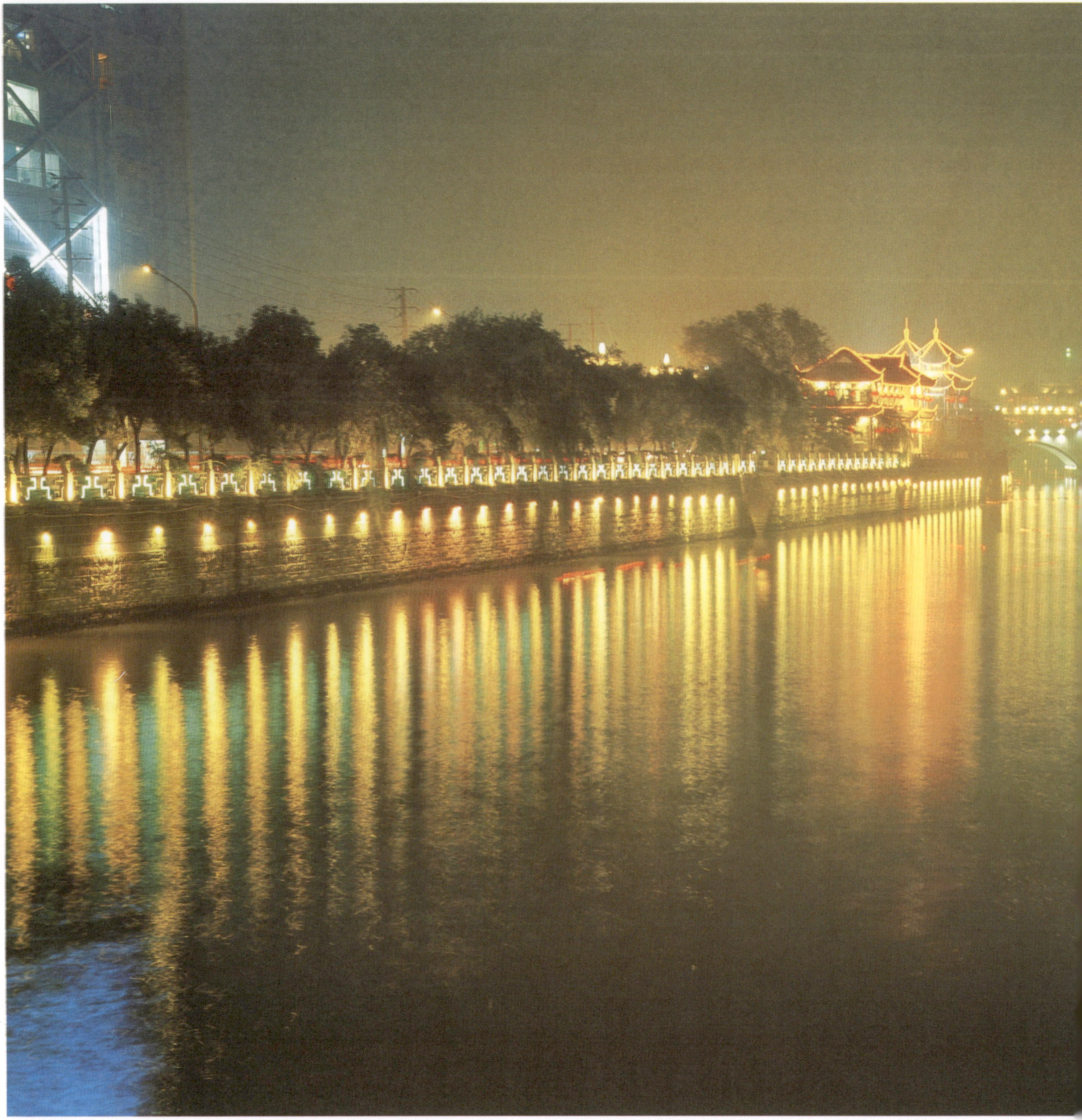

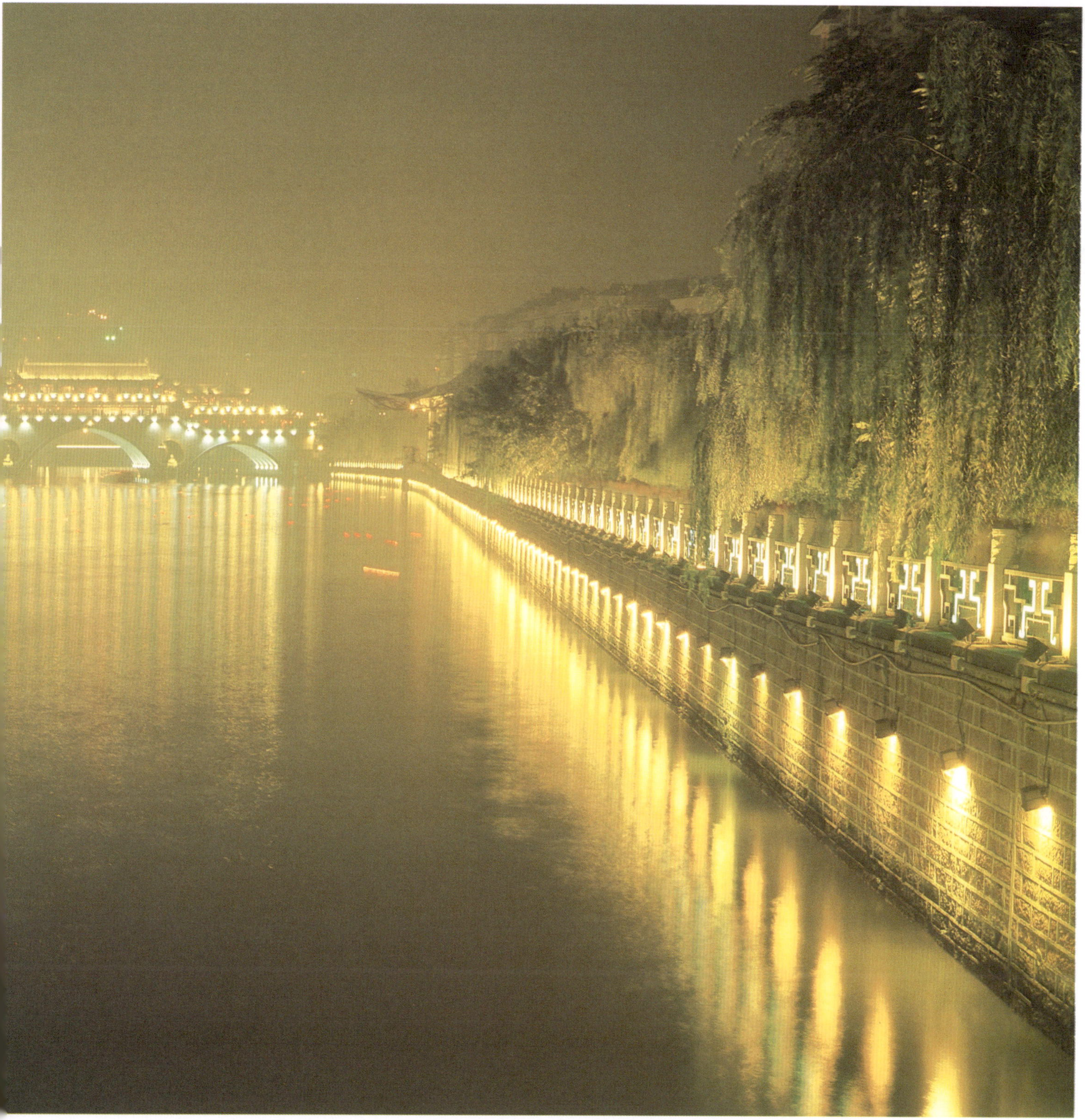

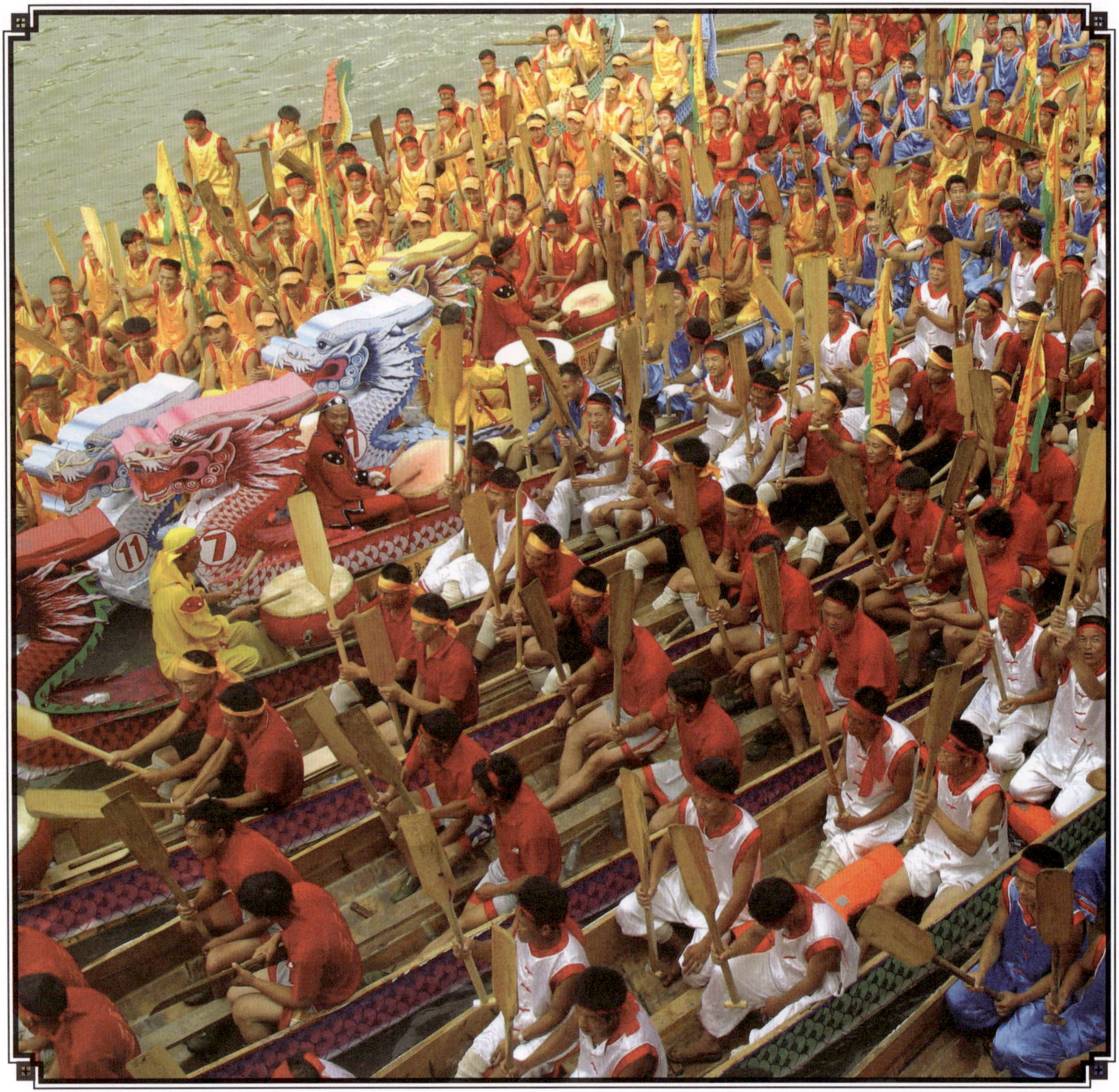

"What's that?" I asked.

"A roofed bridge, Anshun Bridge," Our driver answered.

Anshun Bridge? Marco Polo, who traveled throughout China, wrote of four Chinese bridges and one of them was Anshun Bridge in Chengdu. Our driver said Anshun Bridge had collapsed long before due to wind and rain and in 2003, the municipal government of Chengdu had it rebuilt. Li Chuncheng, the then mayor of Chengdu adopted a surprisingly original approach and succeeded in having this roofed bridge completed, which can keep out wind and rain and has since become the most beautiful view on the Fu-Nan River. And as a result, the people of Chengdu began to look at their mayor with new eyes.

Chengdu is a city surrounded by water and with so much of it, the resulting bridges have developed into one of the characteristics of Chengdu. In the city, men and women live happily by a sea of water. If water can be said to have moistened the soul of the people of Chengdu and endowed them with energy and vigor, then bridges have become indispensable links between different places in and around Chengdu. The outside world is no longer remote, and bridges, waterways, and mountain paths may lead you anywhere. The fragrance of flowers, which permeates the everyday life of the people of Chengdu, can float along mountain paths and waterways to faraway places. The bridges in Chengdu are very interesting. Some of them are named after numbers, such as One Heart Bridge, Two Immortals Bridge, Three Openings Bridge, Five Laurels Bridge, Nine Openings Bridge, and Twelve Bridge; some are named after images, for example, Jade Belt Bridge, Rainbow Bridge, and Crouching Dragon Bridge. Some of the names are very simple and even casual, such as Bridge No. 1 and Bridge No. 2; and some are natural and unadorned, for example, North Gate Grand Bridge, South Gate Grand Bridge, and Jinjiang Grand Bridge. And there are still some other bridges that exist only in name, such as Cyan Stone Bridge, Face Washing Bridge, and Milling Tools Bridge. All these bridges have witnessed the historical changes in Chengdu.

Chengdu abounds with stories about bridges, some of which are well grounded in history, while some are fictional and others half true, half false. Nine Openings Bridge was once the seat of the biggest market for used books, labor, and cheap small commodities in Chengdu, but along with the lapse of time, it has been gradually reduced to only one function: transportation. A new Nine Openings Bridge has been built two or three kilometers away from the old one down the Jinjiang River. The new Nine Openings Bridge is more ancient-looking and antique-flavored than the old one, and as it links Sichuan University and Wangjianglou Park, many people like to go there for a walk after supper.

Under the bridges there is flowing water and on the bridges, time passes by. Today's urbanists spare no efforts in placing the folk customs, practices, and historical memories, of which they cannot let go, under the bridges of armored concrete, such as the Old Chengdu Folk-Custom Park below the South People's Road Flyover and the Venerable Theater below the Su Po Flyover; in this way, they have created many a unique sight in the city.

Our car came to a halt right before a traffic light, when the rain suddenly stopped.

"The rain stopped with showing any sign," I said in surprise.

Our drivers said that in Chengdu, almost invariably the rain came quietly at night and stopped at daybreak. More often than not, people did not know it rained the night before until they opened the windows to observe the weather early in the morning.

As it had stopped raining, we decided to go to Dujiang Weirs with a history of 2,000 years. Washed clean by the rain, the streets in Chengdu appeared exceedingly fresh and new; verdant trees looked like girls who had just taken a bath, standing tall and erect in a straight line, presenting their beauty gracefully and silently, and intoxicating you immensely. As we drove into the downtown area of Dujiangyan, it seemed more beautiful than I had imagined: The streets were broad and clean and the residential sections were surrounded by green mountains. Located on the border area between Chengdu Plain and Mount Longmen, the city of Dujiangyan was originally named Guan County and later renamed after Dujiang Weirs. You can imagine the benefits that the irrigation project has brought to this city as well as the good fortune it has brought to the whole Chengdu Basin: With it have come the vast fertile farmlands; with it has come the laudatory title "the land of abundance." Led by our driver, we walked through the ancient-looking gate of the scenic spot of Dujiang Weirs. Although I had tried to prepare myself for the great surprise at seeing Dujiang Weirs, when I finally stood right in its presence, I still felt a stream of warm blood surging to my head…Looking down from the top of Mount Yulei at the rushing water of the roaring Minjiang River, I seemed to hear an echo from the depth of history. The heart quake caused by Dujiang Weirs was beyond description and the most heart-stirring was its great momentum, which, notably, had continued unabated for thousands of years. My train of thoughts could not help but sail against the current that kept surging forward endlessly and trace back to the historical origin of Dujiang Weirs…

The Minjiang River in the west of Dujiangyan tops all the rivers inside Sichuan in the amount of water; it rushes down from Mount Min and winds through many mountains and ravines. In ancient times, while nourishing the splendid Ba-Shu culture in the plain in west Sichuan, the Minjiang River also brought about rampant droughts and floods. The consequent droughts in the east and floods in the west had always been plaguing the people in west Sichuan. In 256 B.C., in order to bring the river under control, the then prefect of Shu prefecture in Qin state Li Bing and his son led the people to cut Li Dui (an Isolated Hill) from the mountain and build Dujiang Weirs in the middle of the river; the Minjiang River was divided into two and the torrential water was harnessed by Dujiang Weirs. Both floods and droughts were brought under control and calamities were turned into blessings; the plain in west Sichuan thus became a vast fertile land, there were no more famine years, and Dujiang Weirs served as the wellspring of life in Chengdu Plain.

Dujiang Weirs consists of three main parts: the Fish Mouth Water-Dividing Dyke, the Flying Sand Spillway, and the Precious Bottle Neck Water Inlet. The Fish Mouth is a water-dividing dyke in the middle of the river, which divides the onrushing Minjiang River into the inner river and the outer river, the former serving as a drainage system to prevent floods and the latter leading water off to irrigate farmlands. The Flying Sand Spillway functions to discharge floodwater, tackle silt sedimentation

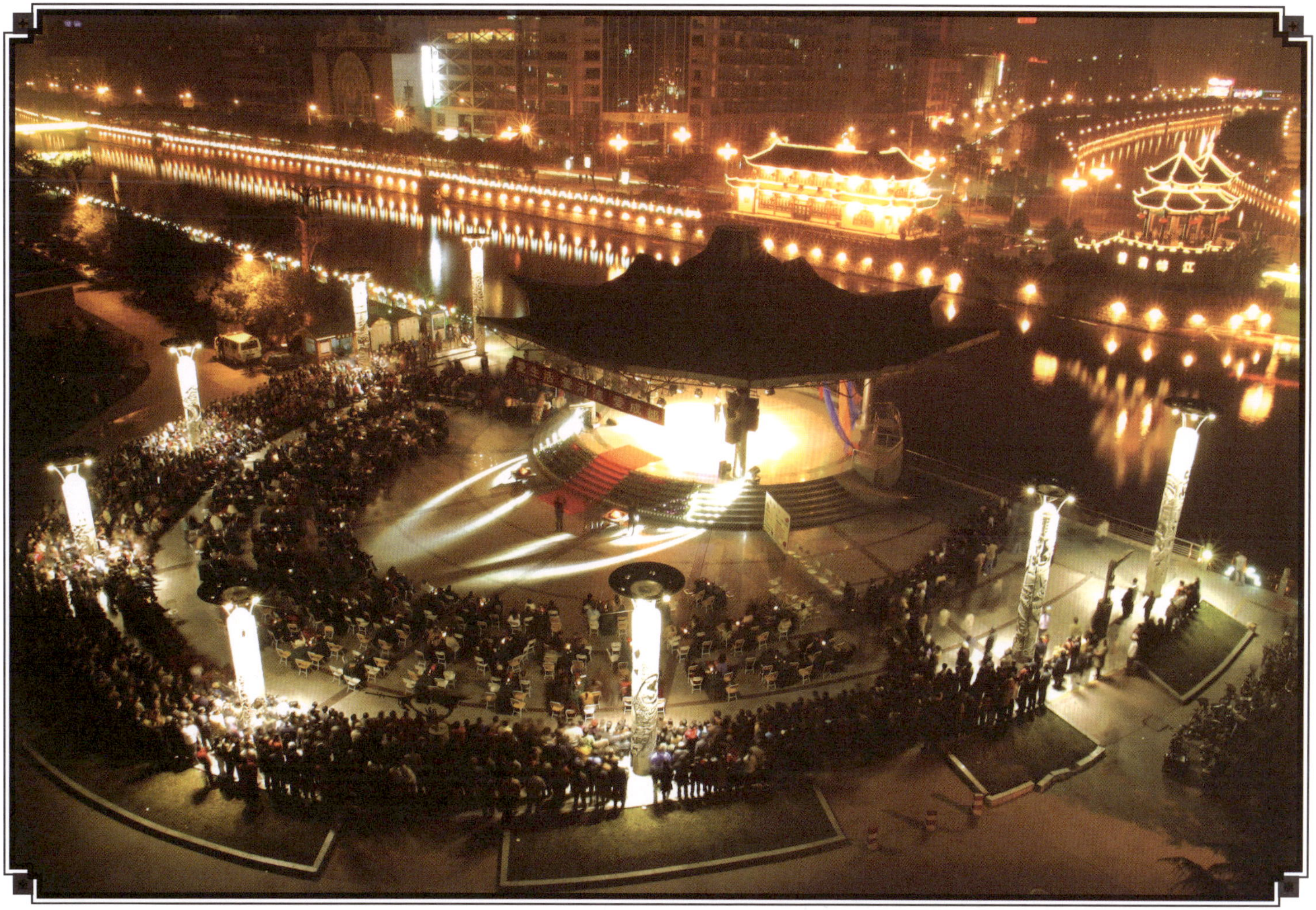

and control the flow of water. The Precious Bottle Neck controls the flow of water into the inner river and looks like the neck of a bottle, which is the origin of its name. The water of the inner river flows through the Precious Bottle Neck into the plain in west Sichuan for irrigation. Looking down from the mountain top, you can see owing to the diversion of Dujiang Weirs, many a irrigation channel spread out like a fan, crisscross evenly like leaf veins and water the entire plain in west Sichuan. If Chengdu is "a city of paradise," it is largely owing to Dujiang Weirs. A contemporary writer once said, "Thanks to Dujiang Weirs, the Sichuan plain which had been plagued by unmanageable droughts and floods became a land of abundance. Whenever we, the Chinese Nation, were hit by life-and-death disasters, the land of abundance could always stay calm and provide us with refuge and sustenance. Therefore it is safe to say Dujiang Weirs has been irrigating the Chinese Nation to make her go on generation after generation. Without it there would not have been the great talent and bold vision of Zhuge Liang and Liu Bei; without it there would not have been the brilliant works of Li Bai, Du Fu and Lu You written after they arrived in Sichuan. To be nearer in time, without it China in the Anti-Japanese War would not have had a relatively safe rear area."

Walking down the steps from Qinyan (the Weirs of the Qin State) Tower, we arrived first at the Erwang (Two Kings') Temple. This temple was first built in the Southern and Northern Dynasties (421-580) to commemorate the water-control exploit of

Li Bing and his son and originally named the "Chongde (Revering Men of Great Virtue) Temple"; after the Song Dynasty, Li Bing and his son were granted the posthumous title "King" and it was thus renamed the "Erwang Temple." The existent architecture was rebuilt during the Qing Dynasty. The temple makes the best of the topography of the mountain and tiers upward, which impresses the visitors as magnificent and beautiful; surrounded by ancient trees and a dense shrubs, it boasts a sequestered and pleasant environment. There are the statues of Li Bing and Li Erlang inside the main hall and the rear hall. On the stone tablets are engraved Li Bing's mnemonic rhymes about water-control, such as "Dredge the riverbed and build low dykes," "Remove the surface soil at the turn of a river and the islet in a river to make the water flow smoothly," and the like. Further down there is Anlan (Appeasing Billows) Bridge, Danny's favorite. He walked on the bridge back and forth to enjoy himself wobbling over the flowing water. Anlan Bridge is a chain bridge that spans both the inner river and the outer river. The chain bridge was previously supported by wooden and stone piers, bamboo cables with a diameter as long as the mouth of a rice bowl flied across the river and bamboo chains served as bridge railings on both sides. The whole length was about 500 meters. The present bridge moved down over 100 meters and the bamboo cables and chains were replaced by steel ones, and the wooden piers, by concrete ones. Afar off, it looked like a rainbow hanging on the sky; near by, it seemed like a net dried in the sun by a fisherman. Strolling on the bridge and looking west, I saw the raging Minjiang River roaring through the mountain; looking east, I saw irrigation channels stretching in a crisscross pattern. The functions of Dujiang Weirs were clear at a glance. Across Anlan Bridge there is Li Dui. Just as the name indicates, Li Dui refers to a hill that has been cut away from a mountain. According to historical records, it took Li Bing and his people eight years to cut this Li Dui from the mountain opposite. At that time, there were neither gunpowder nor advanced tools, but Li Bing thought out a way: They burned the hard rocks with fire and then poured cold water, which caused the rocks to expand and shrink time and again and at last give way. The Fulong (Taming the Dragon) Temple is a three-tier complex that ascends along the mountainside tier upon tier. In 1974 when a control gate was built on the outer river, a stone sculpture of Li Bing was dug up from the riverbed and was henceforth displayed in the front hall. The sculpture, which was built in the first year under Emperor Ling's reign during the Eastern Han Dynasty, stands three meters tall and weighs four tons. On the left of the Fulong Temple there is the Precious Bottle Neck Water Inlet, through which the river water surges forward and gains great momentum. At the apex of Li Dui there is Guan Lan (Watching Billows) Pavilion of two tiers and eight corners. Looking far into the distance, you can see the Fish Mouth Water-Dividing Dyke, Anlan Bridge, the rip current of the Minjiang River, and the snow-clad mountaintop of Mount Xiling.

In the Fulong Temple, people bowed and kowtowed to the stone sculpture of Li Bing reverentially to express their gratitude to him for his tremendous contribution. As a matter of fact, Li Bing had just performed his duty as a government official. His six-character and eight-character mnemonic rhymes "Dredge the riverbed and build low dykes" and "Remove the surface soil at the turn of a river and the islet in a river to make the water flow smoothly" are not just rules for harnessing water but also imply the philosophy of being a government official. Every government official should follow the example of Li Bing and do everything with the view of benefiting contemporaries and later generations as well. It would be best if he or she can achieve success, win recognition and leave a good name to posterity; if not, he or she could still be a worthy person with a clear conscience who stands tall and upright between heaven and earth!

We spent the whole afternoon sauntering in the scenic spot of Dujiang Weirs, looking at the riverside compounds where gloriettes and pavilions of long standing rose tier upon tier and age-old trees looked vigorous and curled upward, and at the torrential Minjiang River roaring and surging forward…Whether we overlooked the ancient weirs or stood by the river, the exuberant interest and charm of ancient times would blow on our face along with the wind and the torrential river seemed to be still telling about the remarkable people through the ages. If I could live a leisurely life in this serene and beautiful place for some time, doing some reading in the garden and listening to the wind on the mountain every day, I would wish for nothing else for my life…Walking out of Dujiang Weirs along the Yangong Path (a path in memory of those who made great contributions to the building and maintenance of Dujiang Weirs), which was lined on both sides by many a sculpture, I felt as if stepping on the spirits of water-control personages in past dynasties. There were so many generals after Li Bing who guarded and maintained this grand project. As a matter of fact, without Zhuge Liang and all the other successors, the entire Chinese civilization, not to mention Dujiang Weirs, would have crumbled and vanished silently long before as the civilizations of ancient Babylon and ancient Egypt did. There are many archaic objects in the world that can be used only for people to visit and ponder on the past, but it is not the case with Dujiang Weirs. Its antiquity can be of great benefit; its antiquity is still in full vigor. The smoke and dust of history have buried in oblivion many grand projects such as the famous ancient irrigation projects of the Hammurabi Channel in the Kingdom of Babylon and the man-made channels in ancient Rome have long before fallen into disuse. But Dujiang Weirs is the only exception: It has surpassed the endless flow of history and its ancient blood vessels are still pulsating with inexhaustible energy, just like the river that surges forward ceaselessly. At the gate of Dujiang Weirs, there is a stele erected by the World Heritage Committee of UNESCO. Danny looked at it attentively and exclaimed with admiration now and then, while I tried to imprint the inscriptions on my mind:

Built in the third century B.C., and located on the Minjiang River in the west of Chengdu Plain in

Sichuan, Dujiang Weirs is a large-scale irrigation project whose construction was directed by prefect of the Shu prefecture Li Bing of Qin state and his son during the Warring States Period in Chinese history. Up to the present it has remained the oldest and the only grand irrigation project in the world that is characterized by leading off water without a diversion dam. From over 2200 years ago till now, it has been bringing immense benefits. Li Bing's water-control project is a heroic achievement in his time and a beneficial exploit for thousands of years to come. It proves to be a great masterpiece of human civilization and a great irrigation project that benefits the people…

Tender was the night in Dujiangyan City, but tenderer were the undulating ripples of water under the moon. When I looked far into the distance, the river seemed to have rested its head on the dazzling neon lights of the city and gone to sleep; when I looked near, customers were still drinking to their hearts' content at the riverside *lengdanbei* restaurants with many shining lights. The people of Chengdu refer to midnight snacks as *lengdanbei*. Sitting on a bamboo chair by the river and looking around, I felt nice and cool as the wind blew on my face. Myriads of twinkling lights along the banks were being reflected by the rushing water and looked as if the river was overflowing with colorful light; intermittent string music, to the accompaniment of the roaring water, was floating on the surface of the river and sounded like heavenly music. Such a wonderful scene was already enchanting enough, not to mention the iced beer and various aromatic and delicious snacks served by the waiters or waitresses. Many hawkers walked here and there inside the bar, calling out to sell *bingfen* (a curd made from malaxis bancanoides), cooked corn cobs, fried dough twists, crisp sesame seed cakes, big grapes, and many other local delicacies and various kinds of fruits and by no means could anybody resist the temptation to have a try. Some people say, "Without visiting Dujiangyan, your trip to Chengdu won't be complete and without drinking beer on the riverside at night, your trip to Dujiangyan won't be complete." Even if you get as drunk as a fish on this age-old riverside and sleep away the night in the cold wind on the side of the street, you will feel pleased. We ordered stir-fried field snails, fried crawfish in soy sauce, various fresh fishes, green soy beans, pot-stewed spiced meat, beer, red wine, and the like and had a wonderful time through the night, eating and listening to the surfs of the Minjiang River breaking on the shore. Danny strolled about happily, exploring the beautiful views by the river. Our driver said, come and settle in Dujiangyan; every evening, you can enjoy the blood-red setting sun with a draft of beer in the hand, or scoop up a handful of clear water to wash your sleepy face. Small as it is, Dujiangyan is nevertheless a garden city with mountains and rivers. Five rivers pass through the city and add much charm to it; the air in the city is extraordinarily pure and fresh and you may feel as if you're inside a natural oxygen bar…

Chengdu is really a city tied up closely with water, which cannot be denied any more after a visit to Dujiangyan. Thanks to historical figures like Da Yu, Li Bing and his son, Chengdu was able to grow and prosper in the embrace of tamed running water. A city nourished by water as such breathes in even rhythm and looks leisurely; not tyrannous or very aggressive in character, it can always modestly absorb anything foreign and in the way of genic mutation, transform them into things of its own before making use of them. As water is pliable and lovely, so the inhabitants of this city are easy-going, not obstinate, nor antiforeign; they are self-confident and modest as well." Actually, many of the famous names in Chengdu's history were not born in Chengdu, such as Li Bing, Zhuge Liang, Li Bai, and Du Fu, who, for one reason or another, formed certain ties with this city, leaving behind good deeds and merits or literary works. The natives of Chengdu have never regarded them as outsiders; instead, they have not only glorified them by erecting monuments to them and writing their biographies, but also considered them part of Chengdu's history. Many of the government officials in today's Chengdu are not natives, either. Perhaps many years later, they will also occupy a segment in the history of this city. Such are the natives of Chengdu; they will never forget any person who has spared no efforts in performing his or her duty to Chengdu. Its historical profundity, strong cultural flavors, and the tea culture that has been moistening the land of Ba-Shu, have resulted in the water-like comprehensive and tolerant mind of the natives of Chengdu...

It is said that God created the world by an unwritten rule: Every city must be given some water. The water of Chengdu flows from Dujiangyan City, whose water, in turn, comes from boundless snow-capped mountains. With water God has not only nourished life but also cultivated multifarious interests and charms in Chengdu.

Built in 1998, Chengdu Flowing Water Park is the first theme park in the world aiming at a comprehensive urban environmental education. Designed jointly by Chinese, American, and Korean environmental artists, it has won two awards from relevant world organizations: Waterfront Top Honor Award and Environment and Region Design Award. Shaped like a fish by the Fu River, the Flowing Water Park demonstrates the water-purifying process: Water is pumped from the Fu River and after sedimentation, it flows past a pond where reeds and sweet flags grow and then a fish pond turns from muddy to clear. In cities worldwide, there are few projects like the Chengdu Flowing Water Park, which enjoys great fame at home and abroad and receives both official and popular recognition. Chengdu Flowing Water Park registers the glory and the dream of the people of Chengdu: The glory lies in the fact that the Fu-Nan River Project has been constructed to tackle silt sedimentation and drain sand, river embankments and green belts have been built, and thus the so-called "rotten river" has been turned into a gold girdle of Chengdu (the Comprehensive Control Project of the Fu-Nan River has successively won the UN-Habitat Scroll of Honor Award, UN Award for Best Practices in Human Settlements Improvement, and Local Initiative Award); their dream is to make the Fu-Nan River limpid and clear.

For the people of Chengdu, Chengdu Flowing Water Park is not just an object lesson of environmental education but also a scenic spot. A bird's-eye view from a helicopter will enable you to see the fine and ingenious layout that combines both Chinese and Western characteristics; and sauntering through the park, you can enjoy its beauty in detail. In the park, there are such simulated scenic spots as the central garden, the fountains in sculptures, the vegetation on Mount E'mei, and the rainbow pond in Huanglong Scenic Resort. On summer nights, the fragrance of sweet flags and the croaking of frogs will make you feel as if you are in the countryside. Reportedly, on the night of every dragon boat festival, many visitors will drift lanterns, which bear their good wishes, downstream from here. As such, with water, Chengdu has developed a character of its own: leisurely, tolerant, enterprising, and so on. In Chengdu, your senses of sight, taste, smell, touch, and hearing can be properly cared for by water. And thanks to water, no day is "unfit to travel around" in Chengdu. When it is hot, you can come to Chengdu to escape the heat; when it is cold, to eat hot pots; when it is neither hot nor cold, you can drink tea. In addition, you can come to Chengdu to enjoy the sight of peach blossoms in spring, lotuses in summer, sweet-scented osmanthuses in autumn, and plum blossoms in winter...

Late at night, my friend drove me to the place where the Fu River and the Nan River join up. Under the dim light, I could see the river flowing slowly, with dense small ripples on the surface. The Fu River and the Nan River are two man-made rivers that surround the city of Chengdu. The Nan River is a tributary that was separated from the Minjiang River when Li Bing had Dujiang Weirs constructed; it flows around the west and the south of Chengdu and then goes east. The Fu River is a moat that passes under the prefectural city. The Fu-Nan River has not only brought economic prosperity to Chengdu Plain but also nourished Chengdu's civilized history of over 2,000 years. The two rivers join up with each other in front of Anshun Bridge and broaden out at this point. Looking south at the end of the bridge, I saw the river disappearing into the distance amid boundless mist and clouds, just as Du Fu aptly described in a poem, "The beauty of spring flows along with the Jinjiang River and pervades the whole universe; / The floating clouds over Mount Yulei have become the past, the present, and the future." Reportedly, the municipal government of Chengdu has recently decided to call the Fu River and the Nan River by a joint name "the Jinjiang River." This joint name corresponds not only with its designation in the poems and other literary works in past dynasties but also with that in the folklore of Chengdu. The Jinjiang River may seem too noisy in the daytime, but at night, especially when the moonlight softly shines on the surface of the river, it is the most romantic place in Chengdu.

We walked by the river, chatting…I exclaimed over the drastic change in Chengdu, and my friend said, let alone you, even a person who grew up in Chengdu will get lost when he or she has left Chengdu for several years and now returns; even those who have never left Chengdu for a single day will be very surprised to find a new road or a new building if they have not moved about for some time. As such, changes take place in Chengdu every day, ranging from the Fu-Nan River project to the construction of five roads and one bridge, from the broadening and greening of one road after another to the clearing of the Fu River, the Nan River, the Sha River, the Qingshui River, the Jinma River, and the Huanhua Brook…The ancient city of Chengdu is now writing a history of the most rapid development since its founding. Looking at the babbling water of the Jinjiang River, I was reminded of a night at the Seine River in Paris a year ago. It was also in June and it was also by the most beautiful river in a city. Those sculptures of great originality were so much alike and the mountain stones, rare trees, and fresh flowers seemed so familiar. No wonder the United Nations awarded the UN-Habitat Scroll of Honor Award to both Paris and Chengdu…Facing the lowering clouds, we walked slowly in the breeze; partly hidden and partly visible, the moon was shining on the dark river, which seemed as if having accumulated too many histories or too many past events…Unknowingly, it rained and we dodged into a small teahouse in a hurry. I ordered a cup of weak scented tea, leaned on the muntin, watched the rain floating down before my eyes, and touched the traces of water on the glass; my thread of thoughts seemed to be elongated by strings of rain and float to nowhere along with them…I felt as if having returned to a certain moment in my prelife; a hallucinatory effect took place and I thought all the rain water had been accumulated for many years and would not cease. Suddenly, my mobile phone received a short message—the reasons for liking Chengdu:

1. The romantic atmosphere, chance encounters, beer, pretty girls, old movies, and parties—you will find Chengdu lacking in none of them.

2. The Fu-Nan River is the belt of Chengdu, but Liushahe (a famous writer in Sichuan whose name means "a river in which sand drifts") is not a river in Chengdu.

3. What can you buy with one *jiao* Renminbi? With it, you can eat with relish a bunch of *chuanchuanxiang* (bunches of food cooked in a hot pot) in Chengdu.

4. We all take a sunbath. It takes one hour to get suntanned in Hainan but in Chengdu, it takes one week.

5. How does it feel to have your ears cleaned while drinking tea? You ears tickle while your heart smiles.

6. In Chengdu everything can be "goudui (negotiable)."

7. In Chengdu, you can always get the best books and videodisks without having to pay one more *fen* Renminbi.

8. Don't be afraid to argue with the people of Chengdu, for under no circumstances will they raise a hand to strike you.

9. You won't know that you have gotten married too early until you come to Chengdu, for strolling in the streets, you will see pretty girls everywhere!

10. Do you need reasons for liking Chengdu? You will find the answer after staying in Chengdu for only several days!

Tips:

Dujiang Weirs:
Spanning the Minjiang River 56 kilometers away from Chengdu, Dujiang Weirs is the irrigation project with the longest history in the world that is still in use today. As one of the World Cultural Heritage sites, the irrigation project has been rendering an immense service for more than 2,200 years. It consists of three main parts: the Fish Mouth Water-Dividing Dyke, the Flying Sand Spillway, and the Precious Bottle Neck Water Inlet.
Website: www.dujiangyan,org
Phone: 028-87120836
Transportation: Special buses depart every day from Chengdu Railway Station and the West Gate Bus Station to Dujiang Weirs, and the ride takes about one hour and a half.
Accommodation: Guoyan Hotel (add: Central Section, Guanjing Road, Dujiangyan; phone: 028-87146666); Jinye Hotel (add: Lower Section, Guanjing Road, Dujiangyan; phone: 028-87119999)
Food and drink: The Rens' assorted handmade sweets and red plums are famous local delicacies.

Mount Qingcheng:
Situated in the south of Dujiangyan City, over 60 kilometers away from Chengdu, Mount Qingcheng is one of the cradles of Taoism in China and one of the most important scenic spots in the list of World Cultural Heritage sites. The entire mountain is covered with flourishing green trees and sprinkled with gurgling springs and cliff-side waterfalls; verdant ridges and peaks overlap each other and look like city walls; hence the name "Qingcheng (Green Wall)." There are altogether 36 peaks and the highest one is over 1,600 meters high above sea level. Walking up the winding stone steps, you can see 38 Taoist temples and may lose yourself in the deep, quiet and beautiful scenery.
Website: www.qcs.cn
Phone: 028-87218228
Transportation: Special buses set out for the front entrance to Mount Qingcheng from the New South Gate Bus Station. There are also sightseeing buses from Chengdu Railway Station and Chadianzi Bus Station.
Accommodation: You can put up for the night in the Temple of the Highest Clarity, the Celestial Masters' Grotto, and the other Taoist temples. It is quite cheap, 25 *yuan* per night for a double room.
Food and drink: *Kuding* tea, stewed chicken with gingko nuts, cured meat, the Fifth Grotto Heaven Chinese gooseberry wine, and Taoist pickles are strongly recommended.

Where to enjoy the sight of the Jinjiang River:

Wanli Passenger Liner:
Wanli Passenger Liner is a new ship-shaped building by the Jinjiang River near Wanli Bridge. There is an open-air teahouse on the top floor, where it would be best to have afternoon tea at four or five pm. You may choose a seat overlooking the river, order a Green Mountain and Blue Water tea, and savor every sip. At the moment, the setting sun is hanging on the west of the sky

and the clouds there have turned red; looking down, you will see the Jinjiang River at its best, shining bright and exceedingly charming. As you sit high, you can look far; the Jinjiang River seems to be vanishing like a curve into the distant tall buildings that stand in great numbers. Since it is a "passenger liner," you can see a "mast." Looking down the Jinjiang River, you may feel as if riding on a ship and drinking tea that calls for song cup to cup.

As the night falls, you may order several bottles of beer and a plate of grill and watch the Jinjiang River that looks much gentler and lovelier under the dim light of night. Now the lights along the river are on, so are those on the automobiles and in the tall buildings as well as the streetlights. The lights along the river can change constantly from red to blue to purple, dazzling and fascinating.
Add: No. 29, Jiangxi Street, Chengdu
Phone: 028-85588833

Hexin Tea Garden:
Hexin (the Heart of the River) Tea Garden is a peninsula-shaped open-air teahouse that sits by the Riverside Impressions Neighborhood on the opposite side of Wangjianglou Park. The triangular land, on the forepart of which lies Hexin Tea Garden, cuts into the Jinjiang River and divides it into two. As the tea garden is surrounded by water on three sides, it feels extraordinarily cool. If you stand against the wind on the tip of the tea garden, you will see the Jinjiang River rolling right before your eyes.
Add: Group 3, Hexin Village, Jinjiang District, Chengdu
Phone: 028-87763507

VII. A Romantic City

In *Historical Records*, Sima Qian, a historian in ancient China, described Chengdu as "out of the ordinary and free from vulgarity, beautiful, charming, and refined," for the charm of Chengdu can neither be fully attributed to its splendid long history nor to her fast-paced urban construction and modernization. Its strongest attraction issues from something that you can neither see nor touch, something that, however, affects you deeply; and that is the leisurely and romantic charm that permeates its high streets and back lanes, its ancient temples and new buildings, its night rain and morning air. It is the trademark of today's Chengdu and the lifestyle of its inhabitants, who quest after style in drinking tea in teahouses and chatting with each other, after prosperity on the basis of preserving the essence of classic culture, and after romanticism in the delicate and smooth brocades of Shu embroidery, which, in an unaffected and easy-going way, fascinates you to such an extent that you will surely lose self-control.

"What's that?" Danny's exclamation of surprise awoke me from a reverie and I saw our car passing through a tall memorial archway on which is written "Old Qintai Road." Inside the archway, an imposing brass horse-drawn carriage caught Danny's eye: A fine horse was lifting its feet high up, the wheels seemed to be rolling fast, and a serious-looking high-ranking official in the imperial court was holding the reins in one hand and the top cover in the other. As I had done an adequate homework, I knew now we arrived at the famous Qintai Road in Chengdu; so I said smilingly, "This is an very old story and the man on the carriage is called Sima Xiangru." Tradition has it that during the Western Han Dynasty, Sima Xiangru, a poor scholar, met Zhuo Wenjun, a young widow from a rich family who could play *qin* and write poems. The man immediately fell for the woman's good looks and literary talent; he composed a song *A Male Phoenix Wooing a Female One* on the spot and won the woman's heart. Later, for all the heavy pressure brought on her by her family and society, Zhuo Wenjun eloped to Chengdu with Sima Xiangru, where she assisted her husband by selling wine and playing *qin*. After Sima Xiangru won the favor of the emperor and was appointed capital official thanks to his work *Fu by Zi Xu*, for five years he had not returned home. He wrote Zhuo Wenjun, who had stayed in Chengdu, old and no longer pretty now, a letter of no words and intended to marry a concubine. Overwhelmed by grief, Zhuo Wenjun wrote a heartrending poem in reply. After reading it, Sima Xiangru felt extremely ashamed and at last, with a grand carriage drawn by four horses, he returned home and took Zhuo Wenjun, who had stayed with him in adversity, to the capital with him; hence a much-told love story through the ages. This sculpture of a horse-drawn carriage is actually an artistic presentation of the romantic story.

On both sides of the sculpture there is a long row of buildings in the style of the Ming and Qing Dynasties. Under the eaves there are a great variety of Chinese palace lanterns, including white square ones, dark red diamond-shaped ones, big ball-like ones and some other unique ones. Hung on the façade along the street, they set off the outline of the flying eaves and suspending beams and make all the buildings splendid in green and gold, leading visitors into an age with strong antique flavors. Between the sidewalks and the driveway, there is a belt of brick painting about the Han Dynasty. We walked along the belt and people

Jack Quian

in the Han Dynasty, who were drinking together in a party, singing and dancing, daggering and shooting, riding in horse-drawn carriages on a tour of inspection, came alive in our eyes, together with the social reality and imaginary paradise from over 2,000 years ago. A friend of mine who was accompanying us said, "Paved with 160,000 natural bluestone bricks, this belt is the longest brick painting in the world up to now."

I have been to many cities in the world and found it hard to judge which city is pleasant and which is not, for each city has a unique culture and architectural concept of its own. But I believe that culture requires creative exploitation, which has already attained perfection in Chengdu…Sauntering in these streets full of antique flavors and thinking about the historical stories that had come down to us, I felt an increase of emotional stirrings in my heart: Chengdu was really an all-inclusive and tolerant city; it not only allowed Sima Xiangru and Zhuo Wenjun, a couple who eloped against social morality at that time, to open a wine shop in public, but also built a platform for playing *qin* and a landscape garden in memory of them; besides, there are Four Horses Bridge, Qintai Road, Wenjun Street, Xiangru Memorial Archway, and many other streets whose names have their origins in this story. It proves, to my surprise, that Chengdu had been a romantic and open city from time immemorial. By the end of Qintai Road, I saw a sculpture of Sima Xiangru and Zhuo Wenjun dancing to the accompaniment of *zheng*: "The male phoenix returns to his hometown, and he has traveled around the world in quest of the female phoenix." How many beautiful and talented girls' heartstrings have been tugged at by the song *A Male Phoenix Wooing a Female One*! And how many visitors have been infatuated with it!...

Chengdu has been a city of immigrants since its founding and welcoming people all over the world, can be regarded as one of the characteristics of this city. Whether you were born in Chengdu or somewhere else, this city will receive you with open arms as long as you have lived and exerted yourself here. As a matter of fact, many of the great writers in history whom the people of Chengdu have glorified by erecting temples were not natives of Sichuan, neither are the majority of capable entrepreneurs in today's Chengdu; but the people here still regard them as the pride of this city. Mr. Gao, CEO of Kingsoft Corporation in Chengdu, said to me over tea, "Of all the cities where I've been, Chengdu is the least antiforeign; I've settled in Chengdu without regret, partly because of the beautiful environment in Chengdu and its outskirts, the agreeable living conditions, and the hospitality and cordiality of the people of Chengdu. It is rightly said that even if you have lived in Beijing for ten years, you still remain an outsider; but only after a two months' stay in Chengdu, you can safely regard yourself as a native of Chengdu." He said how Kingsoft had chosen Chengdu as the seat of its research and development center of online games was a good story. Kingsoft had planned to base the research and development center in Shenzhen, but in hunting for relevant talents, a group of outstanding software programmers were discovered in Chengdu. Kingsoft had thought of attracting them to Shenzhen with a high salary, but unexpectedly they did not want to leave Chengdu. When Kingsoft turned to Chengdu, it was greeted with tremendous warm attention from both the municipal government and the Internet users, which moved the leadership of Kingsoft deeply. Mr. Gao said, "Our decision was truly influenced by the sincerity of the municipal government of Chengdu in inviting us again and again and by the personal charm of the leaders. Of all the cities in China, the leadership of Chengdu is a rare team of elites with excellent educational background, who have not only created a favorable environment for investment but also inherited and carried on the traditional characteristic of Chengdu, that is, to welcome people all over the world into its bosom."

Such hankering for high-tech products and such favorable investment environment have paid off: Nearly 100 of the world's 500 biggest corporations have established their factories or branch offices in Chengdu, such as Motorola, Toyota, Sony, and Microsoft. Reportedly, it was owing to two department managers' travel to Chengdu in 2001 that Intel decided to base its chip packaging factory in this city and invest hundreds of millions of dollars here. The outcome of that routine investigation was a visit to Silicon Valley, USA by a delegation headed by Li Chuncheng, the then mayor of Chengdu, who presented to Intel headquarters the report *A Comparative Analysis of Investment in Chengdu* and the sincerity and hospitality of the people of Chengdu. Such "Chengdu-style quick response" amazed the leadership of Intel and when its CEO Mr. Barrett came to Chengdu and saw tens of thousands of hands waving at him in the Computer Street, his amazement gained the power to move…As the CEO of one of the world's biggest companies paid two successive visits to this city in west China, the analysts in Wall Street soon realized that Intel had finalized its decision to invest in Chengdu. Today, a popular saying among investors in Chengdu goes like this: "Chengdu means success."

I can be called a veteran user of the Internet; ever since 1988, I have created online writings that amount to several million characters; as a result, I have been granted the "inflated" title, "the Grandfather of Online Chinese Literature" and written into almost all the academic and non-academic works about the history of online Chinese literature. I had thought that I knew the Internet like the palm of my hand, but in face of the online games that had appeared suddenly in the past two years, especially when I heard such titles as *Warcraft, The Legend of Mir II, Tomb Raider, Commandos, Championship Manager* that Danny blurted out, I was at a loss. In Chengdu Digital Entertainment Software Park, I saw a scene of great vitality; the young and energetic IT workers, the agreeable working environment, and the innovation-oriented research and development strategy assured me that online games would bring an immense opportunity to the digital entertainment industry in Chengdu. As we all know, along with the development and application of new technologies and relevant industries, people will allocate more time for rest and recreation and the makeup of China's population and its economic development ensure that China will become one of the biggest consumer markets in the world for entertainment products. It, undoubtedly, means business openings and favorable opportunities. In this era of information technology, as the market of TV and computer games is dominated by Nintendo and Sony, online games will become a sharp sword that will help China and its enterprises prize open the door to digital entertainment industry and even mainstream economy in the 21st century. Once the door is open, in face of people's thirst for rest and recreation, Chengdu's digital entertainment industry will take the world by pleasant surprise.

Reputedly, Chengdu boasts the most of online game players in China, and the people of Chengdu even believe Shanda Interactive Entertainment Limited Corporation that came into the market in Wall Street owes its prosperity to *The Legend of Mir II*, which became a hot multiplayer online role-playing game first in Chengdu. It may be safe to say that of all the cities in China, the inhabitants of Chengdu are the best at seeking pleasure. During its long history of 3,000 years, scholars and men of letters have appeared in great numbers, beauties and talented women have gathered in large groups; there are plentiful oases of human culture such as Dujiang Weirs, Mount Qingcheng, Sanxingdui Ruins, the Wuhou Temple, the Wenshu Temple, in addition to the highly developed and constantly innovative service industry as represented by Sichuan dishes, Sichuan spirits, Sichuan tea, Sichuan opera, and the like. The people here, whether rich or poor, quest after a *bashi* (comfortable) life while seeking a successful career. Under their natural and easy-going appearance, there is an undercurrent of passion and wisdom inside the people of Chengdu that cannot be entirely contained. The men of Chengdu always like to get together with their friends in threes or fives, which impresses visitors from elsewhere most favorably and easily tempts them to blend in. The men of Chengdu mostly look quite happy; they are dressed neatly and their faces glow with ruddy health. They are neither as opinionated as the men in the north nor as sensitive as those in the south; but when the situation demands that they should assert themselves, they will never give the impression of being weak, and when they become as gentle as a lamb back at home, they take it as a show of gentlemanship. A common saying goes like this: "Different climates breed different people." The lofty mountains and precipitous peaks surrounding Sichuan Basin help keep out the cold front from the north, which not only results in the fine, smooth, soft, and delicate skin of the women of Chengdu, but also in the leisureliness peculiar to the men of Chengdu but strange to those outside Sichuan Basin.

Once I went to have breakfast in a snack bar opposite the hotel. There were only four or five sets of tables and chairs inside the snack bar but it looked neat and clean and the sweet bean jelly was delicious. I was told to finish my meal before eight o'clock for the snack bar would be closed by then. The bar keeper was a middle-aged man of about forty years old. When some customers suggested that the snack bar should sell deep-fried twisted dough sticks and soybean milk, the keeper responded with no words but a smile. I asked him curiously, "Why don't you sell more varieties?" He answered that although now he only sold bean jelly, life was already good enough; after eight, he would go to drink tea, play mah-jongg, and chat with others, and he felt his life was very comfortable. I stared at him with surprised wide eyes, for it was the first time that I had heard someone would rather drink tea and play mah-jongg than make money. This, actually, is the lifestyle of many men of Chengdu. In Chengdu, *bashi* (ease) always comes before other considerations. If you take a walk outside, from the Jinjiang River to the Wenshu Temple, from the Zhaojue Temple to the Qingyang Temple, from high streets to back lanes, you can see many men of Chengdu holding a cup of tea in the hand, or playing mah-jongg, or chatting with others. The men of Chengdu look mostly gentle and elegant, slim and lean, comely and cultured if not dazzlingly handsome, and give the impression of being mild and placid. With a cup of tea, a newspaper, and one or two friends, they can stay in a teahouse for most of the day, happy and contented. While reading a newspaper, the men of Chengdu start from the masthead to the last page and miss no word at all. This partly accounts for the fact that newspapering in Chengdu runs neck and neck with that in Guangzhou and Beijing. In Beijing, time is opportunity;

in Shanghai, time is vogue; in Guangzhou, time is money; and in Chengdu, time is living. Historical sites, natural sceneries, and mild climate are the highlights of Chengdu. In high streets, in back lanes, and in teahouses, men's attitude toward life truly reflects the nature of this city. One day, while riding in a taxi, I saw a sentence pasted on the rear window of an Alto: "I grow up to be a Cadillac." Smilingly, I picked up a back issue of *Chengdu Daily* from my seat and read an essay on six reasons for marrying a man of Chengdu:

Mildness—The men of Chengdu are as mild as the climate of Chengdu, moist and moderate.

Humor—The men of Chengdu are very humorous! They can chat ceaselessly whether on formal or informal occasions. From heaven to earth, from north to south, the men of Chengdu seem to have an inexhaustible list of topics.

Faithfulness—The men of Chengdu are the most faithful! If you are their girlfriend or wife and want to shop around, they will willingly accompany you no matter how busy they are.

Forthrightness—The men of Chengdu are forthright! They like to speak their minds out and never act like a base person who stabs or shots someone from the back, plots in secret against someone, sets up defenses, and engages in secret activities designed to hurt someone.

Diligence—The men of Chengdu are very diligent! They busy themselves the whole day with trying to carve out a career for themselves. They never make money for the purpose of seeking pleasure for themselves; instead, they turn every cent over to their wife back at home!

Cooking—The men of Chengdu are good at cooking! Married to a man of Chengdu, you will never have to worry about what to eat and how to eat for today.

For women, the men of Chengdu are like Sichuan dishes, which, complete with tongue-numbing, hot, fresh, and aromatic flavors, taste delicious and smell fragrant. The men of Chengdu are also like tea served in a teacup with lid and saucer peculiar to Sichuan, which has a strong bitter taste and a light fragrance; neither ostentatious, nor irritable, nor quick-tempered, they let their pleasure, anger, sorrow, and joy evaporate along with the floating scent of tea. They like to lead a routine life: Going to work, returning from work, going to the food market, going to teahouses, returning home, all of them are followed with pleasure and bring them great joy. They like *bailongmenzhen* (chatting), and their topics cover a wide variety of things, none of which seem too strange for them: "historical topics about ancient times, extremely remote areas beyond China, secret stories and anecdotes about the Man nationality and the Han nationality in the Qing Dynasty, as well as very up-to-date, very fresh topics about things near at hand; rustic topics with pastoral sentiments and local flavors that were talked about while smoking a pipe in the past, as well as fashionable topics about motley, bizarre, and mysterious things permeated with the redolence of coffee; serious, profound, solemn, meaningful topics, as well as topics a bit on the pornographic side dotted with cheeky grins and cynical remarks." They start to chat away as soon as they sit down and they eat and chat wherever they go. Richly endowed by nature, Chengdu abounds with produces, which ensures a comfortable life for its inhabitants and explains why the men of Chengdu attach great importance to enjoyments. If eating can be counted an enjoyment in Chengdu, then chatting is another, which brings about a leisurely and carefree mood. The former is an enjoyment of the tongue while the latter, an enjoyment of the ears.

In Chengdu, there is a story-teller Li Boqing, who is widely known as "Master Li." Many listeners, whether they are taxi drivers, tricycle drivers, vegetable vendors or civil servants, white-collar workers in foreign enterprises, employers, are fascinated with Li Boqing's *Sanda*. The so-called *Sanda* actually refers to a kind of storytelling derived from traditional Sichuan storytelling, which, in a humorous and witty way, criticizes and derides every aspect of life. Naturally, as a man of Chengdu, Li Boqing can tell remarkably true-to-life stories about the men of Chengdu. Yet more surprisingly, while Master Li spares no effort in satirizing and mocking the men of Chengdu, which is enough to make a saint swear, he nevertheless is extremely popular in Chengdu. In the high streets and back lanes, people who listen to his storytelling split their sides with laughter and even get infatuated with it; they curse him after listening and yet still want to have a listen after cursing; poor people buy a piratic CD, and rich people follow Master Li from Jinjiang Theater to Jincheng Palace of Arts…For the people of Chengdu, like *chuanchuanxiang*, *lengdanbei*, and small mah-jongg, Li Boqing is addicting…

A friend of mine who had come from the USA to work in Chengdu for many years told me, Chengdu is slow-paced on the surface and a tolerant attitude toward life can be seen on everyone's face. As a result, Chengdu boasts well-known delicious food, mah-jongg houses and teahouses representative of its unique urban culture, pretty charming girls like lotus flowers in full bloom, and a sense of leisureliness and ease rooted deep in everyone's heart. Many people call Chengdu the most leisurely city, but below the surface, Chengdu is a city full of passion: The people of Chengdu were the first to issue stocks, the first to reopen a pawnshop, and so on. In this city have appeared the most avant-garde painters and poets, which attests to its open, unconventional, and unorthodox character as a city. If you want to classify the people of Chengdu, you will find that they fall into two entirely different categories: the busy and the leisurely. This busy-leisurely opposition arises from the fact that out-of-towners see only fragments of the city. When these fragments are pieced together, you will discover that the person who is busy right now actually lay back relaxed on a bamboo chair a moment ago. The people of Chengdu like the leisure after work and their ultimate goal is be content with their lot. After busying themselves for some time, they often hold a cup of tea in the hand and look at the mist and clouds of this world indifferently, but they still value friendly feelings and are no less courageous and upright…

Jack Quian

For thousands of years, Chengdu has been the focal point of Ba-Shu culture and through the ages, Chengdu has been teeming with poets; it is from such a highbrow cultural tradition that the Chengdu-style romanticism has arisen. Such is the characteristic of Chengdu: Its distinctive mountains and rivers have given shape to a distinctive region, and this distinctive region has, in turn, nourished a distinctive group of people, who have been living there generations after generations and evolved their distinctive identity and idiosyncrasies. An ancient saying goes like this: "A young man must not go to Sichuan," for it is feared that the *bashi* (comfortable) life in Chengdu may fritter away the young man's great aspiration and more importantly, that the pretty girls there may make him reluctant to return home from Sichuan. I have been to many places and met many beautiful women both in the south and in the north. But during my stay in Chengdu, I found that the pretty girls in Chengdu could truly be described as "a sea of clouds." Walking in the streets of Chengdu, I could see stylishly dressed women here and there and long black or pink hair floating everywhere; especially in Chunxi Street and Zongfu Street, pretty women gathered in crowds. The women of Chengdu are of medium height and proportional build, about 1.62 or 1.63 meters tall and 50 kilograms in weight, with a face on the round side like a hibiscus flower, bright eyes, lips like megranate flowers, bright and clean skin like white jade, and in the words of a local writer, "with such a well-proportioned and curvaceous figure that no one will have the heart to take his eyes off it." They have a beautiful and shining long hair, which they never use to hide their faces; instead, they are genial and easy-going, ready to smile at others at any time and at any place. They are dressed in good taste and look very appealing. They often carry a dainty purse on the shoulder, walk through the high streets and back lanes like a dream, slightly open their red lips like a dream, and blink their bright and intelligent eyes like a dream…And you feel as if enjoying a beautiful painting. Looking at them walking past you in twos and threes, you will surely think that it is so easy to be happy. Reportedly, in summer the pretty girls of Chengdu like going to the city of Dujiangyan most, where they order a draft of German black beer in a open-air riverside teahouse and drink over a plate of cashew nuts or pickles to such a degree that their eyes look misty.

Many foreign tourists come to Chengdu mainly to feast their eyes. They can feast their eyes on three kinds of beautiful sights: The first includes the beauty spots in and around Chengdu such as Mount E'mei and the Scenic Area of Jiuzhaigou, the second, famous Chengdu snacks such as *fuqi feipian* (husband and wife's sliced pot-stewed entrails of oxen), pockmarked woman's bean curd, and *dandan* noodles, and the third, pretty women. Beautiful sceneries are pleasing both to the eye and the mind; local delicacies are delightful both to the eye and the taste buds; and pretty women in Chengdu can keep the eyeballs of out-of-towners rolling all the time. Psychologists claim that looking at pretty women can produce the same effect as listening to melodious music; that is, one's life will be prolonged, for every kind of aesthetic feeling can conduce to physical and mental health.

The beauty of the women of Chengdu lies first on their skin; their facial features are pretty and their skin is as fine and smooth as china. In addition, they are pretty and coquettish, good at making up their faces and dressing themselves appropriately, fond of delicious food, skillful in communicating with others, and bold to project themselves, which adequately displays their taste and style. The women of Chengdu are straightforward, daring, and vigorous and always wear a cool expression; yet in the meantime, they are sweet and charming, like honey covered with chili oil. Their voice has a lingering appeal, as soft as a spring breeze that brushes through poplar and willow trees. Especially when they want to say something but smile instead, their expression is a mixture of coolness, sweetness, brightness, mischievousness, simplicity, forthrightness, self-confidence, romantism, considerateness, joy, passion, heroism, chivalry, elegance, stylishness, kind-heartedness, and innocence, which reveals that they are indeed favorably endowed, both physically and spiritually. The women of Chengdu are beautiful in their hearts; charming and gentle but with a bit of masculinity, they look like water on the surface, but beneath the surface, they are loyal to friends and generous in aiding needy people. They can "entertain guests in the main hall and cook meals in the kitchen"; when anything crops up, they remain smart and capable, as cool as a cucumber…A poem by Du Fu reads like this: "There is a thatched cottage to the west of Wanli Bridge, and inside Baihua Pond, dark green waves arise. Brushed by a breeze, the green branches look graceful and beautiful, and moistened by rain, red lotus flowers give off a continuous fragrance…" It is from such lovely watersides that the pretty girls of Chengdu come. As a matter of fact, the women of Chengdu are like this city with a history of over 2,000 years, both ancient and modern, both traditional and up-to-date; they are like the mist in Chengdu, full of mysterious allure as well as tender feelings.

A book entitled *A Map of "Pretty Girls" in China* has been published in China. It discusses the relation between a few big cities in China and the pretty girls there, puts forward the theory that different cities breed different types of pretty girls, and analyzes the pretty girls in many Chinese cities with the aid of index numbers. The women of Chengdu come top in the list.

The women of Chengdu are like tea served in a teacup with lid and saucer unique to Sichuan, which, steaming hot and lightly fragrant, can only unveil its quiet, elegant, harmonious, and romantic nature after you have fully tasted it. The people of Chengdu call women "fenzi," which means that women's skin is fine, delicate, smooth, and soft, somewhat like *fenzi* (a snack made of glutinous rice powder). Therefore, generally speaking, only pretty women are qualified for the title "fenzi" and according to the level of beauty, they can be classified into three categories: small "fenzi," medium "fenzi," and big "fenzi." "Every spring, Chengdu is teeming with luxuriant trees and bushes, just like the 'fenzi' of Chengdu that we admire ardently, beautiful in the daytime and moist in the nighttime…" *Chengdu Fenzi*, an online novel that hundreds of thousands of Internet users have read in China, makes a romantic representation of the pretty women in Chengdu. In the streets of Chengdu, there are too many pretty women for the eye to take in and it seems as if red powder is floating ceaselessly down from the sky to this ancient city. The great number and the high rate of pretty girls in Chengdu are unimaginable for out-of-towners, but for local inhabitants, it is nothing surprising but much too familiar. There are many rivers and plentiful rainfall in Chengdu and that is why the girls of Chengdu all look fresh and juicy, or in Chengdu dialect, "shuisehao (fair-complexioned)."

The pretty girls of Chengdu are sweeter and more delicate than those of Beijing, plumper and more curvaceous than those of Shanghai, bolder and more vigorous than those of the south of the Yangtze River, and gentler and tenderer than those of Chongqing. Meanwhile, they are as wise as the women of Beijing, as tasteful and romantic as those of Shanghai, as smart and capable as those of Wuhan. Walk at random into a teahouse, sit down, and look at the flowing beauties in the streets, and you will surely feel as if belonging to the previous generation. Now the word "fenzi" has made its way to Beijing, and Feng Xiaogang, a famous Chinese movie director, called his wife "cleansing *fen*" in his book *Devoting My Youth to You*. Human beings are products of geographical environments, history and culture, and habits and customs. The female inhabitants of a certain place are always its calling card and mirror, who enrich men's dreamland, display the kernel of local culture, and manifest the future of this place. They are the motor power of their hometown.

It is said that Sichuan is the biggest basin in China, Chengdu the biggest flowerpot in the basin, and the women of Chengdu the flowers in the pot. Couldn't the most beautiful rare flowers grow in this pot, which has been nourished by the history of over 4,000 years as the base fertilizer, irrigated by the age-old Minjiang River and irradiated by the light of future? Every time

I rode in our car, I frequently looked at the girls walking gracefully with red, yellow, blue, or green umbrellas in the hand under the Chinese parasol trees that interweaved with one another on both sides of the street, and as they glanced back with a sweet smile, I could not help but exclaim over their beauty. The girls of Chengdu are mostly delicate and exquisite and seldom apply powder and paint, but they look fine and tasteful in appearance. And they always look younger than their age: College students look like high school students and high school students, like middle school students. The distinctive geographical and cultural environments have nourished the pretty girls of Chengdu; gentle and cultivated, lovely and charming, tender and loving, with a soft and lingering voice, full of feminine beauty, they are like a glass of pure red wine: The more you drink, the mellower it tastes, and the more moved with admiration you are…

Chengdu dialect is a branch of the southwestern Chinese mandarin, a subdivision of the northern dialect. Its speech sounds are somewhat different from Mandarin Chinese: There are no retroflexes but blade-alveolars in Chengdu dialect and [n] and [l] are indistinguishable. Chengdu dialect is a bit low-pitched than Mandarin Chinese and winding its way to the tips of tongues of the girls of Chengdu, it sounds soft, pleasantly sweet, and agreeable. "You won't know you're too low in official ranking until you go to Beijing; you won't know you aren't rich enough until you go to Guangdong; you won't know your health isn't good enough until you go to Hainan; and you won't know you've got married too early until you go to Chengdu." This doggerel, in a way, reveals how pretty, intelligent, elegant, and gentle the girls of Chengdu are. However, what is the most laudable about the women of Chengdu are their self-confidence and intelligence and their well-grounded desire to show their talents and abilities. In the streets of Chengdu, you can often see a fashionably dressed girl with a bunch of *chuanchuanxiang* in the hand, eating while walking as if there is no one else present; after eating the bunch of *chuanchuanxiang*, she wipes her mouth clean, then takes out a powder box, puts on her face, and turns into a gentlewoman again three or five minutes later. The girls of Chengdu like to follow the vogue; they wear clothes in the height of fashion, drive the latest model of car, and eat in the latest style…My friends said, few out-of-towners know that as far as women are concerned, Chengdu is a rather open and free city. In many common households, the husband takes charge of domestic chores such as cooking while the wife works outside and thus enjoys quite a large sphere of activities; as a result, the women of today's Chengdu are free, easy, independent, and self-confident in aspiring after self-development.

Ever since the new century dawned, the girls of Chengdu have been engaged in many eye-opening activities. TV contests and selective competitions of every description, such as "the Super-Girl Singing Contest," are extremely popular throughout the country and most of the contestants are pretty girls from Chengdu. Their desire to show their talents and abilities pay off most satisfactorily in this era, and the beauty and style of the girls of Chengdu have the tendency to set the nationwide trend. A magazine based in Guangzhong claimed that the pretty girls of Chengdu boast ten strong points: First, they are good at dressing themselves and making up their faces to their advantage; second, they know the art of living; third, they are very cordial and kindly; fourth, they know how to carve out a career for themselves; fifth, they know how to mold the minds of men; sixth, they know how to educate children; seventh, they know how to create a romantic atmosphere; eighth, they can endure hardships; ninth, they have the virtue of filial piety; tenth, they know how to look younger than their age. As a matter of fact, the women of Chengdu are like this city with a history of over 2,000 years, both ancient and modern, both traditional and up-to-date; they are like the rain in Chengdu, full of mysterious allure as well as tender feelings…

Jack Quian

A popular saying in China goes like this: "Mountainside places abound with handsome boys and waterside places teem with pretty girls." As there are many rivers and more rainy days than sunny days in Chengdu, the girls here are bright and beautiful. If you drop in a teahouse, take a seat facing the street, and look outside, you will see unadorned or flamboyant beauties all over the street. If Chengdu can be said to be a city steeped in water, then the women of Chengdu are made of water. The girls of Chengdu are not only full of water-like tender feelings, but also boast a voice as mellow as pearls, as smooth as jade, and so soft that it seems as if going to melt away. Even when they are quarreling, if you just listen to the sounds and ignore the meaning, you will think they are singing. As the gentlest water, to be sure, may freeze sometimes, so the girls of Chengdu are also hot-blooded, bold and tough. They are called "pepper girls," who love tongue-numbing, hot and steaming food. In Chengdu, there is nothing secret or embarrassing about the fact that men are henpecked. Not long ago, a great number of men took part in a contest for the most henpecked man in Chengdu sponsored by the media of Chengdu.

In Chengdu, pretty girls and delicious food usually go with each other in mutual promotion. If many pretty girls frequent a restaurant, the food there must be tasty; the pretty girls of Chengdu are actually guideposts to local delicacies. They may straighten their clothes, sit properly, and taste meticulously prepared Sichuan dishes in famous restaurants, or pitch into smoky grills and drip wet with sweat in roadside snack bars, or even concentrate upon gobbling down peasants' snacks in a back lane. While enjoying everything there is in Chengdu, they beautify the city.

According to one of my local friends, looking at pretty girls is called "dawang" in Chengdu dialect, which means "looking from a distance" with neither amorous indication nor improper familiarity. He suggested that visitors who did not know Chengdu well enough should first go to Qingqing (Green) Teahouse, Good Wood Coffee, or Impressions Bookstore in Chunxi Street or Hongxing Street, for these businesses were located on the second floor and could provide the best view of pretty girls in the streets. You may take a seat facing the street, order a cup of tea or coffee, and take your time drinking and looking at pretty girls. Through French windows, pretty girls pass like a movie before your eyes; sometimes, at the tables around yours are seated several peerlessly beautiful girls. In Lingshiguan Road, North Kehua Road, Qintai Road, and Shuangnan Neighborhood, it would be better to look at pretty women while walking along the streets. As you walk into stores or in streets, you will discover so many pretty girls—some of them are dazzlingly beautiful and bold, and others are delicate and graceful—going into or out of name brand or quality goods stores and brushing past you that rouge and powder seem to scent the air. As a matter of fact, not just customers but also many of the proprietresses are pretty women. To chat with a pretty proprietress as long as possible, you may discuss with her the styles, quality, workmanship, and prices of the goods again and again. But you should avoid irritating her, for a pretty woman of Chengdu is gentle on the one hand and hot-blooded on the other and you may regret having offended her so rashly. Only after you have stricken up a friendship with them that you will find their toughness and hot-bloodedness are actually quite fascinating.

Anyone well-versed in classic music knows that Johann Straus composed *Wein, Weib und Gesang* (Wine, Women and Song), a waltz that has enjoyed great popularity. No words can summarize the characteristics of Chengdu more aptly than the title of this waltz, for delicious food, beautiful sceneries, and pretty women have gradually become new points of economic growth in Chengdu during the 21st century as well as the highlights of Chengdu that most strongly attract worldwide tourists.

If you have never been to Chengdu, you will by no means have any idea of how many pretty women there are in this city. The pretty women of Chengdu are neither like lilies whose fragrance assails one's nostrils nor like those tender narcissi on the desk. They are like those common dewy roses in flower stalls, who give off refreshing and romantic fragrance, whether it is a sunny day or a moonlit starry night, whether in lush spring or in foggy winter. Or rather, they are like cups of lightly fragrant jasmine tea that stand slim and graceful on the antique square table; and we are required to calm down before we can smell with heart and soul its fragrance that savors of health and freedom and fully appreciate the current of beauty in uneventful daily life. The gentleness of the women of Chengdu resembles the Jinjiang River that flows through this city, graceful, charming, and enduring, merging quietly and slowly into the blood vessels of this city and moistening the hearts of the men.

As a matter of fact, the women of Chengdu are like this city with a history of over 2,000 years, both ancient and modern, both traditional and up-to-date; they are like the mist in Chengdu, full of mysterious allure as well as tender feelings. Living in this city full of pretty women and shuttling back and forth in this world brimming over with beauty, vibrancy, youth, and vigor, the men of Chengdu find themselves pleased both to the eye and the mind and never get tired…

Jack Quian

Tips:

Jinsha, a song and dance drama
You will be deeply impressed by the costumes that mingle ancient-style simplicity and modern ingenuity, exquisite masks, colorful background pictures, designs in imitation of unearthed gold, jade, copper, stone, ivory, earthen wares, and the like. The play centers upon the heartrending but beautiful and eternal love between the male protagonist Sha and the female protagonist Jin that spans 3,000 years; the audience are brought back to ancient times to experience the primitive and mysterious sacrificial ceremonies 3,000 years ago, the war in ancient Shu Kingdom 2,000 years ago, wrathful thunder and lightning, shining spears and armored horses, and the heavenly music of a band of 24 female players. The play is really a heart-stirring spectacle and a veritable feast for the eyes and it might be safe to call it the song and dance drama of the biggest production in China.
Add: No. 48, Shuinianhe Road, Chengdu
Phone: 028-84456688
Time: 8:00-10:00 pm

Sichuan opera:
Gongs and drums play a vital role in Sichuan opera. A side drum, a barrel-shaped drum, a large gong, a large cymbal, a small gong, a stringed instrument, and *suona* (a woodwind instrument) form an orchestra conducted by the side drum. The performance of Sichuan opera follows a profound realistic tradition that boasts a set of unique and perfect conventions, realistic and exquisite renderings, humor and witticism, and the rich appeals of life. Such consummate skills as partner stunts, eye-opening, face-changing, fire hoop-jumping, and broadsword-hiding add much color, mystery, and changeability to the stage. The Wuhou Temple is among the most famous places where Sichuan operas are performed.
Add: The Open-Air Grand Theater, the Wuhou Temple, Chengdu
Time: 8:00-10:00 pm

The Purple Castle:
It is a house on a small hill, made of deep purple-red rocks. A sign at its entrance reads "Sichuan Color Wash Painting Research Institute," but it is actually the private villa of a painter whose surname is Qiu. Beyond the entrance gate, there are two ways leading to the Purple Castle proper: One of them is made up of tens of stone steps and the other is a "railway." The guests always choose the latter: They get on a railcar, flick open the power supply button, and arrive at the villa in a moment. With only a departure station and a destination station, this "railway" may be the shortest one in the world; with a low starting point and a high end point, it may also be the railway with the biggest slope in the world. The railway cuts through a grove of bamboos and trees and the ride is really a great joy. Green Boston ivies are exerting themselves to cover the purple outer walls of the villa. There are a lotus pond, a vegetable garden, pavilions and bowers, an artificial brook and waterfall inside the yard, which make a unique view. You can see many inscriptions, some of which sound solemn, and others are humorous. A stone bench is placed in a pavilion and named by the painter "cold bench" to mark his bitter memories. The studio is located on the third floor and named "September." Hanging on the walls of the showroom are many paintings and group photos of the painter with celebrities.
Add: Near Longquan Park, Longquanyi District, Chengdu

Lingke (Water Chestnuts' Nest):
Lingke is the former residence of Li Zheren, a famous writer in Chengdu. It is quite small and simple, composed of only a two-storied building, a pond, and a few ancient trees. Li Zheren's white marble bust radiates much vigor and on the back there is an inscription: "A man of letter who stood out in his time in the paradise-like land of Ba-Shu." The first floor is where Mr. Li and his family lived their daily life and the second floor serves as a showroom where the visitors can see an introduction to his life and an exhibition of his works. Mr. Li's works belong to the school of naturalism and literary critics call him "the Chinese Zola." His most famous works include *Ripples across Stagnant Water, Before the Rainstorm*, and *Great Waves*, which realistically depict in Chengdu dialect what life was like in Chengdu and its neighboring country. *Ripples across Stagnant Water* ranks 17 among the "100 most famous Chinese novels in the 20th century" selected by experts from Mainland China, Hongkong, Taiwan, Singapore, the United States, and other countries.
Add: Shahebao, the East Gate, Jinjiang District, Chengdu
Phone: 028-84674112

The Lius' Manor:
With an area of over 70,000 square meters, the Lius's Manor is an important historical site and one of the representative architectural structures of modern China. Built in the late period of the Qing Dynasty and the early years of the Republic of China, it comprises two complexes with the total area of over 20,000 square meters that face each other from south and north. It is a manor of great dimensions that keeps more than 20,000 cultural relics and collected wares. The well-preserved manor houses, the large amounts of historical objects and literature, and the unique layout of the demesne constitute an organic whole, which in turn can be regarded as a miniature of the countryside in Old China and a section of China's social development. The sculpture *Rent Collecting Courtyard* is well known far and near.
Add: Anren Town, Dayi County, Chengdu (about 52 kilometers away from Chengdu)
Phone: 028-88315113
Transportation: Nonstop buses depart from the New South Gate Bus Station for the Lius' Manor

Chengdu Ebony Arts Museum:
A popular saying goes like this: "Ebony of a cubic meter is more valuable than a chest of jewelry." Thousands of years ago, due to natural disasters, many trees were buried in ancient riverbeds and turned into ebony woods. Ebony is very hard and dense and varies from ocher to taupe to livid. The section of ebony is smooth but the bark is variegated and rough. Ebony wood is peculiar to Chengdu Plain. In the past dry seasons, the locals might stumble across an ebony wood in a queer shape, and some of them were curious enough to make the wood into everyday wares such as Chinese chess, pencil vases, and the like.
Add: Opposite to Gold Oxen Hotel, Jinquan Road, Chengdu

Old Chengdu Folk-Custom Park:
It is located below the South People's Road Flyover, which is the only way to downtown Chengdu for any traveler who comes by air. It would be best to go to Old Chengdu Folk-Custom Park at dusk; in gathering darkness lights are turned on and the old bridges and streets of Old Chengdu appear before your eyes one after another. The old streets are actually a series of relievos and

the old bridges are miniatures hanging over a brook. You can also see copper sculptures featuring the folk practices of Chengdu: pushing the *Jigong* cart (a wheelbarrow in the shape of a cock's head), cleaning ears, *zhuantangban'er* (spinning the sugar wheel), sawing a log, singing to the accompaniment of angklung, trundling iron hoops, and so on. If you like, you can sit on a copper chair and have your ears cleaned by an old man whose face is full of wrinkles. The pillars of the flyover are inscribed with lines on Chengdu written by such famous poets as Li Bai, Du Fu, Lu You, and Su Shi. On a stone tablet is engraved a map of Old Chengdu, which shows the size of the old city and the directions of the flowing rivers are quite different from today. When tired, you can drink tea in Old Chengdu Teahouse or go to stores that sell calligraphies, paintings, and curios. To learn about the folkways and morals of Old Chengdu, out-of-town travelers cannot afford to miss Old Chengdu Folk-Custom Park.
Add: Below the South People's Road Flyover

The most charming historical and cultural sites:
Du Fu's Thatched Cottage, the Wuhou Temple, Mount Qingcheng, Dujiang Weirs, the Qingyang Temple, the Wenshu Temple

The most charming teahouses and cafés:
Shunxing Old Teahouse, Shanxi Guildhall Teahouse, Good Wood Coffee, *Sanyi* (Three Arts) Teahouse

The most charming scenic spots:
Snow-Capped Mount Xiling, Mount Tiantai, Shixiang Lake

The most charming streets:
Chunxi Street, Qintai Road, the Ancient Street in Luodai Town, the Ancient Wenjun Street in Qionglai County, Hongmin Food Center in Shuangliu County, Binghe Road in Dujiangyan City

The most charming shopping centers:
Chengdu Guomei Electrical Appliances Store, Chengdu Suning Electrical Appliances Store, Chengdu Ito Yokado Department Store, Chengbai Yongle Electrical Appliances Store, Chengdu Pacific Department Store

The most charming fitness centers:
Sichuan International Golf Club, Longquan Sunshine Sports Center, the Champion's Night Climbing Club, Wuhou District Recreation and Sports Center, 6250 Club

The most charming leisure centers:
Daweiying International Club, Beisen Leisure Plaza, Hailanyuntian Bathhouse, Chengdu Xianshe Feet-Bathing Center, Chengdu Hongqiao Health Center

The most charming resorts/happy rural resorts:
Mount Qingcheng Hexiang Resort, Nancaoping Resort, Jiufeng Resort, Yinrongyuan Ecological Resort, Yongyashanfang Resort

The most charming places of entertainment:
One-Way Street Club Discotheque, Sounds of Nature KTV Center, Empty Bottle Pub

The most trustworthy travel agencies:
Sichuan China Youth Travel Service Corporation, Ltd, Sichuan Kanghui International Travel Service Corporation, Ltd, Chengdu China Travel Service Corporation, Ltd

VIII. A Nightless City

As night falls, the lights in Chengdu are turned on gradually from far to near and add a touch of charm and warmth to this city. The air irradiated by neon lights is mild and lovely, just like a woman who gets exceedingly gentle after having drunk some wine. Daytime busyness, purposefulness, methodicalness, and orderliness are laid aside for tomorrow. The night is gathering around us and cannot be driven away. For us out-of-town tourists, it would be best to melt the long night into drinks drop by drop and spend at leisure the unscheduled time.

There are a wide choice of places to go; in such a leisurely city as Chengdu, hundreds of bars attract numerous night owls. If you are just fond of drinking, then you do not have to go to a bar; instead, you may as well stay at home, drink with restraint and chant in a low voice, or you may drink to excess, sing like mad, play finger-guessing game and drinkers' wager game with your companions and flash goblets from hand to hand. Perhaps we are tempted to go to a bar by its color, the color interwoven and intermixed by light and shadow.

The lighting in a bar is invariably designed to be neither bright nor dark; therefore, the color of a bar takes on transitional nuances. You do not have to distinguish between the bar's inherent color and that of lighting or of environment; perhaps it is just the color that appears in your eyes after you have got tipsy. Most of the bars present an intimate warm color: orange, tangerine, or coffee. Amid various sources of steady lighting, the flickering candlelight and the glimmering cigarette butts seem to be alive with motion. Inside such an atmosphere, misty eyes are made mistier, and unsteady footsteps more unsteady.

A few of the bars, to be sure, present a cool color, such as dark blue and silvery white. Inside such a bar, with wisps of cigarettes' smoke floating about, if you drink a glass of Chivas a bit on the bitter and astringent side and listen to sentimental blues, you may feel that the air is permeated with melancholy.

Neither the drinks in the glasses nor the paintings on the walls look what they are originally. Just like your mood at the moment, with a common grounding, they have blurred their own boundaries and hidden their own characters. You will discover that in a bar, two colors can always blend into each other. Meanwhile, you will find that no color can be replicated or reproduced, and this is exactly why you go to the same bar time and again.

Chengdu's bars are concentrated in the south and west of the city. Yulin Neighborhood and Section Four of South People's Road have the reputation of being Sanlitun (the famous street of bars in Beijing) in Chengdu. The proprietors of the bars there have racked their brains, finally got a sudden inspiration and created half-real half-imaginary scenes, with 40% romance, 30% uniqueness, 20% artistry, and 10% artificiality. There, you have every reason to look forward to a beautiful chance encounter and a hundred reencounters, with all sorts of feelings welling up in your heart.

I sent Danny to sleep over in the home of one of my friends, for he would go to the amusement park with my friend's child the next day. Upon my return to the hotel, it was the right time for night owls. Therefore, against the wind I walked on my shadow into a bar called "Happy Capital" in North Kehua Road. It had a very bright neon sign and from afar, I could see its slogan: "Let's Meet in Happy Capital." The style of the bar was more Western than Eastern and it looked quite wonderful. This impression became stronger when I walked into the hall. The windows in the walls were of Western style, square in the lower part and round in the upper; they were decorated with iron openwork and the finishing touch was the gilded leaves in the iron openwork, which looked majestic. The lights were embedded in the ceiling, soft and not protrudent. One of the corners where the ceiling and the wall joined together was also decorated with iron openwork, which was in no sense anything superfluous that ruined the whole effect, for it was in perfect harmony with the overall style of the hall. I took a seat and on my right there was the rather long bar counter. A great variety of bottles stood on the liquor cabinet in twos and threes but did not look crowded. As the light was quite dim, I took a careful look at the ceiling, which was layered in good order. The out-of-the-ordinary lights shone through the novel grids and the hall was made soft-colored and very comfortable. The innermost section of the hall was a bit higher than the rest. Leaning on the wall were a row of soft fabric sofas and between them were

interposed green potted plants. Here you could also get a good view of the performances. The stage was on the other end of the hall, where you could see two high chairs with a low backrest and two microphones. A chanteuse was singing a sad song from the bottom of her heart. She looked clearly different from those girls who liked to idle away the hours in bars as well as those women at the bar counter whose beauty struck me as commercial and professional.

Amid the alluring colors, light and music, some customers were sitting alone in corners, some talking and laughing loudly, some drinking to the limit of their capacity, some smoking, and still some whispering gentle and nice words to each other. To the accompaniment of the chanteuse's light and sad song, both the time in the air and the drinks on the table were disappearing slowly. With a bottle in the left hand and a tin in the right, the bartender was busy making a show of his forte before the customers. Under the dim light, I saw him hurl a bottle up into the air, and the bottle spiraled up and then down at high speed. He turned about and extended his right hand behind his back, the stainless steel tin was reflecting dazzling silvery light, and with a clear bang, the bottle fell right into the tin. In face of the loud "Bravos" and ambiguous smiles of the customers, especially the pretty women, the bartender quickened his movements. He bared his strong arms and hurled the bottle up backward and the bottle flew over his head and drew a beautiful curve in the air. He stretched out one of his arms, the bottle fell down and stood firm on it, then he jerked his arm upward, the bottle jumped to the air and fell down again on the other arm—it was repeated several times. In the twinkling of an eye, a dark golden water column thrust itself from the bottleneck into the tin, which looked very fascinating. Hardly had the applauses subsided when four bottles suddenly appeared in the air, rising and falling one after another and none of them fell down to the ground. Below the flying bottles, the bartender remained calm throughout, his hands hurling at astonishing speed, which was a dazzling display of acrobatics.

In an age overrun with commercialism and desire for material wealth, Chengdu's bars have been pervaded with an unruly, leisurely, marginal, and hedonic atmosphere from the very beginning. The most distinctive or unique fashion stores, hot pot restaurants, taverns, cafés, video stores, and the like are concentrated in East Yulin Road, near Sichuan Province Athletics Center and Sichuan Province Museum. And in West Yulin Road cluster together bars of various styles, where people interested in poetry, movies, rock-n-roll, fine arts, architecture, and so on gather in groups.

At night, the singers in this city, pretty women who sleep by day and become active by night, and poets with crumpled manuscripts of poems in the hands, begin to go in and out of "Empty Bottle," "Music House," "Coordinate," and other bars in Yulin Road. Under the dim light, they pour out their inner thoughts to each other, or murmur to themselves. Strong beer, weak chrysanthemum tea, South American coffee that has crossed seas and oceans to Chengdu, rich and gaudy facial makeup, strange and exotic magazines, and the singers' screaming, all of them are blended together wonderfully.

Here, poets are passing on writings, rock-n-roll singers communicating with each other with sounds, painters and sculptors looking for inspiration, and artists from south and north and visitors of this city collecting vital energy. It is a special circle that exists for the "countless minority" in this city. Meanwhile, Yulin Road is the last stronghold of flashy secular life before inlanders enter Tibet. On the last night of their stopover in Chengdu, those foreign tourists who are going to trudge up the Qinghai-Tibet Plateau, the so-called "Roof of the World" with much reverence, will take out a map of this city from their backpacks, find their way to the bars in Yulin Road that have already been circled on the map, and listen to the strong accent peculiar to this city there.

Undoubtedly, bars are important places for the unconventional life in this city. In a sense, they are also the secret "middle belt" between inland cities in China and Tibet, the "Roof of the World," which display, most thoroughly, the rich and complicated artistic life and pleasure-seeking activities of this city. These bars have their own strong accents, unique colors, leisurely movements, and good drinks, tea and food in which customers may indulge themselves. They are the musical circles, the poetic community, as well as a map of the city in which both arts and commerce are flourishing. On this map, various cultural and artistic genealogies are juxtaposed more randomly amid the tide of globalization. As a matter of fact, you may find the weather of this city hard to understand, but you cannot help but like the atmosphere here.

Beer, art, love, and life always exist synchronously in Chengdu's bars, places that cannot do without alcohol or cappuccino at any time. Despite the prevalence of disco and rave culture, bars have not declined in Chengdu, and on the contrary, they are more popular with the young people. Opposite the American Consulate stands a conspicuous red building named "Red Age," which evokes a certain strong atmosphere. A group of local DJs play an active role here, and more often than not, famous DJs come here from all round the world to give performances. New styles of enjoyments are being produced here. Red Age is one of the biggest bars in Chengdu, where enlarged pictures of Mao Zedong, Lenin, Lu Xun, and other old revolutionists hang on the walls. Every night, they will be woken and rocked by the quick-rhythm electronic music and can do nothing but helplessly watch their offspring put into practice their instruction: "Make foreign things serve China."

I am a traveler who likes to explore a city thoroughly; once in a city, I would like to see its sights, read its history, taste its food, drink in its bars…It does not necessarily mean that I am fond of the lively and jolly atmosphere in a bar; but instead, bars in a city and the people killing time there can often reflect the living habits and public feelings that permeate this city. I went to a tall building in Yulin Living Plaza on Section Three of the South Second Ring Road. It was a bar with an empty bottle painted on the entrance gate. From a distance, I saw a group of young people swinging their bodies to the accompaniment of dance music. They found their selves in the bouquet of wine; whether chatting with friends or experiencing loneliness by staying alone, they felt quite *bashi* (at ease) in bars, as if birds were experiencing the tenderness and mystery of night. It was a typical gathering of the young people; I defined myself as a spectator and walked in like a detective. It was a big open bar partitioned into several areas and with a capacity of several hundred customers, where you could sing and dance wildly to the accompaniment of exciting music. Everywhere in the bar, you could see pretty girls with a willowy figure who wore unconventional costumes and a makeup in vogue; sitting alone beside a window, they were drinking a glass of red wine and skillfully puffing rings of cigarette smoke, with a lonely, proud and aloof expression on their faces. Youngsters with their hairs dyed blonde could also be found indulging themselves here occasionally by guzzling and getting drunk. Certainly, there were quite a few people who came here with two or four friends after the strain and constraint of a whole day's work; in the bar they could return to their real selves and seek their true being cloaked in mundane affairs. Let the noisy metallic music drown the pandemonium; let the blurred and dim light screen frailness and loneliness; and let the flowing florid red wine conceal the lonely young faces. In such a nebulous and confusing state, they could experience a flashy and foaming life under the dim light of night.

I was drinking a beverage unique to Chengdu: Chivas mixed with iced green tea. A strong liquor as Chivas is, when mixed with the same amount of green tea, it begins to have a taste unique to Chengdu. Unknowingly, you let alcohol into your stomach along with the scented tea and soon reach the highest state aspired to by bar frequenters: being tipsy. At the table next to mine, a man who called himself a frequenter of this bar said that he once owned a bar and that he would not feel awake until he took a glass of drink from the bar counter. After so many years had elapsed, he still clearly remembered those bars that he saw in foreign movies as a teenager and in that era of scanty material and cultural life, he had dreamt of sitting at leisure in a bar someday and idling away several happy hours. From South People's Road, Xiyu Street, Yulin Neighborhood, to Zijing Neighborhood, from Half a Dozen, Moulin Rouge, Western Cowboy, 360°, Bistro, Empty Bottle, Sounds, to Music House, Coordinate, and Handsome Friends, he had been frequenting bars for 20 years since the middle of the 1980s. He said the most unforgettable bar was Half a Dozen around 1990. Then it was located near Minshan Hotel in South People's Road and there, you could see a comedian good at telling jokes, a man with a beard playing the accordion, a singer wearing a long scarf playing the guitar, and so on. He said that music was the soul of a bar and a bar was soulless without music.

In Half a Dozen, what I saw could almost be called a gathering of purely white-collar workers in Chengdu, who kept swimming in and out of the bar like fish. It was a typical "petty bourgeois" bar, and the customers' clothing and behavior told everything. They had an adequate sense of propriety: The most ostentatious were pioneers and avant-garde; the least were vulgar clodhoppers; and in between them were petty bourgeois with appropriate manners. I felt like the oldest among them and compared with their formal clothes and dresses, my T-shirt and jeans seemed quite out of place, which made me ill at ease all through the night. On such an occasion two things must be kept in mind: First, wear a smile all the time; second, speak English. While going to the bar counter to order a drink or something else, you must nod and smile at anyone in your way and always avoid walking with long and fast strides. And you must say to the waiter, "A glass of juice" or "A glass of whiskey"; or if at a loss for the right English word, its replacement in Sichuan dialect will also suffice; but Mandarin Chinese is definitely out of place here.

After observing closely for a while, I discovered the flaw of Chengdu's petty bourgeoisie. That is, they were lacking in the open-minded "Beijing mentality"; the mindset typical of inhabitants of a provincial capital still remained in their innermost nature and they had not got used to chatting with people other than their acquaintances. Unlike the bars in Sanlitun Street in Beijing, there were no gentlemen hunting around for beauties with a glass of wine in the hand; the girls here were neither so proud and aloof as those in Beijing nor very friendly to strangers and ready to make new friends. The so-called "Beijing mentality" implied an ability to get acquainted with strangers and move on to a friendly relationship right away. The petty bourgeoisie in Beijing's bars had already acquired this mentality and they were bolder and more utilitarian than Chengdu's petty bourgeoisie who valued feelings and affections. "Petty bourgeoisie" had been a derogatory term in China before. If you were said to be full of petty bourgeois sentiments in a year-end summing-up, then you were a dead duck, for it meant that you lacked the sentiments of the leading working class and peasants and must be subject to education and remolding. Although according to the theory of class differentiation, petty bourgeoisie tended to neither exploit others nor be exploited by others, their way of expressing thoughts and feelings, their aesthetic taste and attitude toward life were extremely problematic. In the past, it was out of keeping with the times to attach great importance to personal feelings, thoughts, sentiments, interests, and preferences.

Today's petty bourgeoisie do not have to fear the criticism from the working class or peasants any more, but they have aggrandized to the utmost their personal way of expressing thoughts and feelings, their aesthetic taste and attitude toward life. They tend to divide social classes according to something illusory that can neither be seen nor touched. For instance, while drinking a cup of coffee, you value the taste, they, the emotional appeal; while watching TV, you focus on whether the plot is thrilling or not, they, whether the program is of superb taste or not, just like a true artist. They read novels written by Kundera, Calvino, and Zhang Ailing; they watch movies directed by Wang Jiawei, Hou Xiaoxian, and Buñuel; they eat Häagen-Dazs ice creams; and they can tell the real name brand clothing from the fake…If we judge by means of production in control, a part of today's petty bourgeoisie in China may even be counted among the proletarian. Meanwhile, some employers who control means of production and wring surplus value out of their employees may meet none of the basic requirements of petty bourgeoisie and therefore, they are regarded as clodhoppers. The amount of wealth can be changed through individual endeavors and even through dishonest practices, but the petty bourgeois mentality cannot be acquired at your free will. The petty bourgeoisie class is enlarging by leaps and bounds. They write about their feelings and thoughts in a tempting language, which, publicized by media, not only appeals to the young people and some trendy peasants, but also brings spiritual and cultural pressure on those uncultured upstarts.

In Chengdu's bars, you can clearly feel the presence of such petty bourgeois interests and feelings, but it does not mean that you fully understand them. Only when you are on the scene in person and catch their high spirits, can you discover that the customers here are a group of people that deserve much attention. They are young, intelligent, and full of vigor; many of them are the backbone of the high-tech industry in Chengdu and the trendsetters in this city as well. Although they have no intent to influence others, nor want to be influenced by others, their thoughts and feelings, aesthetic perception, and even attitudes toward life all demand sufficient attention from society. There are a variety of thoughts and feelings left out in the corners of this city in hopes of being wakened by the giddy alcohol. As far as this group of people are concerned, they can find in bars the lingering charm and interest that cannot be drunk away, alluring smiling faces set off by the hop, a musical feast for the mind, and a certain sweet solace that helps them to forget the stress of work…They regard frequenting the bar as an expression of their self-consciousness and stubbornly cling to it, determined to aggrandize their personal way of expressing thoughts and feelings, their aesthetic taste and attitude toward life. Such illusory stuff has been termed "the urban sub-culture."

With a glass of rum with cola in the hand, a white-collar worker with Intel told me that he liked the feeling of having a drink in a bar, the fun of the finger-guessing game, and the attempt to chat with strangers, and he also enjoyed sitting at the bar counter and staring blankly, listening to the sweet-sounding deep low voice of the guitar singers, taking a taste of new beverages recommended by bartenders, and feeling rather light and relaxed after having had a certain amount of drinks. He said it was not because he was an alcoholic that he came to bars; rather, he just wanted to sit in a clean and elegant corner in this modern city and relax himself in such noisy nights when he felt fidgety and lonely in the gathering darkness, letting his thoughts and feelings float aimlessly in the air along with the faint scent of beverages, and trying to boost his spirits for tomorrow with his sereneness and leisureliness this night. Along with the arrival of more and more transnational corporations and high-tech industries in Chengdu, this group of young people is enlarging by leaps and bounds and appearing in newspapers and other kinds of media. They write about their lifestyle in a tempting language, which, publicized by media, not only appeals to the young people and some trendy peasants, but also brings spiritual suffering and cultural pressure to those uncultured upstarts.

A bar is a second living room for urban young people. On the surface, a bar seems to be where the Eastern culture and the Western culture interchange; but in the nighttime of Chengdu, a bar is not just something in front of you but a space that invites you to enter…The dim halo is overflowing with drifting fragrance of Vodka and lemon; the smell of Havana cigars is becoming dense and filling the air to the accompaniment of music. Here, you can savor the trumpet, saxophone, and electric guitar played by Louis Armstrong, John Coltrane, and Miles Davis; you can also search for your favorite books such as *One Hundred Years of Solitude* by Marquez and *Norwegian Wood* by Haruki Murakami under the dim light…Here, you can be made to feel serene and sorrowful and recall the perplexity and agony that you have experienced at a certain stage of your life; here, you can also be made to feel inexplicably intoxicated and at ease after unloading the heavy burden of reality. These vigorous well-paid young people, eager to disport themselves to their hearts' content, act the parts of office worker and night owls at once. Every day each of them is engaged in two activities: working and having fun. They convert life into the froth of beer and aspirations into the green tea in Chivas whiskey, and prolong their pursuit…

While leaving the bar, I looked at the quiet streets and the silk-like rain curtain and did not know until now that Chengdu had so much charm suggestive of poetry and painting. Thanks to the noise and excitement in the nightless bars, Chengdu has become as beautiful as the graceful blush of a maiden who lowers her head. I allowed my thoughts and feelings to roam in the long night, accompanied by the sound of raindrops hitting the ground. Finally they also dropped to the ground and stayed overnight in the hometown of Xue Tao, a talented woman in the Tang Dynasty…When I woke up amid the fragrance of tea and bouquet of liquor, the sky was already sending out a twilight glow; I swept my eyes over the architecture of this city, and those poets who got tipsy in Chengdu just as I did flashed across my mind, such as Du Fu, Li Bai, Lu You, and Xue Tao…

Tips:

The business hours of Chengdu's bars: 18:00 pm-4:00 am
Prices: The usual prices of beers are 180-240 *yuan* Renminbi per dozen and those of red wines are 120-250 *yuan* Renminbi per bottle.
Brandies and Whiskeys:
Remy Martin Louis XIII: 11,000 *yuan* Renmibi per bottle
Hennessy XO: 1280 *yuan* Renminbi per bottle
Hennessy V.S.O.P.: 488 *yuan* Renminbi per bottle
Remy Martin XO: 1480 *yuan* Renminbi per bottle
Martell Condon Blue: 1080 *yuan* Renminbi per bottle
Royal Salute 21s': 1488 *yuan* Renminbi per bottle
Chivas Regal 12s': 280 *yuan* Renminbi per bottle
J/W Black Label: 380 *yuan* Renminbi per bottle
Jack Danniel's: 380 *yuan* Renminbi per bottle
Gordon's Dry Gin: 320 *yuan* Renminbi per bottle

The in drinks in Chengdu's bars:

1. **Vodka + Orange juice:** It is the most fashionable drink. Vodka never fails to remind the drinker of the desolate vastness of Siberia and the orange juice adds a touch of gentleness to vodka's unruliness.

2. **Chivas + Iced green tea + Soda:** Whiskey is a strong liquor, which, if drunk alone, will almost burn your throat, so liquor dealers always advise you to add the same amount of soda. The mixing of this drink in bars is quite interesting, for it requires iced green tea instead of iced red tea and the brand of green tea had better be "Master Kang." As a result, alcohol slips into your stomach along with the transcendental flavor of tea.

3. **Hennessy Pure White + Soda:** Hennessy is one of the four famous brands of French brandies. What would the narcissistic French people think if they know that Hennessy is used to mix such a drink?

4. **Jack Danniel's + Cola:** Reputedly, this drink was invented by one of the leaders of China and therefore was named "No. 1 in Heaven and Earth." Whether it is good to drink or not depends upon one's own taste. And it is said that a product similar to "No. 1 in Heaven and Earth" has come on the market and its main ingredients include Jack Danniel's and cola.

5. **Rum + Gin + Tonic:** Both rum and gin are strong alcohol and mixed together, they can take fire. Both are also transparent alcohol and mixed together, they still look as clear as water. That is to say, there is no distinction between water and fire in the eyes of drinkers.

6. **Bailey's + Soda:** Women take a risk in drinking alcohol: They look either exceedingly depraved or extraordinarily beautiful. Any drink with Bailey's as the main ingredient caters to the needs of women. Other than soda, even milk can be mixed together with Bailey's!

7. **Rum Bacardi + Cola:** Although my eyes were blurred with the effects of alcohol, I was still taken by surprise: How could there be such a cocktail full of revolutionary passion? After a careful look I got the answer: Rum Bacardi made in Cuba meets the free cola made in the USA and the outcome proves that some lovely harmony exists in the maelstrom of conflicts in the world. Besides this cocktail of "Free Cuba," the fact that both Castro and Clinton love cigars is a case in point.

8. **Tequila + Lemon + Salt:** It is actually the most orthodox way of drinking tequila. This drink is included in this list because you will feel quite like a knight-errant in drinking it.

Recommended bars:

Half a Dozen:
"Music bands, romantic atmosphere, chance encounters, stories, beers, foreigners, games, pretty women, the new generation, none of them are lacking in 15-year-old Half a Dozen," the bar advertises itself as such. Its nostalgic style and music selection service appeal to successful white-collar workers of about 30 years old and consequently, the bar is playfully called "the recreation center of middle-aged and old people" by the younger generation of Chengdu. At the weekend, there are no empty seats in this bar, even around the bar counter.
Add: No. 26, Fangcao Street, Chengdu
Phone: 028-85176969

Empty Bottle:
With the total area of over 1,000 square meters, it is a grand English-style bar that can accommodate four or five hundred customers. The extra-large area is partitioned into several sections: the game section that offers customers various kinds of English-style games and entertainments; the Internet section where consumers of different levels can log on to the Internet while drinking beverages at the same time; and the open section of high bar where professional music bands give a series of performances. The bar features an authentic style, decorations with a strong flavor of culture, delicious snacks, and beverages most popular in Europe and the USA.
Add: The third floor, Yulin Living Plaza, Section 3, South Second Ring Road, Chengdu
Phone: 028-85599798

Jack Quian

Blue Bird:
Not a big bar, it is nevertheless one of the strongholds of travel lovers in Chengdu. The proprietor himself is extremely fond of traveling. Here customers give slide shows and tell interesting stories about their journeys. On the walls hang many big and small photos, favorite ones taken by the proprietor and frequenters in places all over the country as well as postcards mailed from places all over the country; on the corner shelves there are travel books. Here you also see advertisements for traveling companions, introductions to traveler's outfits, schedules of upcoming activities, and the like.
Add: No. 4, Fanglin Road, Chengdu
Phone: 028-87034530

Carlo Western-Style Food Bar:
It is located by Jinjiang Hotel, near Jinjiang Bridge. I had not expected that the bar, especially the dance pool as small as a palm was thickly packed with so many people. The melodious music, inexpensive drinks, and many foreigners impressed me most deeply. I went there later because I wanted to listen to the music. I like the DJ there very much, who always plays the in pub music in foreign countries. Customers from abroad all said Carlo was just like those pubs in foreign countries. After a day's work, it is very relaxing to go to drink, dance, and listen to music in Carlo, where you can give vent to your pent-up feelings.
Add: No. 2, Linjiang Road, Chengdu
Phone: 028-85444639

Allen's Stories:
The pitch of the bar goes like this: "Accepts romance reservations but sell no love." It is a bar aimed at helping its customers make friends with each other. On every table, there is a phone and a map of all the seats in the bar. Every customer can make friends on his or her own, by dialing to introduce himself or herself or chatting through a particular BBS. The proprietor has written *Who Says Gentlewomen Never Go to a Bar?*, *I'm a Good Citizen, Please Love Me* and other novels, which enjoy great popularity on the Internet.
Add: No. 107, Shuangyuan Street, Shuangnan Neighborhood, Chengdu
Phone: 028-85550978

White Night:
Everything in the bar is white: a white bar counter, white bookshelves, white chairs, white decorations, and so on. Bright and dainty, it is one of the important strongholds of poetry and arts in Chengdu, where poetry readings and arts exhibitions are held aperiodically. On the bookshelves that hang on two walls, you can find almost all the magazines on Chinese poetry, either coarsely or beautifully printed. Below the two enthralling purple-light lamps, lines of characters on the magazines are brought into relief as if by magic and you cannot help but glue your eyes on them.
Add: No. 85, West Yulin Road, Chengdu
Phone: 028-85594861

Music House:
The proprietor is a young man who aspires zgotealously after great music. Therefore every weekend, the DJ, whether he is from Chengdu or other places, will shake up everything inside the bar with electronic music to create a dreamland of music lovers. The relationships between hosts and guests are quite close and harmonious. When the singer sings a well-known song, all customers under the stage, while drinking with each other, will sing together with the singer. A customer who has requested a song from the singer often goes onto the stage with two drinks and toasts him or her.
Add: No. 305, Yulin Living Plaza, South Yulin Road, Chengdu
Phone: 028-85510227

***Shifeng* Multiple Concept Shop:**
Perhaps it is a luxury to stay overnight in the bar, but unknowingly you may experience a moment of ease in tranquility. Customers who value originality and thinking will be attracted to those idiosyncratic rooms that are designed in neat and tight lines and give a strong impression of silvery metals. The so-called "concept" emphasizes the fact that everything in the bar—clothes, music, books, electrical equipments, computer games, sights, and the like—is of great originality and unique design. In the bar there is a small showroom, where many unknown new brands and limited-edition special products are on display. From the bookshelves filled with various books on design trends, you can pick one and read it while listening to the music as fluid as the light. The strong coffee, cool beer, and even the smell of cigarettes here will all make you quiet and placid.
Add: No. 73, West Yulin Road, Chengdu
Phone: 028-85580662

Post-Jazz Pub:
It is a work of installation art, the combined effort of three women. With music, books and drinks, these three Eastern women attempt to display in this space what they understand to be Western modern music, modern arts, and modern culture. On the surface, Post-Jazz seems to be a change in time and place of the two different Eastern and Western cultures, like the dissimilation and syncretism as a result of cultural importation and exportation. They intend to create a sense of reality in the wake of mutual influence and restraint, integration and disintegration, assimilation and dissimilation between human beings of different colors, between societies, science and cultures of different political imports, and between different forms of art in the present era of postmodernism. At night, under the dim light, the bouquet of vodka with lemon and the redolence of Havana cigars float about and permeate Post-Jazz.
Add: No. 96, South Yulin Road, Chengdu
Phone: 028-85173809

Twelve Oaks:
It is a bar in the style typical of country clubs in American West. The most eye-catching is the glass cabinet by the gate, in which a great many bottles lie in disorder, manifesting the rich connotations of alcohol. Every piece of jazz music is so stirring that you have the impulse to dance. Swinging to and fro in your seat, wagging your head, and beating time with your hands, you seem to be reveling in some vague feelings of your own and the unusual joy of loneliness, immune to boredom. If you dislike

dancing like mad in an uproarious discotheque or those uninteresting programs in a nightclub, you can choose such a tasteful bar as Twelve Oaks, for you will feel at home here, and besides, the singers here always sing old songs and love songs.
Add: Attached Building No. 6, No. 12, Section 4, South People's Road, Chengdu
Phone: 028-85563607

Home Base:
Typical of sports pubs, it is permeated with a bold and unrestrained atmosphere and the charm of sports. Various soccer team jerseys and logos of Manchester United, Arsenal and other teams fill your eye. Together with your friends, you may sip a refreshing drink and cry out while watching an intense and exciting match of Chinese First Division Soccer League, UEFA Cup, World Cup, UEFA Champions League, and the like. Here you can indulge yourself in your love of sports and games. It is the best choice for customers who want to comment on, chat about, and watch soccer matches.
Add: Attached Building No. 4, No. 1, Fanglin Road, Chengdu
Phone: 028-87026888

Languifang **(Orchid and Osmanthus):**
Built of coarse stones, the outer walls look very plain and unpretentious. Inside the bar, the lampshades are all made of big and small shells, and on the four walls hang guitars, violins, and discs. All of them, together with the wooden-framed paintings and photos on the walls and pillars and the dark brown wooden tables and chairs, create a unique atmosphere. You may drink a draft of beer brewed by the proprietor, listen to jolly jazz blues and get tipsy. And if you still feel lonely, you may use the "friend-making hot line" to call customers seated at other tables and chat to your heart's content.
Add: No. 15, Shaocheng Road, Chengdu
Phone: 028-86263626

The Street of Coordinate European- and Asian-Style Pubs:
The street consists of six bars named after things of different cultures. Their respective pitches are as follows:
St. Petersburg: St. Petersburg was once the symbol of tsarist Russia at the height of power and splendor and the red capital of revolution, where all the glories and dreams have been buried. Your arrival will get them unearthed. St. Petersburg that has witnessed the great changes of the world, as well as Russian pubs of various styles, is concentrated here into a long stage for your feelings and thoughts. Through the blurred time and space, you seem to see Lenin in 1918 refracted by vodka.
Champs Elysées: Champs Elysées is a synonym for fashion and romance. Traversing Paris, the world-famous city of flowers, Avenue des Champs Elysées is likely to throng your mind with reveries. Do you remember the photo *Le Baiser de l'Hotel de Ville, Paris*? Do you remember the reversed Eiffel Tower? The charm of the capital of arts is fully presented inside this French-style bar, where you can fully appreciate the vogue and the avant-garde and mixed flavors of French culture and world cultures.
Cherry Blossom: It is a Japanese-style bar named after cherry blossoms, which wither overnight and evoke a sad and mournful feeling. They are revered in Japan as the most sacred and civilized national flower that can fully represent the feelings and sensibilities of the Japanese people. There are 28 cherry trees in front of the bar and every April or May when they come into full bloom, it gets more beautiful and more romantic here.

Pattaya: Inside this bar named after Pattaya, a famous scenic spot in Thailand, you can experience the mystery and splendid romantic appeal of the Buddhist country. The charming tropical customs and practices are seductively beautiful. Decorated with Buddhist statues, myths and legends, pictures of transvestites, masks made of gamecock feathers, and the like, this bar boasts a style of its own.

Greenwich: Greenwich is an English-style pub where you can fully appreciate the tradition and genteel culture of Britain.

Frankfurt: Inside this bar named after a famous German city, you can fully experience the preciseness and boldness typical of the German people and think freely about soccer and beer amid glasses, cups, bowls, and dishes.

Add: Shaziyanzhong Alley, West Yulin Road, Chengdu
Phone: 028-85577799

And more...

Red Age:
Add: No. 30, Section 4, South People's Road, Chengdu
Phone: 028-88074548

No Distance:
Add: No. 2, North Jiulidi Road, Chengdu
Phone: 028-87610035

One-Way Street:
Add: Inside the Light Industry Building, Section 2, Central People's Road, Chengdu
Phone: 028-87650545

Hundred-Year-Old Mill:
Add: No. 12, Alley No. 8, Central Yulin Road, Chengdu
Phone: 028-85556019

Fontainebleau:
Add: No. 80, Section 2, South People's Road, Chengdu
Phone: 028-85506666

Bistro:
Add: No. 3, Xuefu Garden, Hongwasi Street, Chengdu
Phone: 028-85253829

Heaven's Eyes:
Add: Attached Building No. 18, No. 117, Wuhouci Street, Chengdu
Phone: 028-85567336

Half-a-Cigarette Lovers' Bar:
Add: Attached Building No. 8, No. 18, Qingyang Street, Chengdu
Phone: 028-84471368

The Seventh Sense:
Add: No. 12, Section 4, South People's Road, Chengdu
Phone: 028-85539243

Carpe Diem:
Add: No. 13, Central Yulin Road, Chengdu
Phone: 028-85567725

IX. An Unforgettable City

Chengdu is a city very fit for habitation and a city worthy of a walking tour as well. Reportedly, in Chengdu, it is quite common for men and women in love to walk from *Shengtianlu* Teahouse to *Shengtaoshao* Teahouse, or from Hongxing Street to Shuangnan Neighborhood. And I found asking the way in Chengdu was very different from that in Beijing: In Beijing, the locals would tell you to walk 200 meters to the North and then 40 meters to the West, but in Chengdu, you were told to walk along till you come to the end of the road, turn left, and then walk a bit further.

Following such directions of "walking along till you come to the end of the road and then making a turn," I went to look for Sophia in the places where she had worked or studied and visited three universities on the way: Sichuan University, Sichuan Normal University, and Southwest Jiaotong University.

Located next to Wangjianglou Park near Jiuyan (Nine Eyes) Bridge, Sichuan University is the largest university in Chengdu, where there are not only majestic teaching buildings and libraries, but also inexpensive tasty snacks and big or small quality goods stores and bookstores. But more importantly, cheap teahouses and bars stand side by side like fish scales. In those pairs of love-struck university students walking hand in hand under the Chinese parasol trees in the dazzling sunshine, I felt as if seeing myself in my youth and could not help but sigh over the ruthlessness of time. The most eye-catching were those pretty girls writing a paper or reading a book inside a teahouse, where they had met, fallen in love, and then parted with some boy. In two bars named respectively Let's Drink and 1812, I met many foreign people. These two bars sold beer at 5 *yuan* per bottle and customers could stand on the tables and sing a song.

Patrick came from Sweden and had studied with Sophia in the same elementary chinese class in Sichuan University. He could not tell me for certain where Sophia was now, but he told me rather elatedly that he lived in a small room on the second floor of an old quadrangle at a very low price of only 200 *yuan* every month. He got up at noon, went out to eat a bowl of noodles, and then came back to take Chinese lessons—surely in the company of pretty girls. At 4 or 5 in the afternoon, he would invite several friends over and drink tea together in the courtyard below at 2 *yuan* per cup. In the evening, he would eat a bowl of stir-fried rice in any restaurant and then went to have some drinks in a bar. Sometimes he would go to eat "ghost food"— that is: soup with boiled scalloped pig's feet and noodles with beef, which were so called because they were offered late into the night—in the Niuwang (King of Oxen) Temple. After returning to his room if he was not yet tired, he would watch a cult movie. If he was in the red, he would restrain himself, endure a month or half a month of suffering, and then continue as always. He said both Sweden and China were socialist countries, but authentic socialism resided only in China, especially in Chengdu.

Patrick told me to go to Sichuan Normal University where according to him, Sophia probably was teaching French. But I was told by the office in charge of foreign teachers that she had worked in the university only for a month and left long before. Sichuan Normal University is located in a place called Lion Hill. The so-called "hill" is actually a slightly sloping field. A railway passes through the hill and on both sides it stands tall and dense with poplar trees and Chinese scholartrees. It is said that in former times when in spring, all flowers were in bloom and the air was saturated with the fragrance of the flowers of Chinese scholartrees, *baxian* tables (an old-fashioned square table for eight people) and bamboo chairs could be laid in the wood and people could sit back in the bamboo chairs to watch small cracks of light and shadow drifting about. In addition to present and former university students, many inhabitants of Chengdu also come here on a picnic with their families and treated the place as a free park. Later as the university authorities drew up an overall plan and set aside this place for other uses, the students made a protest. As a result, the university authorities had a four-storied "campus plaza" built in compensation and concentrated all rest and recreation businesses in this new building. Here you can find *Lengdanbei* (midnight snacks, especially offered in summer), Chinese meals, hot pots, grills, snacks, cold drinks, internet bars, pubs, teahouses and everything, and all of them are always crowded with customers. The names of these businesses sound pleasing in a popular style: *Feilengcui* (Cold Jadeite), *Shuimu Nianhua* (Age of Water and Wood), *Yimulin* (One-Tree Wood), *Zaishuiyifang* (Somewhere along the River), *Jiulongding* (Tripod Caldron Carved with Nine Dragons), *Toufaluanle* (Dishevelled Hair).

In the foreign students' dormitory, I found Robert from Missouri University, USA, who, according to a teacher in the office in charge of foreign teachers, was a good friend of Sophia's. I told Robert that I could not get into contact with Sophia because I had deleted her E-mail address by accident and I dialed the phone number she had given before but could not get through. Robert told me exactly where Sophia was and then said in awkward Chinese even with a touch of Chengdu dialect, "Since you've come here, why don't you have a look around?" He told me that Sichuan Normal University was the university with the most pretty girl students and numerous pretty girls could be seen in the "campus plaza." He said to me with a cunning look, "You'd better wash your eyes thoroughly here before you find Sophia." I knew "to wash one's eyes" means "to look at pretty girls" in Chengdu dialect, but why did I need to protect my eyes by washing them? I was so grateful to him for his "considerate" suggestion and his valuable information about Sophia's whereabouts that I treated him in *Haiteng* (Surging Sea) Restaurant on the top floor. There was a gurgling brook and luxuriant green bamboos and trees inside the restaurant, but I followed Robert's advice and concentrated on looking around to "wash my eyes"…

At last I found Sophia in Southwest Jiaotong University in the Northwest of Chengdu. After staying for some time in several universities in Chengdu, she had finally chosen to teach in this university. For unknown reasons, there are more students from other provinces than Sichuan Province in Southwest Jiaotong University; therefore, it is not bustling with so much local color as Sichuan University and Sichuan Normal University. But as it is located by the Fu-Nan River, it feels uniquely pleasant to take a walk, read a book, and look at pretty girls on the broad open-air plaza. Reportedly, open-air movies are often shown here. You can buy some Leshan grills, *Laoma Tihua* (boiled scalloped pig's feet), *boboji* (bunches of chicken boiled in an earthen bowl) with green Sichuan pepper, several bottles of iced beer, and several dishes with or without meat from the snack-bars inside the university; while eating, you can enjoy such old movies as *Heroic Sons and Daughters*, *Scouting across the Yangtze River* and *Bathing Beauty*, and feel exceptionally satisfied. When Sophia was telling me about all these in idiomatic Chinese, Coca Cola nearly spurted out from my mouth. You know, it was just a year and a half before that she had left France for Chengdu, but now she could speak better Mandarin Chinese than a native of Chengdu. I really admired the high level of Chinese teaching in Southwest Jiaotong University that highlighted science and engineering education.

Two years ago when I was drinking coffee with Sophia in Rive Gauche, Paris, she just played with the idea of learning the Chinese language. And it was chance that finally led her to Chengdu. In her hometown Montpellier, a sister city of Chengdu, there is a street and a square named after Chengdu; and as a girl who grew up by the Mediterranean Sea, she got her first impression of Chengdu from tens of photos about Chengdu that were hung in the city hall of Montpellier. But now she had become an old hand at Chengdu able to serve as my guide in Chengdu temporarily, just as she had years before in Paris.

She said she liked the climate of Chengdu most, which, quite like that of Paris, was conducive not only to good health, but also to the growth of flowers. Thanks to its mild and moist climate, the women of Chengdu all had a fair complexion and the men of Chengdu all had a gentle, honest and sincere character. Both the women and men of Chengdu contented themselves with a leisurely life; they did not care so much about domestic and international affairs as the people of Beijing, nor haggle over every penny like the people of Shanghai. Flowers and grass benefited most from the mild and moist climate of Chengdu. Sophia said that plum blossoms in many other places were red in color, but in Chengdu, they were almost invariably light yellow. When plums were in full bloom, a faint fragrance would permeate the back lanes and high streets of Chengdu. No other flowers could be so prevalent in Chengdu as plum blossoms. All food markets, flower stalls, and flower peddle cars were filled with bunches of plum twigs already in bloom or merely in bud. Housewives, white-collar workers, young petty bourgeois and other lovers of plum blossoms would spend several *yuan* on bunches of plum twigs, put them in vases and decorate living rooms, bedrooms, studies, bars, teahouses, or restaurants with them. For many days after, the faint fragrance of plum blossoms would linger in these places. For a whole season, Chengdu would be saturated with the fragrance of plum blossoms, which enabled the inhabitants to experience spotless romances and affections that could stand trials and tribulations.

Sophia said, "You mustn't miss Happiness Plum Wood in the neighboring country of Chengdu. It's the biggest plum wood in Chengdu, where over 200,000 plum trees of over 200 varieties grow. There's also a plum blossom museum. It's the most beautiful rural area I've seen in China." We went to Happiness Village, Sansheng Township and seated ourselves in a peasant's courtyard of a unique style, but plum blossoms were already out of season. Instead we saw stretches of yellow flowers that got us into ecstasies. Sophia said we could not sit here to appreciate yellow flowers. It would be best to ride a bicycle toward the west or south of Chengdu, then walk on any tractor-plowing path and enjoy the beauty of tracts of dazzling yellow flowers that would intoxicate you. She said once she lay alone in a field of yellow flowers and felt extraordinary: All her thoughts and feelings were being embraced by yellow flowers and even the passing birds overhead were chirping happily at her. Nestled among the yellow tracts, she felt her youth and passion that had been kept in store for a whole winter were all set free at the moment.

Although Chengdu is called "The City of Hibiscus", hibiscus flowers are rarely seen in the city except for few places such as Yongling Mausoleum and the Wuhou Temple. Du Fu once wrote, "Looking around in the morning, you will see / Wet heavy red flowers all over the city of brocade officials," but now these two lines can only evoke poetic memories…As a matter of fact, although you can hardly see hibiscus flowers in Chengdu, you can feast your eyes on peonies, the queen of flowers. In Mount Danjing north of Chengdu, peonies have been planted on a large scale for more than 1,000 years; there are peonies of over 200 varieties and in red, white, yellow, purple, and various other colors. And at the end of March and the beginning of April, millions of tulips in Shixiang Lake burst into bloom together and look peerlessly magnificent.

And peach blossoms contend with each other in beauty and fascination on luxuriant branches all over the hills and dales in Longquan County. Moreover, you can see pear blossoms in Xinjin County.

Sophia said, "Chengdu was actually a city of flowers and in this respect, it even outshone Paris that called itself "the city of flowers." She told me, "In Chengdu, if you drive out of any exit to any place where you've never been before, you'll find a pleasant surprise is waiting for you." When we rode in our car out of Sansheng Township along a cement road that was not quite wide, we saw towering upright unknown trees on either side with dark green old leaves and light yellow new leaves. By the roadside there were crops in all shades of green, ridges and fields alternated with each other, and occasionally, we could see exposed brown mud. In the sunshine, everything was tinged with a warm color and looked like a French landscape oil painting. We asked the driver to drive as slowly as possible along this road, which was flanked with bright-colored wild flowers.

Thanks to its profound history and culture, many historical sites have been preserved in Chengdu, and historical and cultural marks have been left on many of the streets. For example, Tidu Street, Duyuan Street, Zongfu Street, Xuedao Street, Yandao Street, Fanshu Street, and the like were named after the government offices located in these streets in history; Front Wenmiao Street, Rear Wenmiao Street, Chenghuangmiao Street, Lingguanmiao Street, Kanggongmiao Street, Luogongci Street, and so on were named after some temples. In Chengdu there is a very famous street, Chunxi Street; its name has its origin in Lao-tzu's _The Book of Tao and Its Virtue_: "People are bustling around, as if visiting a beauty spot," which reveals the business prosperity in this street.

Sophia said, "If you don't go to Chunxi Street during your stay in Chengdu, you'll feel as much regret as you will if you don't go to Wangfujing Street while in Beijing, or to Nanjing Road while in Shanghai." Chunxi Street was originally built in 1924 by Yang Sen, a warlord in Sichuan and named "Senwei Street" after his title "General Senwei"; later it was changed into today's name. When I first came to Chengdu early in the 1980s, Chunxi Street was already the commercial center of this city, where you could find the time-honored Huntley Watches and Clocks Firm, the first department store complete with everything ranging from soup to nuts, many snack bars, and what not. Many mini-stores were located in the seat of today's Pacific Department Store; I still remember one of them with a façade of less than one meter long that sold rubber bands and headbands. I bought a pen at the Hu Kaiwen Stationer's Shop, looked at the four treasures of the study (writing brush, ink stick, ink slab, paper) with relish at *Shibeijia* Store, and visited *Xinhua* Bookstore and Bookstore of Ancient Books. According to one of my friends, the overall expansion and reconstruction of Chunxi Commercial Street for "Foot Passengers Only" started in the spring of 2001, which was the biggest cosmetic surgery in terms of scope and change in the 100-year history of Chunxi Street. The rebuilt Chunxi Street is wider and paved with granites and ancient-style bricks; the streets converge in the main street where the famous Zhongshan Square stands. There are an open-air pond and strips of trees in the expanded square, which serves as a good place for visitors to have a rest. As the most prosperous commercial street in Chengdu, Chunxi Street has always been an important place where people spend money and seek fun; besides, it inherits and transmits the cultural strains unique to this city. My friend said, several years ago, when you came to Chunxi Street in the evening, it was like a night fair where cheap goods were hawked in noisy disorder; but now, when the people of Chengdu suggest going to Chunxi Street, they mean to experience a fashionable and modern way of living. Now Chunxi Street is subdivided into the "name-brands street," the "sportswear street," the "food street," and the like. In terms of types of goods, today's Chunxi Street commercial circle has become a shopping center of top quality. Yet that is not the only value of Chunxi Street; along with this city, the street has been undergoing some unprecedented changes of historical significance and it is going to exert itself further in consolidating culture.

What fascinated me was the "relievo wall" at the northern end of Chunxi Street. On a polished wall of white granite there were carved in intaglio the old stores, old streets, and old people in the old marketplace of Old Chengdu, which, indistinctly visible, represented a memory of years past. This relievo wall, set against the colorful and dazzling Chunxi Street, produced a visual impact. Especially when people stopped to appreciate the relievos, their shadows were cast on the polished surface of the stones, as if the shadows of humankind and history were blended together. Another cast copper relievo *Glimpses of Time-honored Stores in Chunxi Street*, which kept Sophia looking for the right angles to take photos, presented scenes inside Guanggong Cutlers' Store, *Xinxin* News Agency, *Sanyigong* Theater and altogether 16 time-honored stores. A novel work that did not take much space, it was also like a genre painting that concentrated the commercial history of Chunxi Street since its opening,

Full of curiosity and pleasant surprise, Danny, who had now returned from my friend's home and joined us, watched the hustle and bustle in this Street for Foot Passengers Only; in the USA, he had never seen so many stores that were crowded together and so many people that flowed past like an endless stream. Groups of middle-school students after class wore a prideful and indifferent expression typical of adolescence; in front of fashion stores where popular music was playing, fashionable-looking shop assistants were waving their hands and shouting "Welcome to have a look!"; the brass statue of Sun Yat-sen in the middle of the square looked lean but calm; among the copper carvings at the crossroads, there were posters of *Waterloo Bridge* and other movies shown in the moviehouses of Old Chengdu…Everything here could arouse his curiosity, but there were too many things for him to take in at once…When tired, we sat down at an open-air café, where we got a panoramic view of the prosperity of today's Chunxi Street. Looking at the rare sun and the streams of people, I felt as if sitting in a street in Paris or Vienna. Thinking of the coarseness and shabbiness of this city more than 20 years ago, I seemed to be measuring its growth with the eye and found that it was more dazzling, more shining, and more cosmopolitan than ever…Chengdu is not a lead city in China. It boasts neither the rich political and economic resources of Beijing, nor the large gathering of foreign investment and financial organs in Shanghai, nor the rapid increase of GDP in Guangzhou. Nevertheless, it is an extraordinarily promising city, profound, self-determining, independent, growing at a steady pace by tameless, proud, and aloof perseverance, and creating the most *bashi* (comfortable) life for men and women of this land. Could you think of any other city in China as miraculous as Chengdu? It has never been plagued by war or famine, but instead, it has been enjoying the resource endowment of the "land of abundance"; more importantly, it has not indulged itself in a life of ease and comfort, but instead, in self-examination it has been developing and rising with force and spirit…

As a tourist from abroad, I was quite happy to regale myself on Chengdu's consumption products oriented toward the common people and experience the locals' service consciousness in "fulfilling a gigantic task with a small amount of money." I even would like to say that Chengdu is really a city that centers on human beings and their needs. The consciousness of serving the common people rarely perceivable in other cities is prevalent in food, clothing, housing, transportation, tourism, shopping, entertainment and many other aspects. Life in Chengdu has the power to intoxicate you and make you feel at home. People of different social standings are made to sit on the same kind of bamboo chairs, drink a cup of tea at the same price, and idle away the same hours. Teahouses and restaurants welcome all customers, whether employers or common people, whether white collar or laborers working on a public project, whether they come by car or by bicycle. Life in Chengdu has much attraction to out-of-towners. Therefore, passing travellers are often tempted to stay a few days longer and sacrifice health and sleep more willingly, and vagabonds used to a wandering life are lured to linger on and on.

I picked up a magazine that I had just bought a moment before and an article on Chengdu's tourism index caught my eye:

Chengdu's Tourism Index:

Composite index: 8.5. In terms of overall impressions, out-of-towners give higher marks than locals, for which there may be two reasons: First, out-of-towners are willing to save the face of Chengdu, and it is after all a favor done at little cost to them; second, the inhabitants of Chengdu do not appreciate their happy life.

Sight index: 9. Tourists can take much delight in viewing flowers, pretty women, city walls, rivers flowing through the city and real or replicated ancient buildings. And they can go to a quadrangle, sit on a bamboo chair at a *baxian* table, and watch vines climbing up flower racks.

Hearing index: 7.5. Tourists can enjoy Sichuan opera, Li Boqing's storytelling, and comedy shows in Chengdu dialect in bars. Foreign tourists may not understand the language, but just looking at the gestures and expressions, they cannot help laughing.

Taste index: 10. I do not need to give examples, for fear that you will get an insatiable hunger…

Interest index: 8. There are so many pleasure-seeking activities in Chengdu, that you will get tired of deciding what to do first. In terms of rest and recreation, the people of Chengdu are not just good at learning from others but also keen on creating and transforming new styles, of which you will get a thorough grasp during your stay here.

Culture index: 8. There are over ten universities and many museums—not to mention the ancient Shu civilization, the culture of Three Kingdoms, Li Bai, and Du Fu—have made Chengdu into a place where scholars and writers gather together. Reportedly, in Chengdu's Yulin Neighborhood, you will run into nobody other than a poet, or a former poet, or a would-be poet, or at least a friend of a poet.

Art index: 8.5. You can go to watch domestic or foreign cult movies and DV works in Whit Night Bar, or appreciate postmodernist paintings in Blue Peak (a converted studio, originally a factory), or see nostalgic copper relievos in Chunxi Street.

Air index: 7. It is often misty in Chengdu, perhaps because embraced by Sichuan Basin, the air in Chengdu cannot circulate smoothly. But compared with other big cities in China, the air in Chengdu is not bad; besides, it often rains here.

Weather index: 7. Although there are not many sunny days in Chengdu, you can rest assured that your skin will not get browned by the sun.

Pretty women index: 9. There is no place in the world without any pretty women, but pretty women abound in Chengdu. Why? Because there are more cloudy days than sunny days in Chengdu and the air is always damp. Such a climate is conducive to women's fair skin and fair-skinned women always look pretty.

Leisure index: 9.5. You can chat with others over tea, have some rest and recreation while working, and work while having some rest and recreation…Can you find any other cities more satisfying in this respect?

Pleasant surprise index: 9. Chengdu can offer you many pleasant surprises. For example, your expenses turn out to be lower than your budget, there are more enjoyments than you have expected, and so on. I will not list them all, or there will be no pleasant surprises for you.

Romance index: 8. Chengdu is a romantic city in its innermost nature. Somebody paid to advertise his love for his girlfriend on the front page of the local newspaper with the largest circulation; somebody arranged nearly 10,000 potted tulips of different colors on the hillside into "I Love You"…

Wherever you were born or for whatever reason you have come here, Chengdu remains a charming city. This feeling of temptation defies description. From spicy fish head hot pot to light dragon wonton, from the fashion world in Chunxi Street to the drifting bouquet of wine in Yulin Living Plaza, from weak tea in teacups with lid and saucer to the performance of face-changing that makes you clap hands and shout "Bravo", too many bits and pieces like these make up the whole of your impressions of Chengdu. Both what you like and dislike may fill your heart with reluctance to leave. I have come to understand Chengdu as if it were a human being, unfamiliar and puzzled at first and familiar and fascinated now; I have come to love its character and flavor, the inhabitants' open-minded and easeful attitude toward life, the food and drinks here, and everything…Chengdu is a city that you will remember all your life once you have laid a finger on it.

Sophia said, "Like countless people who've been welcomed and seen off by Chengdu, I'm just a sojourner." Yet as an individual with a limited life, every place where I've been will surely transform into the most important musical movement of my own; and that's why my experience of every city will be engraved in the bones and imprinted on the heart. Already an image on my atrium, Chengdu has captured my yearning and I'm so infatuated that I don't want to leave this metropolis in west China with a long history, profound culture, and colorful life. Here I've found too many things that touch me deeply, not just the modern architecture of the city, but also its flavor and character. What underlies the leisurely life in Chengdu is an affluence and opulence since time immemorial, the Jinjiang River that flows through Dujiang Weirs at all seasons, a cup of scented tea in tea houses in the summer, the past events discussed with fervor and assurance, and those local-style dwelling houses with cyan tiles, lofty eaves and carved doors and windows…"

A city is like a human being; cities with a character and temperament of their own are surely the most enjoyable and the most unforgettable as well. The vicissitudes of years cannot ablate her charm but wear away her physical beauty. I cannot exhaust the list of images of Chengdu that have left an ineffaceable mark on my mind: the splendor of the gold foil of "divine sunbirds" in Jinsha Ruins museum, the thousand-year-old wisdom of the ancient Shu people transmitted by the culture of the Three Kingdoms, the poetic songs of the "Sage of Poetry" resounding in Du Fu's Thatched Cottage, the past and present of this city that is flying higher and higher…

It was time to say farewell and Sophia said, "I hope to see you again in Chengdu next year."

"Next year? Are you going to stay permanently in Chengdu?" I asked in surprise.

"Is it so long before next year? I love this city. At least so far, I have found no reason to leave," she answered with a brooding expression, as if my question was "problematic."

It was raining again when we left Chengdu. Bathed in rain, Chengdu gave the impression of "being moistened without any noise." It dawned on me that I had begun to feel everything in this city with my heart. I started to understand why Ruth Harkness wished to be buried here and why Sophia liked this city so much. Although we had stayed in Chengdu for quite a brief time of several days, my heart was already filled with fascination and attachment. Right then, a line in that short movie directed by Zhang Yimou, a famous director in China, occurred to me: "Chengdu is a city where once you've come, you don't want to go…"

A soft song broadcast on the radio was floating about in the car: "Walking out of your light blue room into the rain, /I remember well you said, better to say farewell in a rainy day; / it seems you already knew it would happen someday. / Forgive me for not saying good-bye to you, / for I want to bury this unconsummated love deeply. / I'm going to miss every rainy day…Silently, I gazed at the world outside the window; enveloped in the song as well as the rain, the whole city of Chengdu seemed empty and quiet. It was a far-reaching quietness, which, to the accompaniment of the melodious and slightly sorrowful music, was permeating the infinite time and space; drifting along with it were my endless thoughts and feelings about rain. For a while, I was lost in a trance: I did not know what kind of space it was that had awakened my dormant memories of twenty years ago. Now it was time to say good-bye, and my heart was filled with a sense of loss: All those beautiful things that had belonged to me for once and all my past dreams, could not be brought back home with me. Looking at the threadlike rain sadly, I suddenly found tears were already overflowing Danny's eyes. He, who was only ten years old and came to Chengdu for the first time, looked intently at the city outside the window and murmured: "Chengdu, I miss you!"

Jack Quian

Tips:

Universities in Chengdu:

Sichuan University:
The predecessors of Sichuan University were Jinjiang Academy created in 1704, Zunjing Academy founded in 1874, and Sichuan Chinese and Western School established in 1896. In 1934, it was named National Sichuan University. Later it was integrated with Chengdu University of Science and Technology and West China University of Medical Sciences into the new Sichuan University, presently the largest-scale university in the Chengdu area.
Add: No. 29, Wangjiang Road, Chengdu, Sichuan
Website: www.scu.edu.cn

University of Electronic Science and Technology of China:
In 1956, University of Electronic Science and Technology of China (UESTC) was created by merging the electronic divisions of the then Jiaotong University, Nanjing Institute of Technology and South China Institute of Technology. As one of the earliest national defense universities, UESTC has now developed into a multi-disciplinary university incorporating liberal arts, science, and engineering.
Add: No. 4, Section 2, North Jianshe Road, Chengdu
Website: www.uestc.edu.cn

Sichuan Normal University:
Established in 1946, Sichuan Normal University (SNU) is located on the beautiful and tranquil Lion Hill in the eastern suburbs of Chengdu, with the total area of 3,000 *mu*. It consists of eighteen colleges and three campuses: the main campus, the eastern campus and Caotang campus. More than 200,000 students have graduated from this university in the past years.
Add: No. 5, Jing'an Road, Jinjiang District, Chengdu
Website: www.sicnu.edu.cn

Southwest Jiaotong University:
Founded in Shanhaiguan in 1896, Southwest Jiaotong University (SWJTU) is one of the earliest institutions of higher learning in China and the cradle of civil engineering and transportation engineering education in China. In 1905, it was relocated to Tangshan, Hebei Province and named successively Tangshan Jiaotong University, Tangshan Institute of Technology of China Jiaotong University, and so on. In 1952, it was renamed Tangshan Railway Institute. In 1972, it was relocated inland to Sichuan Province and renamed Southwest Jiaotong University, which has remained unchanged till now.
Add: NO. 111, Section 1, North Second Ring Road, Chengdu
Website: www.swjtu.edu.cn

Chengdu University:
Chengdu University is a new comprehensive university composed of eleven departments: mechanical engineering, architectural engineering, electronic information engineering, computer science and technology, bioengineering, foreign languages, Chinese, design, business administration, economics and law, and tourism.
Add: Shiling Town, Longquan District, Chengdu
Website: www.cdu.edu.cn

The best places in Chengdu to appreciate flowers:

Sansheng Township:
Near the Third Ring Road in Jinjiang District, Sansheng Township boasts six big flower gardens: Zengjiapo Chinese rose garden, Fenfangyan chrysanthemum garden, Happiness winter sweet garden, Wangfu lotus pond garden, and a red sand plantation of ecological technology. You can ride in an electrically operated motorcar to shuttle back and forth in the sea of flowers, or saunter at leisure in the sunshine among various luxuriant flowers. When thirsty, you can drink a cup of green tea in a roadside "happy peasants' inn"; when hungry, you can eat a typical peasants' meal there; and when leaving, you can buy several bunches of fresh flowers at any roadside flower stall and bring them back home…

Peach Blossoms' Home:
Peach Blossoms' Home is located on either side of the old Chengdu-Chongqing Highway in Shanquan Town, 26 kilometers away from the downtown area of Chengdu. It is the cradle of juicy peaches in Longquan and the seat of the former residence of Jin Xitian, who introduced juicy peaches into Longquan. There are 150 peasants' households that receive tourists and all of them are rebuilt in the style of west Sichuan dwelling houses. Peach trees cover an area of over 12,000 *mu* and all the flowers have double petals. As there are both hills and gullies in Shanquan Town, peach trees appear to tier up and as the town sits high, it affords a wonderful bird's-eye view of the peach woods.

Shufang Village:
Two kilometers west of Longquan Town, the village has about 100 peasants' households that receive tourists. Peach trees cover an area of 3,000 *mu* there. Large tracts of peach blossoms stretch along the level ground to the horizon and you can fully enjoy the pleasure of "swimming in a sea of flowers."

Pear Blossom Gully in Xinjin County:
Three kilometers south of the county seat of Xinjin, there is a pear garden of nearly 10,000 *mu*, which is the best place to appreciate pear blossoms in Chengdu. Amid rolling hills, surrounding elevations and winding paths, you will have an eyeful of cloud-like and snow-white flowers. The pear blossoms on thousands of pear trees, in harmony with golden rape flowers, green wheat seedlings, glistening ponds, and peasants' tile and brick houses, make a utopian retreat.

Jack Quian

Peonies in Tianpeng (the former name of Pengzhou City):
On Mount Danjing in Pengzhou, over 30 kilometers north of Chengdu, peonies have been planted for more than 1,000 years. There are red, white, yellow, purple, and other peonies. You have to keep climbing while enjoying the beauty of the flowers, and when you reach Peony Garden breathlessly, you will suddenly see in a clear light a great many of peonies flickering happily in the wind. On Mount Danjing, you can also enjoy the beauty of Chinese herbaceous peonies, azaleas, dahlia pannatas, crape myrtles, winter sweets and other flowers in addition to peonies.

Tulips in Shixiang Lake:
If you drive 86 kilometers along the Chengdu-Ya'an Highway, you will get to a natural lake, where 3,000,000 tulips of 29 kinds grow along the bank. At the end of March and the beginning of April, millions of tulips burst into full bloom, and stretches of yellow, white and red flowers keep spreading along the undulating lakeside with ease and verve, just like a raging fire.

Yellow flowers:
In Chengdu, yellow flowers usually come into bloom in the middle of March. You can see a vast expanse of yellow flowers in the fields of Xinjin County, Shuangliu County and Pixian County. Fiercely blossoming and richly fragrant, they may get you into ecstasies. It would be best to ride a bicycle to appreciate yellow flowers. After you have exited the Third Ring Road and passed the borderline between the city and the countryside, you will arrive at the authentic countryside surrounding Chengdu where stretches of dazzling yellow flowers will intoxicate you. Stop at a certain place and walk into the field along a narrow path, and you will find all of your thoughts and feelings are being embraced by yellow flowers.

Sweet-scented osmanthuses in Xindu County:
Sixteen kilometers north of Chengdu, Osmanthus Lake in Xindu is a famous osmanthus growing area with a history of over 500 years. It is not a big lake, whose banks are shaded by verdant trees and sprinkled with osmanthus gardens. There are five kinds of osmanthuses: orange osmanthus, osmanthus fragrans var. latifolius, osmanthus fragrans var. aurantiacus, osmanthus fragrans var. semperflorens, and cinnamomum tamala. Every August in the lunar calendar, white, golden, and cream-colored osmanthus flowers bloom thickly in clusters among round leaves. Even a gentle breeze can send their sweet and pleasant fragrance to faraway places.

Lotuses in Xinjin County:
In Anxi Town 40 kilometers away from the downtown area of Chengdu, 6 kilometers away from the seat of Xinjin County, there is a lotus village that boasts lotuses of 100 *mu*, 100 fish ponds, and 100 fish restaurants. Looking around, you can see fragrant paddy rice in the surrounding country and lotuses stretching over a length of 10 *li*—what an idyllic picture! Lotuses have the reputation of being "fresh and clean although growing out of mud." In the sunshine, the dewdrops on the lotus leaves are dazzling with brilliance and clustered around by leaves, the flowers seem to be dripping with a delicate charm. There are more flower buds, which hide themselves under lotus leaves, ready to burst.

One-Day Tours of Chengdu :

1.   A bicycle tour of Chengdu's streets:
Reasons for recommendation: Bicycles are a free, handy, convenient, and unpretentious means of transportation. Tourists not only fully enjoy the beauty spots and historical sites, but also thoroughly experience the folk customs and morals in the back lanes and high streets of Chengdu.
In the morning: The Wide Alley—the Narrow Alley—Du Fu's Thatched Cottage
Tourists ride on their bicycles to the Wide and Narrow Alleys, the only well-preserved ancient alleys in Chengdu dating back to the Qing Dynasty. The moment they enter the Wide and Narrow Alleys, they will discover to their surprise that ancient-style streets in Chengdu are unveiling themselves impressively before their eyes. Antique houses, narrow gravel paths, and a succession of snack bars will make them feel carefree and leisurely. Bungalows, gates with two or four door leaves, and motley rusty spots quietly tell their own histories. Seat stones flank the gates, whose lintels are carved with mascots such as pumpkins and fingered citrons. Kylins with bare fangs and brandish claws and uptilting roof corners set off each other and form a pleasing contrast. Cage birds are singing under the eaves of many households. All the inhabitants of the quadrangles raise various kinds of plants, such as bamboos, trees, and flowers and green vines climb over low walls. After the visit to the ancient quadrangles in Chengdu, tourists ride on their bicycles to Du Fu's Thatched Cottage, the former residence of Du Fu, a great poet during the Tang Dynasty. The poet stayed here away from his hometown and wrote over 500 much-relished poems within three years. Finally he drifted south and left behind this thatched cottage in the company of a bright moon and a gentle breeze.
Lunch: Famous Chengdu snacks—Dragon wonton, the Zhongs' dumplings, *Fuqi Feipian* (husband and wife's sliced pot-stewed entrails of oxen), *Suanlafen* (hot and sour Chinese vermicelli) and so on
In the afternoon: Chunxi Street—Tianfu Square—Wangjianglou Park—the Fu-Nan River
Tourists can stroll along the prosperous Chunxi Street, Zongfu Street, and Tianfu Square to get to know a modernized Chengdu, or sit inside a teahouse with a strong flavor of west Sichuan and listen to the locals chatting with each other. Then they go to Wangjianglou Park, where a great variety of famous indigenous and exotic bamboos gather together. It is a beauty spot in memory of Xue Tao, a famous woman poet in the Tang Dynasty. Inside the park, poplars and willows sway with the wind and green bamboos form a dense umbrage. With the total area of 120,000 square meters, the park is mostly covered with bamboos and is therefore called "the world of bamboos." Then tourists ride slowly on their bicycles along the Fu-Nan River, which has won the UN-Habitat Scroll of Honor Award. The most famous beauty spots there include Hejiang Pavilion and the Flowing Water Park.
Supper: Tourists may find a special hot pot restaurant in the back lanes or high streets in Chengdu to have a taste of the tongue-numbing and hot food. Or they may go to a roadside restaurant unique to Chengdu that offers *malatang* (bunches of food with chili pepper cooked in hot pots); there, they can eat steaming and hot food unhurriedly to their heart's content at less than 20 *yuan* per person.
In the evening: Tourists go to *Shufeng Yayun* Teahouse to drink tea and enjoy Sichuan opera, especially the fire-spitting, face-changing, and other consummate skills peculiar to Sichuan opera.
Estimated expenses: About 120 RMB per person

2. A one-day tour of ancient Shu civilization:

Reasons for recommendation: The tour enables tourists to appreciate ancient Shu civilization and enjoy delicious Chengdu food.

In the morning: Jinsha Ruins—Du Fu's Thatched Cottage—the Qingyang Temple

Tourists first go to Jinsha Ruins in the west of Chengdu. Representative of ancient Shu civilization of over 3,000 years ago, it is the most important archaeological discovery since Sanxingdui was unearthed in Sichuan Province and the first one in China since the dawn of the 21st century as well. Then tourists go to Du Fu's Thatched Cottage, the former residence of Du Fu, a poet in the Tang Dynasty during his stay in Chengdu. Typical of landscape gardens, the classic architecture there brims over with a strong cultural flavor. Now it is time to go to the Qingyang Temple. Located quite near Du Fu's Thatched Cottage, it is the earliest and largest-scale Taoist temple in the city of Chengdu. It was originally built during the Tang Dynasty, but the existing buildings such as the *Sanqing* Hall (the Hall of the Three Pristine Ones), the *Doumu* (Big Dipper) Hall, the *Hunyuan* (Original Chaos) Hall, the *Lingzu* (Numinous Patriarch) Hall, the *Zijin* (Purple Gold) Platform, and the *Bagua* (Eight Trigrams) Pavilion were rebuilt during the Qing Dynasty. The most eye-catching are two bronze goats in the *Sanqing* Hall: One of them has two horns and the other, only one horn.

Lunch: Famous Chengdu snacks such as Pockmarked Woman Chen's bean curd sold at the restaurant opposite the Qingyang Temple, dragon wonton, the Zhongs' dumplings, the Hans' steamed buns, the Lais' *Tangyuan* (boiled rice dumplings) and so on

In the afternoon: The Site of Shuijing Street Liquor Workshop—Boat-Shaped Coffins of Ancient Shu Kingdom

The unearthing of the site of Shuijing Street Liquor Workshop, which can be called "the amazing book without words" on Chinese liquor, has filled a gap in archaeological researches on Chinese brewing workshops. In July, 2000, the Boat-Shaped Coffins of Ancient Shu Kingdom made a surprising appearance in Commercial Street in Chengdu and was ranked in the ten most important archaeological discoveries of the year.

Supper: With a long history, Sichuan cuisine is ranked in the four most famous schools of culinary art in China together with Shandong cuisine, Jiangsu cuisine, and Guangdong cuisine. It would be best if tourists go to *Baguo Buyi* Restaurant or *Xianglaokan* Restaurant to fully taste the tongue-numbing and hot, spiced salty, sweet and sour, sour and hot, five-spices, strange-flavored and other flavors of Sichuan cuisine, or go to a hot pot restaurant and eat tongue-numbing and hot food to their heart's content.

In the evening: Tourists can go for a walk along the beautiful Fu-Nan River to *Hejiang* Pavilion, Music Square, or other places to enjoy themselves, or go to drink tea, listen to Sichuan opera and chat with locals in teahouses.

Estimated expenses: About 140 RMB per person

3. A relaxing one-day tour of historical sites:

Reasons for recommendation: The tour can fully display the charm of Chengdu during the Tang Dynasty.

In the morning: Wangjianglou Park—the Daci Temple—the Wenshu Temple

The tour starts at 9:00 am with a visit to Wangjianglou Park, a park shaded by green bamboos where tourists can go to an exhibition of cultural relics bequeathed by Xue Tao or drink tea at leisure. Then tourists take a ride to the Daci Temple, an ancient temple of the Tang Dynasty where tourists can visit Chengdu Historical Museum and an exhibition of cultural relics of the Tang Dynasty. What's more, wooden tables and chairs and long-mouthed copper teapots in this temple enable tourists to fully experience the tea culture of Chengdu. It is followed by a visit to the Wenshu Temple in the north of Chengdu. In this best-preserved Buddhist temple in the city, tourists can see a rich and colorful collection of Buddhist relics, among which copper, iron, painted, wooden and stone sculptures amount to over 450. The temple also boasts fragments of the skull of Xuan Zang, a famous accomplished monk during the Tang Dynasty, the Indian Sanskrit *Pattra-Leaf Stutras*, gilded prayer wheels from Japan, as well as works of famous calligraphers and painters of the Song, Yuan, Ming, Qing Dynasties.

Lunch: Buddhist food in the Wenshu Temple

In the afternoon: After lunch, tourists take a ride north along Chengdu-Pengzhou Highway for 25 kilometers to Xinfan Town, Xindu County and visit East Lake Park, the only well-preserved landscape garden in China dating back to the Tang Dynasty. According to historical records, the lake was dug when Li Deyu, a famous premier during the Tang Dynasty, worked as county magistrate there and expanded by Wang Yide, the father of Wang Anshi, a famous premier of the Song Dynasty. The garden boasts an exquisite layout, brooks winding their way through hills, and tall and elegant pavilions, which combine to present a quiet and refreshing view. Tourists can appreciate inscriptions on tablets and couplets hung on pillars, or drink tea at leisure.

Supper: Xinfan Town can be said to be the place where famous dishes in west Sichuan gather together. Even a common restaurant in Xinfan Town can offer inexpensive but rather delicious food.

Estimated expenses: About 200 RMB per person.

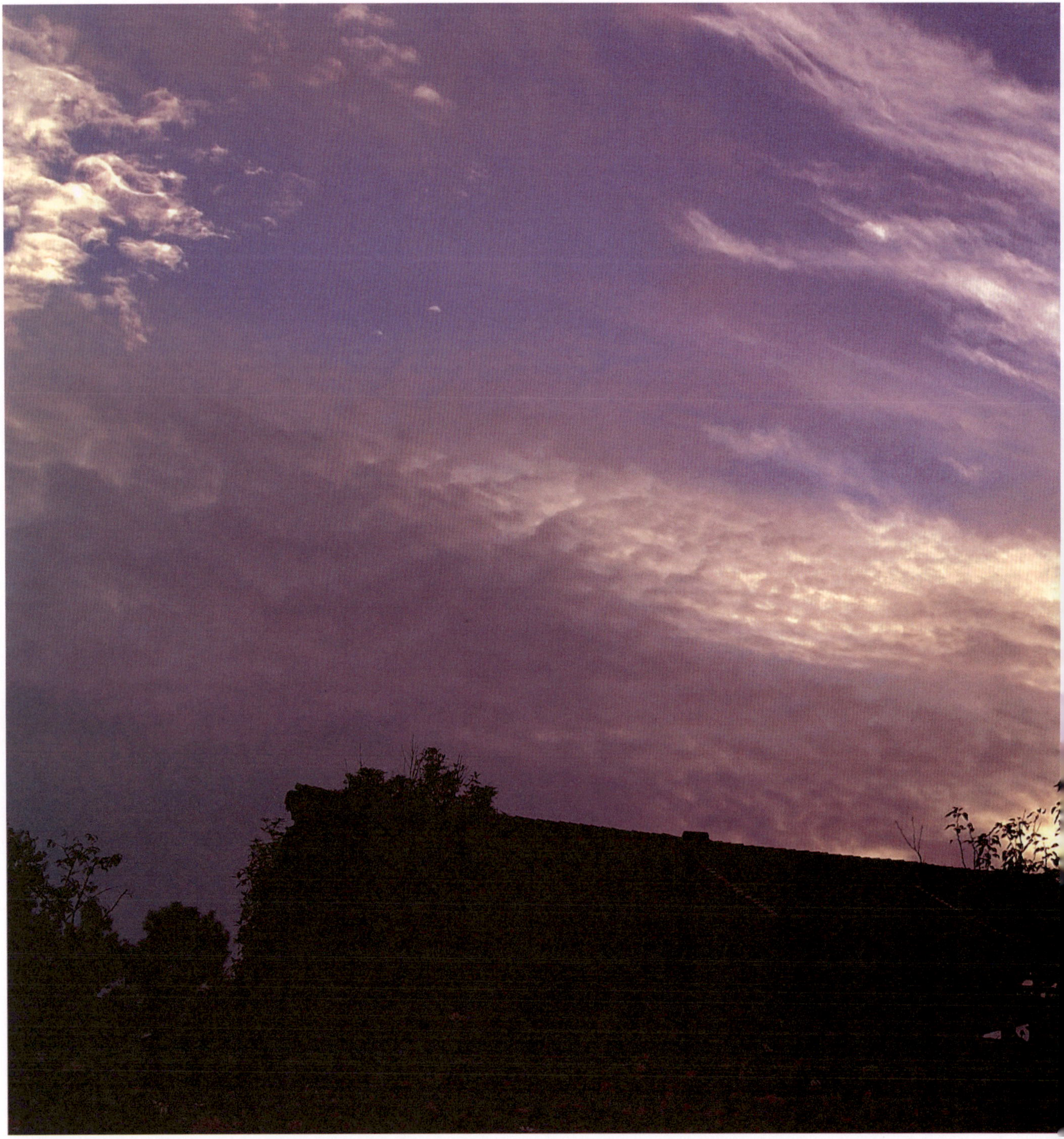

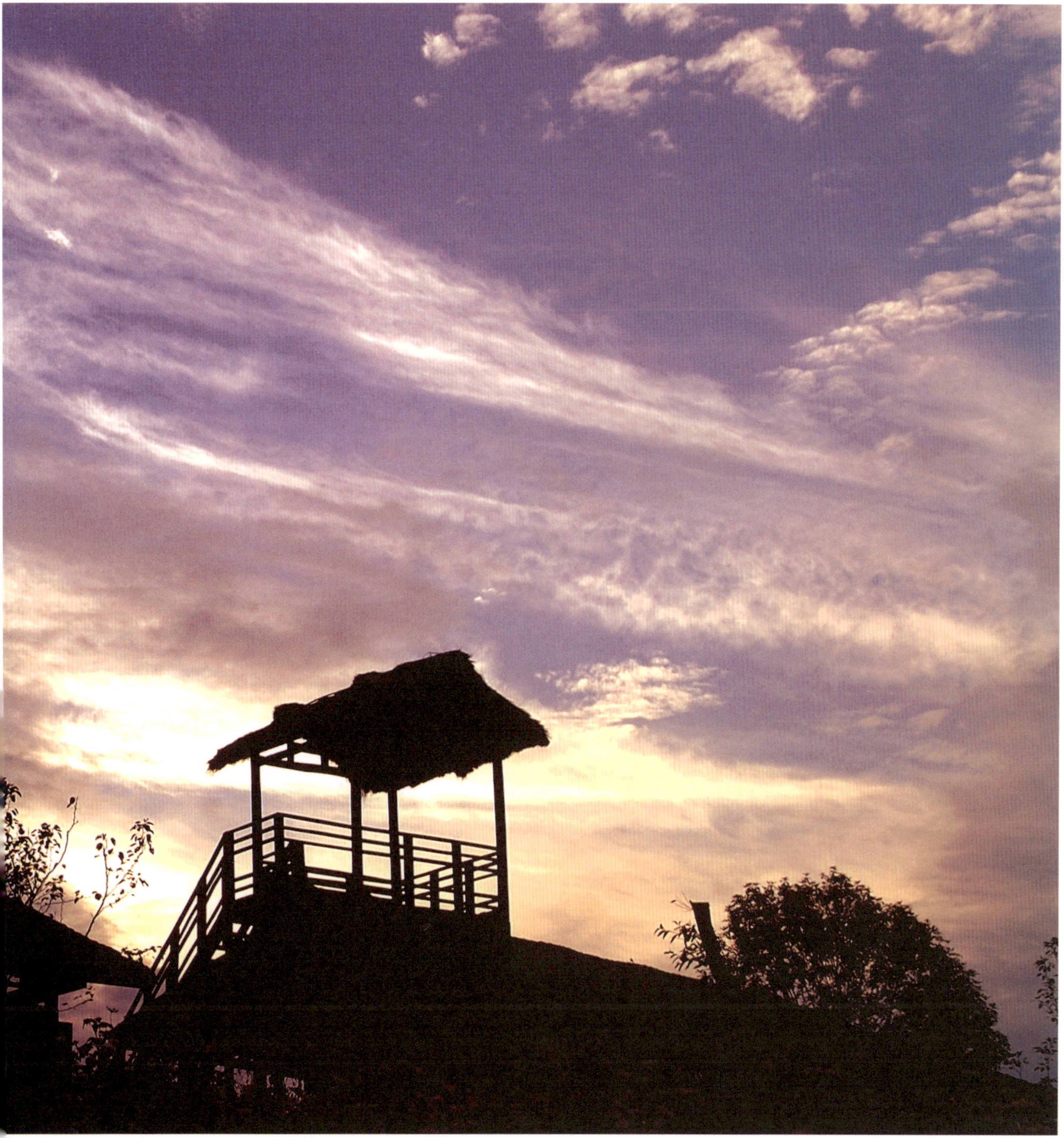